THE COLONIES OF LAW

Colonialism, Zionism and Law in Early Mandate Palestine

Treating law as an essential cultural component in a nation-building project, this book offers a socio-historical analysis of a community-based system of justice under colonial rule. It traces the attempts of Jewish jurist-nationalists to establish a non-religious system of Hebrew courts in British-ruled Palestine. This book analyzes the secular, national and anti-colonial ideology of the Hebrew Law of Peace and shows that Jewish religious groups, secular lawyers and leading Zionist institutions undermined the Hebrew Law project. The book develops the concept of 'dual colonialism' to analyze the complex relations between Jewish settlers and British colonizers, and explores the reluctance of leading Zionists to allow a process of nation-building from below that would have allowed communities, rather than organized quasi-state institutions, to define the trajectory of Jewish nationalism.

RONEN SHAMIR is Associate Professor of Sociology and Anthropology at Tel Aviv University, where he also lectures in the Law School. He was recently a Research Fellow at the American Bar Foundation and is currently serving on the Board of Trustees for the Law and Society Association. He has published articles in leading journals, including the *Law and Society Review*. His previous book, *Managing Legal Uncertainty* (1995), won the annual American Sociological Association award for work in the field of Sociology of Law.

To Omer, Leigh and Yonit

CAMBRIDGE STUDIES IN LAW AND SOCIETY

Series editors:
Chris Arup, Martin Chanock, Pat O'Malley
School of Law and Legal Studies, La Trobe University
Sally Engle Merry, Susan Silbey
Departments of Anthropology and Sociology, Wellesley College

Editorial board:
Richard Abel, Harry Arthurs, Sandra Burman, Peter Fitzpatrick, Marc Galanter, Yash Ghai, Nicola Lacey, Bonaventura da Sousa Santos, Sol Picciotto, Jonathan Simon, Frank Snyder

The broad area of law and society has become a remarkably rich and dynamic field of study. At the same time, the social sciences have increasingly engaged with questions of law. In this process, the borders between legal scholarship and the social, political and cultural sciences have been transcended, and the result is a time of fundamental re-thinking both within and about law. In this vital period, Cambridge Studies in Law and Society provides a significant new book series with an international focus and a concern with the global transformation of the legal arena. The series aims to publish the best scholarly work on legal discourse and practice in social context, combining theoretical insights and empirical research.

Already published:
Anthony Woodiwiss *Globalisation, Human Rights and Labour Law in Pacific Asia*
   0 521 62144 5 hardback 0 521 62883 0 paperback
Mariana Valverde *Diseases of the Will: Alcoholism and the Dilemmas of Freedom*
   0 521 62300 6 hardback 0 521 64469 0 paperback
Alan Hunt *Governing Morals: A Social History of Moral Regulation*
   0 521 64071 7 hardback 0 521 64689 8 paperback
John Torpey *The Invention of the Passport: Surveillance, Citizenship and the State*
   0 521 63249 8 hardback 0 521 63493 8 paperback

Forthcoming titles:
William Walters *Unemployment and Government: Genealogies of the Social*
   0 521 64333 3 hardback 0 521 64414 3 paperback
Christopher Arup *The New World Trade Organisation Agreements: Globalising Law through Services and Intellectual Property*
   0 521 77355 5 hardback 0 521 77408 X paperback

THE COLONIES OF LAW
Colonialism, Zionism and Law
in Early Mandate Palestine

Ronen Shamir
Tel Aviv University

CAMBRIDGE
UNIVERSITY PRESS

University Printing House, Cambridge CB2 8BS, United Kingdom

One Liberty Plaza, 20th Floor, New York, NY 10006, USA

477 Williamstown Road, Port Melbourne, VIC 3207, Australia

314-321, 3rd Floor, Plot 3, Splendor Forum, Jasola District Centre, New Delhi - 110025, India

79 Anson Road, #06-04/06, Singapore 079906

Cambridge University Press is part of the University of Cambridge.

It furthers the University's mission by disseminating knowledge in the pursuit of education, learning and research at the highest international levels of excellence.

www.cambridge.org
Information on this title: www.cambridge.org/9780521631839

© Ronen Shamir 2000

This publication is in copyright. Subject to statutory exception and to the provisions of relevant collective licensing agreements, no reproduction of any part may take place without the written permission of Cambridge University Press.

First published 2000

A catalogue record for this publication is available from the British Library

National Library of Australia Cataloging in Publication data
Shamir, Ronen.
The colonies of law : colonialism, zionism and law in early mandate Palestine
Bibliography.
Includes index.
ISBN 0 521 63183 1 (hbk).
1. Zionism – Palestine – History – 1917–1948. 2. Justice, Administration of – Palestine – History – 1917–1948.
3. Mandates – Palestine. 4. Neighbourhood justice centers – Palestine – History – 1917–1948. 5. Palestine – Foreign relations – Great Britain. I. Title. (Series : Cambridge studies in law and society).
956.9404.

ISBN 978-0-521-63183-9 Hardback

Cambridge University Press has no responsibility for the persistence or accuracy of URLs for external or third-party internet websites referred to in this publication, and does not guarantee that any content on such websites is, or will remain, accurate or appropriate.

CONTENTS

Acknowledgments viii
Mandate Palestine 1914–1936: Some Facts and Figures ix

Introduction 1

1 Mandate Palestine: The Enigma of the Missing Colonial State 6

2 Whose Tradition? Imageries of the Past in Hebrew Law 30

Interregnum 49

3 State Law and Communal Justice 53

4 Celebrating Authenticity and Practicing Hybridity 71

5 Nationalism as a Disciplinary Regime 92

Salle d'Attente 101

6 Lawyering the Nation 108

7 Nation-building and the Containment of Legality 126

8 Dead Law and Statism: A Suggested Lesson 148

Notes 173
Bibliography 205
Index 213

ACKNOWLEDGMENTS

I owe many thanks to the American Bar Foundation for providing me with a research fellowship and an intellectual setting that allowed me to work on this manuscript. In particular, I am grateful to Bryant Garth, whose encouragement was crucial for my work. I also thank John Comaroff, who kept challenging me and offered me his dear friendship; I am very fortunate to have come to know John during the time I spent at the ABF. I also thank Terry Halliday and Bonnie Honig, whose curiosity and ongoing reflections were an essential part of my ability to write. Finally, I thank the administrative staff of the ABF for facilitating my wonderful year in Chicago.

During research and writing, I have had the privilege of presenting my thoughts in some stimulating settings. In particular, I would like to thank Christine Harrington and her colleagues at New York University, Malcolm Feeley and collegues at Berkeley's JSP and David Trubek and colleagues at the University of Wisconsin at Madison. Susan Silbey and Patty Ewick, dear friends who are never tired of stimulating my thoughts, have accompanied this project from the start. Their comments, queries and constructive support provided me with the confidence to keep writing and revising this book. Susan, as one of my editors, kept upgrading my work. Patty, with her insights, kept opening new avenues for my thoughts. Thank you.

I owe Neta Ziv a special debt of gratitude. Her comments, reflections, criticisms and love, provided me with the energy without which I would never have completed this manuscript. I also thank Abraham Cordova, Lawrence Friedman, Pnina Lahav, Assaf Likhovski, and Yehouda Shenhav for their careful reading and helpful comments. Finally, I would like to thank two research assistants: Nelli Elias, who never complained about having to spend hour upon hour in archives and libraries, and Gaby Blum, who was always there for me, fulfilling with a smile every request, capricious as it was, that came to my mind. It is the way of academic writing to ascribe a work to an author. This work carries my name. But I want to testify, fully and wholeheartedly, to a joint project of interaction, dialogue, and support with numerous others.

MANDATE PALESTINE 1914–1936: SOME FACTS AND FIGURES

TABLE 1 Population of Palestine 1919–1936

Year	Moslems	Christians	Jews	Total
1919	515,000	62,500	65,300	647,850
1922	589,000	71,000	83,000	745,000
1936	859,000	77,000	400,000 est.	1,336,518

Source: Peel Report (1937), pp. 43, 156

TABLE 2 Number of Jews in Palestine

Before the First World War	90,000*
At British occupation	55,000
January 1921	64,000
1925	121,000
1926	140,000
1936	370,483**

* 66% of this figure represents non-Zionists
** Does not include an estimated 40,000 illegal residents
Sources: Peel Report (1937); Horowitz & Lissak (1978)

TABLE 3 Jewish immigration into Palestine 1920–1936

Year	Jews	Others	
1920 (Sept.–Oct.)	5,514	202	
1921	9,149	190	
1922	7,844	284	
1923	7,421	570	
1924	12,856	697	
1925	33,801	840	(Jews out: 2,151)
1926	13,081	829	(Jews out: 7,365)
1927	2,713	882	(Jews out: 5,071)
1928	2,178	908	(no data)
1929	5,249	1,317	(Jews out: 1,746)
1930	4,944	1,489	(Jews out: 1,679)
1931	4,075	1,458	(Jews out: 666)
1932	9,553	1,736	
1933	30,327	1,650	
1934	42,359	1,784	
1935	61,854	2,293	
1936	29,727	1,944	

Source: Peel Report (1937)

TABLE 4 Urban population 1931

City	Moslems	Christians	Jews	Total
Jerusalem	173,019	38,488	54,959	266,562 est.
Jaffa	65,478	9,921	69,789	145,502 est.
Haifa	52,830	16,492	23,367	95,472 est.

Source: Peel Report (1937)

TABLE 5 Population of Tel Aviv 1914–1936

1914	2,000
1922	13,000
1926	40,000
1936	150,000 (est)

Source: Peel Report (1937); Yediot, Tel Aviv

TABLE 6   Membership of General Federation of Jewish Labor (Histadrut Ha'Ovdim)

1921 (January)	4,500 *
1923	8,394 (5435 urban)
1926	16,000 *
1927	22,538 (15,325 urban)
1931	30,000 (18,781 urban)
1933	26,500 *
1933	35,389 (21,080 urban)

* Spouses not included
Note: By the second half of the 1920s, 73% of Jewish wage-earners were Histadrut members
By 1928, 70% of all Histadrut members resided in Tel Aviv
Source: Sternhell (1995), p. 228

TABLE 7   Overall rates of litigation 1918–1926, Hebrew Courts of Peace

	Cases	Yearly average
High Court	282	31
Tel Aviv	6,719	746
Jerusalem	2,243	320 (1920–26)
Haifa	2,168	271 (1919–26)
Petah Tiqwa	309	38 (1919–26)
Rishon	1,100	64 (1910–26)
Rehovot	69	16 (1910–26)
Hadera	186	26 (1920–26)
Zichron	283	35 (1919–26)

Source: *Hamishpat* vol. 2

TABLE 8 Number of cases in Tel Aviv instances, Hebrew Law of Peace

1918	171
1919	593 (620)
1920	430 (465)
1921	425 (448)
1922	715 (715)
1923	1,371 (1,480)
1924	1,127 (1,156)
1925	738 (756)
1926	1,092 (1,120)
1927	702 (730)
1928	n/a (471)
1929	n/a (363)
1930	n/a (357)
1931	n/a (326)
1932	n/a (247)

Source: *Hamishpat*

TABLE 9 Proportion of cases by category, District Court, Tel Aviv 1927

17%	Honor claims
6%	Bills
10.5%	Wages
14%	Contracts
10%	Torts
2%	Partnerships
6%	Commercial transactions
14%	Rent and neighbors' transactions
10%	Land

Note: 7.5% shirking (refusing to litigate)

TABLE 10 Comrades Law rates of litigation, Instance A 1923–1927

1923	266
1924	833
1925	508
1926	1,533
1927	520 (Jan.–Aug.)

TABLE 11 Comrades Law cases by category, Tel Aviv 1923–1927

Monetary claims	1,128
Moral claims	250
Monetary–moral	64
Histadrut-related	56
Employment	22
Compensation	33
Contract	21
Partnership	1
Trespass	1
Total	1,576

TABLE 12 The legal profession

1921	1 British, 43 Arabs, 39 Jews
1928	96 Jewish lawyers in Tel Aviv, Jerusalem and Haifa
1936	2 British, 112 Arabs, 264 Jews

Note: The Peel Report (1937) commented that 'this number of advocates seems to be in excess of the needs of the country for strictly professional work' (p. 165)
Source: Strassman (1984)

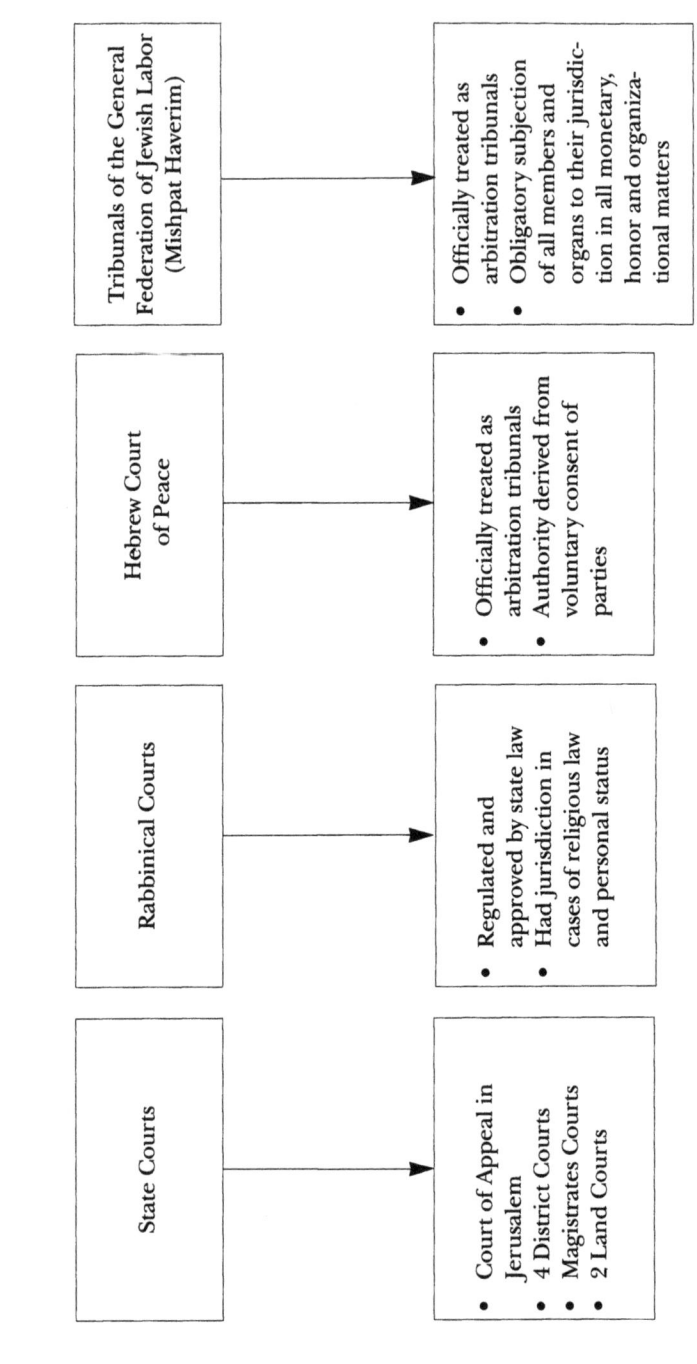

FIGURE 1   Courts for Jewish Population

FIGURE 2 Hebrew Courts of Peace: Organization

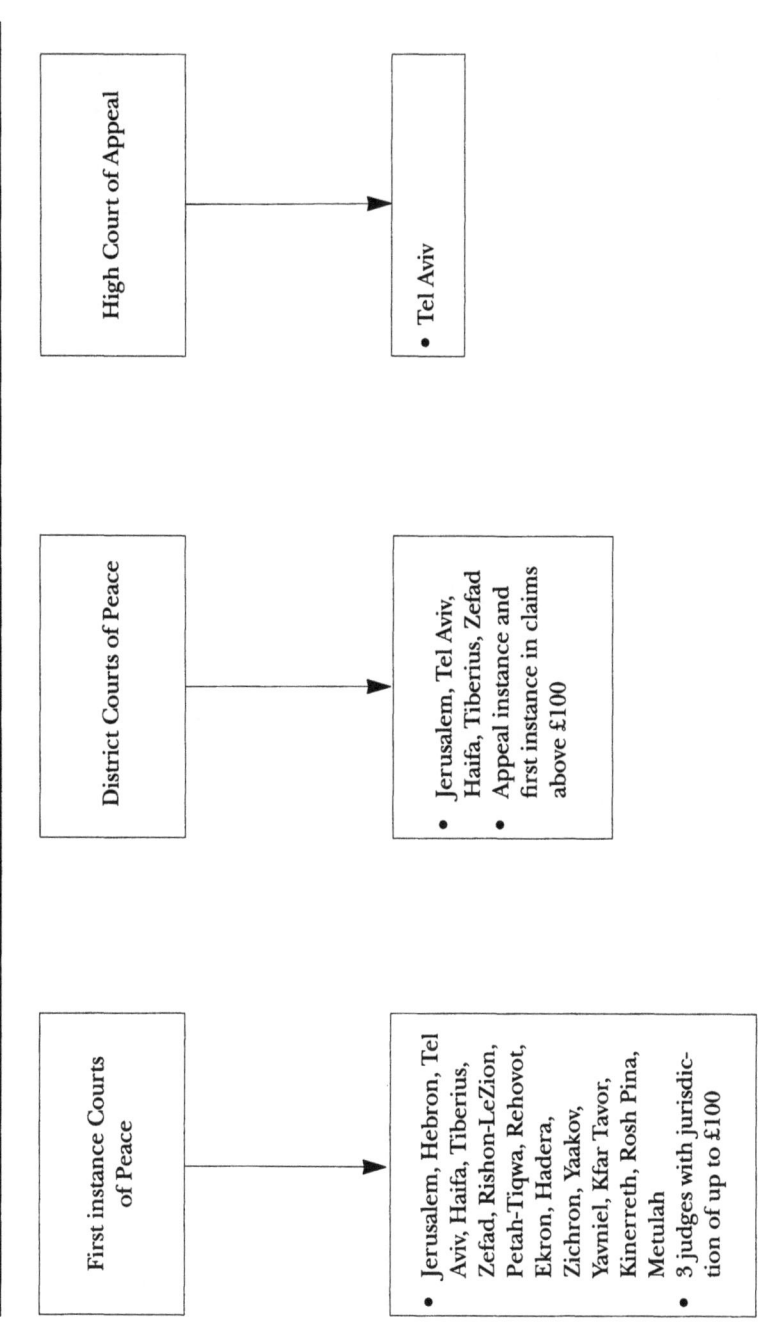

FIGURE 3 Comrades Law: Organization

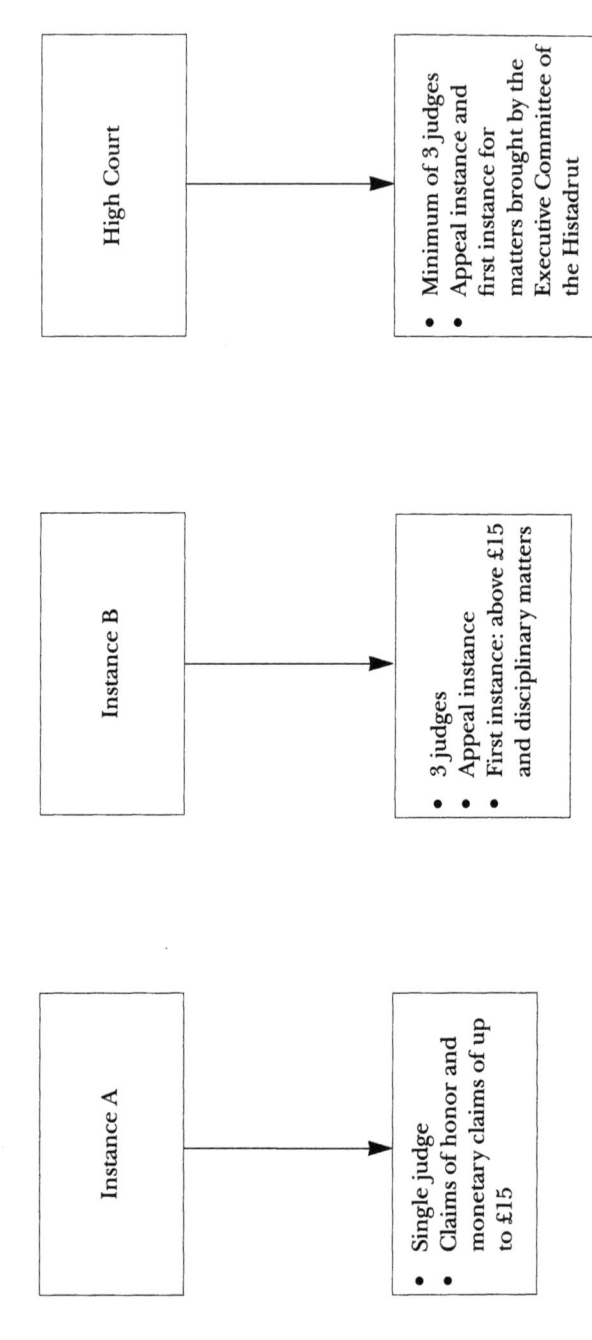

INTRODUCTION

I would like to think of this book as a particular exercise in the sociology of the 'nation.' I am interested in the conceptual and imaginative horizons within which people learn to think of themselves as a nation and learn to act as a nation towards themselves and towards others. Yet in speaking about a project of the imagination I by no means wish to suggest the primacy of ideas over action. On the contrary, I engage in a sociology which radically de-essentializes notions like nation and nationalism. I try to work from within that branch of sociology which seeks to ground the development of such notions in the immediate context of the social relations and concrete practices within which people make sense of the world around them, forever trying to level that 'sense' with the actual conditions and possibilities they confront and create. So when I speak about becoming a nation, or when I discuss versions of nationalism, I have in mind a set of experiences rather than a ready-made and obvious object of discourse. In this book, therefore, I try to develop various loosely connected themes about such competing experiences and the way they shape, and in turn are shaped by, the memory, interests, locations and positions of their carriers and bearers.

I treat law – loosely recognized in the operations of courts, texts, judges and lawyers – as one social arena in which the politics of national construction are enacted and negotiated. This book, in short, traces an attempt to conceive and to execute, through law and legal institutions, the possibility of reviving a nation. Of necessity, this attempt has consisted of a search for the very essence of that nation: locating its spatiality and temporality, its history and trajectory and its relation to others.

I consider a specific geo-social location: 1920s colonial Palestine, a time when, in tandem with the establishment of a British Mandatory government, the Zionist movement acted with new rigor to attain what the British formally promised: a Jewish national home. While this moment in history allows me to elaborate generally on the intersection of law, nationalism and colonialism, it also allows me to elaborate specifically on the intersection of Judaism, Zionism and the British colonial state of Palestine. It is between these two matrices that I move throughout, fusing with my call to bring the colonial state back into the study of Jewish nationalism my attempt to probe the statist trajectory of secular nationalism in Israel. In short, I try to deal with the hybridity of Zionism as a national movement: its ambivalence towards the Jewish religion, yet its inability to create a secular alternative to Judaism qua religion; its ambivalence towards British colonialism, yet its simultaneous construction of the Arab as an inferior being; its hostility towards the 'Jew in exile,' yet its self-perception as a vanguard of 'the West' in 'the East.'

I consider a specific case. I follow a group of jurist-nationalists who tried to establish what they defined as a national–secular legal system that would operate independently of British state law on the one hand and traditional Jewish law on the other. In concrete terms, they operated a set of community-based tribunals that were designed to be user-friendly and to employ relatively informal, yet 'New Hebrew' ways of solving private and public disputes. I show that ardent Zionists as they were, these people found themselves working against the grain, articulating views and making moves that were anathema to some key groups in the emergent Jewish colonizing community in Palestine. Their project, as well as the reactions that it drew from religious Zionists, from the emergent Jewish legal profession and from Zionist institutions at large, established a platform from which to examine some key issues in respect to the interplay of law and nationalism, law and colonialism, state law and alternative law, and, specifically, law and the Zionist–Jewish identity which had been in the process of assuming shape in colonial Palestine.

The book is non-linear in character. First among the set of themes which run throughout the text is my argument about Zionism's statist dispositions; the state, not only in its institutional dimension but also – at times mainly – as a totem and a symbol, became the epitome of the national project. I try to show that both the idea of the state and the disposition towards the state as an organizational matrix are crucial reference points for understanding the unstable Zionist orientation towards law and legality and, by extension, towards the very question of national identity. Within this general theme, I locate Zionist practices in general, and dispositions towards law in particular, in the context of the British colonial state in Palestine. I argue that the presence of the colonial state, materially and symbolically, is crucial for understanding the Zionist national-colonization project as a whole.

A second major theme in this text, which is in constant dialogue with the first, relates to the interplay of religion and secularism in Jewish nationalism. Here, competing narrations of law and about law serve to suggest alternative imaginations of what Judaism is all about. I play out these alternative imaginations (and this is a third theme of the text) while taking a close look at a system of law, the Hebrew Law of Peace. It is one that belongs within the general framework often referred to as an 'alternative,' 'community,' 'popular justice' system, uneasily located and shifting uncomfortably in its self-understanding between the imitation of state law and the invention of local, authentic ordering.

The fusion that ensues from bringing together these three themes serves as my guideline for saying something – insightful, I hope – about a post-colonial experience of law and nationalism. In the Jewish case, this attempt to work through law may turn out to be particularly significant. Consider the following:

> I gaze out over the nations of the modern world, and I see numerous scribblers of laws, but not a single legislator. But among the ancients I find no less than three legislators so outstanding as to deserve our special mention: Moses, Lycurgus, and Numa, all of whom concerned themselves mainly with matters that our doctors of learning would deem absurd. Yet each of them achieved a kind of success which, were it not so thoroughly supported by evidence, we should regard as impossible.
>
> The first of the three conceived and executed this astonishing fact: he founded the body of a nation, using for his materials a swarm of wretched fugitives who possessed no skills, no arms, no talents, no virtues, and no courage, and who, without an inch of territory to call their own, were truly a troop of outcasts upon the face of the earth. Moses made bold to transform this herd of servile emigrants into a political society, a free people; at a moment when it was still wandering about in the wilderness and had not so much as a stone to pillow its head on, he bestowed upon it the enduring legislation – proof against time, fortune, and conquest – that five thousand years have not sufficed to destroy or even weaken. Even today, when that nation no longer exists as a body, its legislation endures and is as strong as ever. Determined that his people should never be absorbed by other peoples, Moses devised for them customs and practices that could not be blended into those of other nations and weighed them down with rites and peculiar ceremonies. He put countless prohibitions upon them, all calculated to keep them constantly on their toes, and to make them, with respect to the rest of mankind, outsiders forever. Each

> fraternal bond that he established among the individual members of his republic became a further barrier, separating them from their neighbors and keeping them from becoming one with those neighbors. That is why this odd nation – so often subjugated, so often dispersed, so often, to all appearances, annihilated, but always utterly faithful to its law – has, scattered among other peoples but not absorbed by them, nevertheless preserved itself down into our own times. And that is why its custom, its laws, and its rites, live on – and, despite the hatred and persecution directed against it by all other men, will live on and on until the end of the world itself.[1]

The above words were written by Jean-Jacques Rousseau and in a way set the scene for this book.[2] Simply put, I pose a conundrum: at the height of establishing, reinventing, and dreaming the resurrection of a Jewish nation in Palestine, many Zionists rejected Jewish law, even at its renewed Hebrew-national appearance, and enthusiastically embraced the law of the British-governed colonial state of Palestine.

In the following chapters, therefore, legal arenas and practices are only a site or useful device, almost an excuse, for thinking about nationalism. Law is at once an expression of violence, an instrument of ordering and control and an expression of aspirations and memories at the collective level. Moreover, law is at once a popular and a professional arena, bringing together, often in tension, lay notions and expectations of justice and expert notions of rules, forms, and techniques. And, where tensions reign, meanings are revealed, allowing for the articulation of different perspectives and opinions and for the destabilization of the taken-for-granted.

As already mentioned, I have written in a non-linear fashion, allowing different chapters to open up new venues of inquiry concerning law and colonialism, law and popular justice, law and nationalism, law and secularism, law and the legal profession, and possible relations among all of these. In the first chapter, I set the stage for the return of the colonial state; in the second chapter I consider the invention of national tradition through law, and in the third chapter I try to establish some links between the first two chapters by looking at the legal ties to the colonial state. I then move to substance: in the fourth and fifth chapters I look at some of the efforts to constitute a national–secular Hebrew law that drew nonetheless on Jewish tradition, exposing the hybridity of the project and accounting for the way nationalism has served as its instrument of regimentation. In the sixth and seventh chapters, I look closely at the response of lawyers and political functionaries to the idea of an autonomous national Hebrew law. And in the final chapter I try to draw a more abstract socio-cultural picture, one which emerges from the story as a whole.

Throughout I integrate law-stories, episodes and at times examples from literary sources. In bringing these together, my intention is to allow readers to draw upon their imaginations and to let them choose from their own scholarly and perhaps literary reflections, without insisting on one single coherent lesson to be drawn from this study. My success in providing this opening is not, of course, for me to judge, yet I feel compelled to articulate this advance warning to readers.

In all probability readers will notice a romantic, possibly a naive, desire for another course that Zionism might have taken. There is a normative desire on my part to celebrate what the Hebrew Law of Peace offered – an opening for an anti-colonialist, non-statist, popular form of justice grounded in an alternative imagined 'authentic' and non-chauvinistic national past. To this extent, then, a certain loss of distance between researcher and subject will be noticeable. Yet, rather than uncritically celebrating a lost possibility, my intention has been to develop a second-order sociological imagination of the visions and projections and practices that accompanied the Hebrew Law of Peace. I base the journey which follows on the understanding that the discourse about community does not necessarily carry a genuine promise of solidarity and is not necessarily more humanizing than a statist discourse. The same principle holds also when applied to the discourse on modernized Judaism. In either case, such projects of the imagination are no less embedded in trajectories of power, jurisdiction, control, interests and authority. Thus, my intention has been not to argue that the possibility which I explore and at times 'help' to imagine would have been a 'better' one, but simply to develop the imagination of this vista as a means of enriching and problematizing the hybridity of Zionism.

CHAPTER 1

MANDATE PALESTINE: THE ENIGMA OF THE MISSING COLONIAL STATE

Zionist historiography rarely engages the constitutive role that the British Mandatory state in Palestine played in the history of Israel. The story of national revival is constructed around the crucial moment of transition from the pre-state period of the Yishuv – literally the Jewish colonizing community that settled in Palestine prior to independence – to that of state sovereignty. This Zionist story is about a radical break with the past. It is often cast in terms of a struggle: Zionists taking their destiny into their own hands and achieving independence by means of a successful struggle against both the Arabs and the British colonizers. The binary imagery underlying the Zionist narrative is strictly related to the political situation of the colonizing settlers: a pre-state state of being versus a state state of being. Consequently, the fact that there had been a fully functioning state in Palestine before 1948 (when the state of Israel was established) has been pushed to the sphere of collective amnesia.

There is a second story, however, one which is told by legal scholars and legal historians, outlined in legal texts and judicial decisions. This is a story about the origins of the Israeli legal system. It follows the law's development by tracing the legal systems and norms that preceded Jewish rule, namely the Ottoman (until 1917) and the British (1917–1948). This story describes Israeli law as primarily grounded in British legal traditions; it accounts for Israel's legal institutions in terms of the legacy of the colonial past, and minutely analyzes the legal mechanisms installed in 1948 in order to secure the smooth absorption of Mandatory law by the state of Israel. In this story, the absorption of British Mandatory law is taken for granted. It is perceived as an inevitable outcome flowing from law's universal commitment to stability, certainty and continuity. So smooth the transition seems to be, so willingly has the former colonial legal system been embraced by both the legal and political elites, that this second story stands in stark contrast to the first: here we are faced with a story which implies that nothing of significance happened in 1948.[1] Here, we have a tale of a smooth transition from one (colonial) state – controlled by the British – to another (colonial?) state – controlled by Jews – with little bearing, if any, on legal and, by extension, social, matters.

It is quite remarkable that the law of the colonial power, so despised and rejected in its last ruling phase, was naturalized in such a taken-for-granted manner. It would be plausible that a national movement, entirely preoccupied with the multiple aspects of national revival, with the reconstruction of the past and with projecting a new future for itself, would consider law to be one of the important mediums through which the national community could, and should, have asserted its vitality. We only need to look at Jewish education under colonial rule in order to get an analogous sense of importance. Although the British established and funded a national educational system, both Zionist and non-Zionist Jews insisted on maintaining their own autonomous schooling system. In fact, not one but four such systems were maintained by the Jewish community in Palestine, all (excluding the non-Zionist ultra-orthodox one) strongly committed to the idea that Hebrew education in general and the revival of the Hebrew language in particular were central components of the national project.

Indeed, colonial experience elsewhere also indicates the relative immunity of colonial law, especially the common law, to otherwise-strong nationalist and anti-colonialist sentiments. As Nathan J. Brown observes, "of all the institutions founded during the era of European imperialism, legal systems and courts have been the most enduring."[2] Still, this observation only begs the question which the following study aspires to address, mainly by looking at the role Zionist elites played in legitimating colonial law and rejecting the possibility of inventing an authentic national Hebrew law.[3]

In short, whereas in the first story the colonial Mandatory state has little relevance for understanding the Zionist project – except as its rejected external 'other' – the second story is grounded in the certainty that a functioning modern state has already been there, offering, among other state-provided goodies, a package deal of ready-made law and intact legal institutions. Whereas the first story portrays revolutionary protagonists whose trademark is the sword, the second story portrays humble state servants whose trademark is their ability to absorb, to inherit, and to serve, pens in their hands, as moderate innovators.

What are we to make of these two different stories? Can they tell us something about the relations of law and nationalism, or the interplay of law and culture? Can they help us in saying something about the nature of Jewish nationalism, that is, Zionism and its revival-of-the-Hebrew, project? The question, of course, is not which of these two stories 'got it right.' Rather, the challenge is to use the one to inform about the other and to thereby enrich and problematize the very notion of Zionism. To state the obvious, there is no single coherent 'Zionist narrative,' nor 'dominant Zionism,' nor 'mainstream Zionism,' and we should approach it as but a linguistic device that compels us, at times, to use such generic notions. What I have in mind, in short, is to look at Zionist versions, at Zionist negotiations over meanings, and at Zionist orientations, exploiting a so-called silenced version to highlight more vocal and arguably powerful ones.

In terms of the two generic stories I outlined above, I would like to use both as means for understanding the roots of a schizophrenic narrativity but also, and more ambitiously, of Israel's mostly silenced colonialist legacy and its bearing on the structure and dispositions of Israeli society.

My entry point is by coming to terms with the (ambiguous) epistemological status, so to speak, of the British Mandatory state that was established in Palestine in the wake of the First World War. On the margins of public and academic discourse, still barely noticeable, two writers have of late voiced a certain puzzlement over the role that England plays in Israel's imagery of its past. One of them, Tom Segev, reviewed an impressive two-volume collection of essays by prominent Israeli historians and sociologists who undertook to offer a fresh look at the 'History of the Jewish Community in Eretz-Israel Since 1882' – literally, a study of Jewish settlement in Palestine from the first wave of colonization in the late nineteenth century, both under Ottoman rule and later under the British Mandate, all the way to 1948, the year of independence.[4] Segev noted that the work's primary flow was that it had remained entirely oblivious to one fundamental question: Could the establishment of a Jewish state have been realized without the active support of Palestine's British rulers? Would it have been realized without the existence of a colonial blueprint that facilitated the operation and development of Zionist self-governing institutions? Ultimately, Segev's question is a call for reflexivity, addressed to the historians and social scientists of contemporary Israel: Do the British deserve the hostility that Zionist historiography typically displays towards them?[5]

Another political analyst, Meron Benvenishti, voiced a similar view. Following a recent visit of Ezer Weitzman – Israel's president and the nephew of Chaim Weitzman, the Zionist leader most clearly associated with an anglophile orientation (and himself Israel's first president) – to the United Kingdom, Benvenishti published an article in the daily,

Ha'Aretz, commenting on the fact that Weitzman's visit to the Queen had barely been noticed in the Israeli press. We live in a land where many are busy inventing and fabricating millennia-old stories and events, Benvenishti lamented, but we hardly give a second thought to our recent past. The whole complex history of relations between Zionism and the British Mandatory State in Palestine has been erased, often simply reduced to being one in which we, the Zionists, managed to kick a foreign invader out of our motherland. This myth of driving out the British empire of evil, he wrote, has been installed in the minds of Israelis by an educational system influenced by politicians whose finest youth memories were associated with their underground activities in the 1940s. Further, he wrote, we are content and comfortable with describing the state of Israel as an anti-colonialist product, aligning ourselves with other colonized peoples who successfully fought European imperialism, whereas

> The State of Israel was established only after the Jewish population had gathered sufficient strength to defeat the national Palestinian community. This acquisition of power would have been impossible if not for British rule over Palestine, and the twilight times of the White Book [British restrictions on Jewish immigration and land acquisition], of the struggle against illegal Jewish immigration, and of Lord Bevin, cannot overrule this fact. One need not be a hopeless anglophile in order to appreciate Britain's role in the history of the Zionist project and the attitude of its leaders to the idea of a Jewish nation returning to its historical land.[6]

It was with and through the existence of a British colonial-style Mandatory regime in Palestine that the Zionist project advanced. It was the might of the British army that crushed the Palestinian national uprising in the second half of the 1930s, and it was British imperialism, Benvenishti observed, that turned a god-forsaken province into a modern state.[7]

The British entered Palestine as an imperial power and established the Mandatory state in line with the administrative blueprint of a Crown colony. The civil administration was composed of experienced civil servants and colonial officers who moved to Palestine from colonies such as Cyprus, Mauritius, Rhodesia, Malta, and Sudan. This administration re-organized Palestine as a distinct geographical entity, giving it coherent spatial dimensions, establishing Jerusalem as an administrative capital, and building an infrastructure of roads, railways and ports in line with colonial interests and imperial strategic imperatives. This colonial legacy of state-formation deeply affected the governmentality of the state of Israel. Not only did it shape the organization of the civil service, the judiciary, the legislature, and the police, writes one enthusiast, but it also infused the "spirit" of British administrative traditions into the state machinery of Israel.[8]

To be sure, Segev and Benvenishti were not disclosing new facts.[9] How could they, in light of the Balfour Declaration and the Mandate for Palestine entrusted to Britain by the Council of the League of Nations? On 2 November 1917, the British government published a statement of policy in the form of a letter from Lord Balfour, Secretary of State for Foreign Affairs, to Lord Rothschild. The letter, known as the Balfour Declaration, expressed His Majesty's government's "sympathy with Jewish Zionist aspirations" and declared that it viewed "with favour the establishment in Palestine of a National Home for the Jewish People" and would "facilitate the achievement of this object." The Mandate for Palestine, as approved by the Council of the League of Nations, endorsed in its preamble the Balfour Declaration. Article 2 of the Mandate stated: "The Mandatory shall be responsible for placing the country under such political, administrative, and economic conditions as will secure the establishment of the Jewish national home, as laid down in the preamble, and the development of self-governing institutions, and also for safeguarding the civil and religious rights of all the inhabitants of Palestine, irrespective of race and religion."[10]

In fact, all major historical studies of Zionism deal, in one way or another, with the nature of the Mandate and with the relations between Zionism and the British government in London and in Palestine. Furthermore, the premise from which at least some analyses take off is that the hegemonic Zionist narrative of conflict with colonial Great Britain is in fact at odds with the most basic orientation of political Zionism. The Zionist national movement always sought the protection of one imperialist power or another, well aware that the Jewish community, being a minority in Palestine, could not have realized its goals without the internationally legitimate physical and material authoritative presence of an imperial power. Zionist leaders, therefore, targeted British policies when these were perceived to be at odds with the Mandate's original commitments, but understood very well the principled necessity of retaining British colonial rule over Palestine. None of the various schools and factions within the Zionist movement, at least until well into the 1940s, ever questioned the necessity of cooperating with Great Britain; and even the most militant wings had more faith in the colonization powers of England than in the colonizing abilities of the Zionists on their own.[11]

How then – in light of the above constitutive documents and the analyses that do exist in regard to the policies to which they gave rise – can one argue that the role of British colonialism in facilitating the

Zionist project has been silenced and ignored? The answer to this question, obviously, does not lie in the mere disclosure of facts, but in understanding the relative weight of these facts in historical studies, the nature of their conceptualization in sociological studies, and the way the facts are inscribed, or dis-scribed, in public memory.

What is most often discussed are British *policies* in Palestine – overwhelmingly those policies with direct bearing on the core business of Zionism: immigration, settlement and land acquisition. It is around the politics of colonization – that touched upon the changing degrees of implementation of the basic British promise to facilitate a Jewish national home – that discussions and studies are organized, mainly analyzing the effect these policies had on the activities of Zionist organizations and movements (e.g., organized 'illegal' Jewish immigration in defiance of governmental restrictions). Little attention had been given to the effect that the colonial experience had, not simply on Zionism's strategic diplomatic possibilities, but on the Palestinian Zionist movement's social and cultural character: the types and structures of social relations that it enabled or dis-abled within the Jewish community, the cultural and political orientations and dispositions it facilitated, and the bearing of these on Israel's relations with its relevant significant 'others', namely, the Arab world and the Palestinians.

Too little attention has also been given to the basic fact that the British, aided by all their colonial experience elsewhere, created and installed a functioning state in Palestine: a rather advanced web of administrative apparatuses and governmental departments, a sound infrastructure and, of course, a fully developed, ready-to-use legal system. The colonial state, whether as an occupational force or civil administrator, became a major player, creating the constitutive blueprint within which other actors moved, acted, and thought; an active player to which one had to respond and whose rules and guidelines one had to follow.[12]

Off-hand remarks beg elaboration. Thus, for example, when historian Anita Shapira writes about the 1920s, she briefly mentions the fact that

> if it had not been for Herbert Samuel [the first High Commissioner for Palestine], who initiated basic infrastructural development projects in Palestine – in particular the construction of a network of roads, a project that provided the majority of Pioneers of the Third Aliah [the Zionist terminology for the early 1920s wave of colonization] with gainful employment in 1920 and 1921 – most of the young immigrants would have been compelled to leave the country.[13]

Yet little is known and understood about the distributive and redistributive functions of the colonial state, about the way its laws shaped communal identities, reorganized and regulated land ownership and control, about the way it regulated labor relations, about the way it orchestrated and helped structure class relations and class divisions, about the way it facilitated, or inhibited, the development of agricultural and industrial cooperatives, about the ways in which it authorized or de-authorized the development of self-governing institutions and loci of political power at the local level (e.g., municipalities), about the way it was conducive to urbanization, about its policies of governmental recruitment (which structured the civil service bureaucratic classes), or about the way it shaped the economic landscape through its system of tariffs and taxation. The works addressing these issues have been undertaken almost exclusively by a handful of economists, while sociologists, political scientists, legal scholars and historians have largely remained silent with respect to all this.[14] Concrete governmental practices – embodying the simple fact that the colonial state was 'there,' not as a passive observer, but as an active player – have been shunned in the history of Jewish nationalism and its state-building project.

The case of law is perhaps one of the most conspicuous examples of this silencing. Law is a primary language of the state and the foundational discursive means for bringing about 'rights, duties and order.' Although the second 'story' referred to at the beginning of this chapter is totally embedded in and indebted to British Mandatory law, that legal scholarship has been predominantly doctrinal and as such entirely ignorant of this law's broader socio-cultural and political implications. Yet imposing a new legal system is arguably one of "the most important, convincing, and successful cultural forms of colonialism."[15] Cultural, writes Dirks, not 'merely' political.

The Palestine Order in Council of 1922 enjoined the civil courts to exercise jurisdiction "in conformity with the Ottoman Law in force in Palestine on 1st November 1914," but it also stipulated that on top of this system of laws the courts were to respect new ordinances and regulations to be enacted by the colonial state in the future and, further, to adjudicate "in conformity with the substance of the common law and the doctrines of equity in force in England."

"By the mid-thirties," writes Shachar, "the law-book of Palestine was equipped with English-oriented 'ordinances' for every aspect of modern commerce."[16] In the law of contracts, English doctrines were superimposed upon the fairly comprehensive Ottoman law which remained in effect. In other areas, like the law of torts, British judges reasoned that the local culture of the native population was too remote from the British one to allow for the imposition of civil remedies for injuries.[17] In either case, British-governed courts were actively dispensing "the new truths of colonial rule."[18]

In India, the introduction of a novel legal system allowed the colonial state to frame a new structure of landholding and property rights. "When the British consolidated their position in South India in the late eighteenth century," writes Dirks, "they immediately began to introduce a political economy in which both relations among Indians themselves and between the Indians and the colonial government would be regulated according to law and new forms of property."[19] In Palestine, the colonial government used the law to regulate and reorganize registration of rights to land and the rules governing their transfer. In fact, the Land Transfer Ordinance of 1920 – which provided that transfer of land should be invalid unless registered in the state-controlled land records[20] – is one of the earliest pieces of legislation enacted by the new colonial rulers.

In the name of imposing order, the British made several efforts to reorganize the system of land transfer, to carry out a land survey, and to establish centralized land registration procedures in Palestine. While these policies were in line with the imperial tradition of bringing a 'Western-type' of order to colonies, the British were also pressured to undertake such tasks by Zionist organizations. Zionist colonizers, it seems, realized the critical importance of this colonialist practice, which would have allowed them to identify lands in which to settle and to locate lands for purchase. "By the end of the 1920s," writes Kedar, "in response to requests from Zionist organizations, the British launched a comprehensive survey and registration of lands in Palestine. This process was based on an Australian method (Torrens) which had been designed to address the needs of colonizing nations." The Torrens method and the colonial ordinances that followed provided the legalistic framework through which Arab–Palestinian lands were to be massively appropriated by the state of Israel in the years to come.[21] In short, the colonial state, through its system of courts, legislative acts, and common-law orientation, played an active part in assigning rights and duties, attributing identities, drawing cultural distinctions, and redistributing social and economic resources. Still, studies of Zionist history by and large relegated the British in Palestine to a passive, background role, as if their presence there constituted no more than the (admittedly) well-choreographed stage upon which the Zionists self-orchestrated and managed the affairs of the nation-and-state-building project.

Nation and narration, as Homi Bhaba suggests, are mutually constitutive. We are faced here with an ideological-methodological bind that needs to be disentangled. Methodologically, the Yishuv – the Jewish settler community in Palestine – has been treated in most studies as the primary unit of analysis, thereby referring both to the Arab–Palestinian community and to the British Mandatory state as "external systems" with little bearing on the internal dynamics of the Yishuv; only the latter considered crucial for making sense of state and society in Israel.

This methodological approach corresponds to a narrative that celebrates the nation's revival as an auto-emancipatory project. State-and-nation-building practices perhaps inevitably require the types of narration that place the nationalist protagonists center-stage. These protagonists – when it comes to imagining an awakening nation – are those who actually settle the land, dream its liberation, and promote the realization of this dream. An essential part of a nation-building process seems to be the idea of taking one's fate into one's own hands; in fact, it is a necessary element in the very ability to imagine the nation and to inscribe its reality into the collective memory and the collective practices of the present.

This narration, moreover, provides a cleansed, self-explanatory and morally justified basis for the construction of a given national identity. This identity is thereby shielded from the exigencies of, say, conflict with hostile or threatening natives, and from being shaped through bonds with other, remote, colonizing powers. Rather, one's identity, as much as one's fate, is solely dependent on one's own deeds and on relations with other brothers and sisters of fate. In such a narration, finally achieving the status of independent state must necessarily be conceived in terms of revolution, the fruit of a struggle, something that had to be won, not granted. And the former rulers, typically, are re-conceived in terms of oppressors, of those with whom one had to struggle to achieve liberation. Such a narration, in short, breeds either the marginalization and silencing of the former rulers' contributions to the national project or their recharacterization as foreign oppressors who had to be overcome. Or both.

Likewise, such narrations of the national self and the collective experience ease the burden of having to come to terms with the fact that one group's story of liberation is, as so often happens, another's story of enslavement. The tragedy of the other is suspended, treated as an external factor to be analyzed and understood and judged without being inscribed into one's national history and identity. In Zionist historiography, this is most evident in the way the Jewish–Palestinian conflict has been analyzed. In fact, the conflict has been dealt with as a separate script, a plot that evolved and developed on the margins of the primary script, one which concerned the actions and interactions of Jews among themselves. The state-building story has often been told from a perspective that does not situate the nature and structure of Jewish society in the context of an ongoing struggle with the Palestinians. Studies of Israeli society often follow one of two lines. One tells the story of Zionist settlers who single-handedly created a Jewish society in Palestine. The other traces the development of the conflict between the Jews and the Arabs, depicting the latter as fundamentally hostile to, or at least suspicious of, Jewish settlement. These two versions rarely intersect, although the Israeli–Arab conflict wrote itself into the culture and institutions of Israeli society, and this inscription is still valid today. The nation-building story is often accounted for in idealistic terms: the nation realizing centuries-old aspirations which came of age with the appearance of modern Jewish nationalism in late-nineteenth-century Europe; and analyses that follow thus 'compare' these ideals with actual 'achievements' and performances.

A number of social thinkers, however, have moved from such idealistic accounts to material analyses, accounting for the actual colonization practices that were invoked in response to material possibilities and political circumstances and evaluating the process of national formation in the context of relations with the Arab Palestinian population.[22] This analytical shift, in turn, situates both Jewish–Arab relations and Jewish nationalism within the theoretical discourse of colonialism, a point to which I shall return shortly. What these thinkers offer is a 'first wave' of sociological and historical revisionism. It is a first wave not in a generational and chronological sense, but in terms of its heightened sensitivity to one major issue: the under-studied relation between the Jewish–Arab conflict (or relations, for that matter) and the social, political, cultural, and economic structure of Israeli society. These scholars critically scrutinize and reevaluate heretofore dominant analytic frameworks for studying the Yishuv, such as the 'dual society' model suggested by functionalist sociologists.

Dan Horowitz and Moshe Lissak, sociologists of the functionalist school, argued that the case of Palestine required a unique (and arguably not comparable) analytic model because of the "significant difference in level of modernization between the Arab majority and the Jewish minority."[23] They ruled out the relevance of Western colonization models because these "described societies with a unified economic structure encompassing parts of the developed and the underdeveloped components."[24] In contrast, they argued that Palestine comprised two national populations radically segregated in all spheres of life: political, economic, cultural, and demographic.

The dual society paradigm, in turn, allowed Horowitz and Lissak to dissociate Zionism from the general history of colonialism. They wrote:

> Two populations so different from one another can exist in the same territorial framework in only one of two ways. The two populations can be aligned in the same hierarchy, with the more

> 'developed' population (according to generally accepted indices of modernization) located in the upper stratum and the less developed in the lower stratum. Or, each population can maintain a hierarchy of its own, which implies that the populations are, to a considerable extent, segregated from each other. The first pattern often developed in areas of European migration and settlement and in colonial societies, such as South Africa and Rhodesia. In Mandatory Palestine, however, a social structure of the second type developed, a circumstance without parallel in the annals of European settlement in the underdeveloped colonial territories. The critical difference between the two patterns may be attributed to the difference between a movement propelled by economic or imperial drives and one motivated by an ideology which combined a call for the political and cultural renaissance of a people and an aspiration for its social and economic transformation.[25]

Thus these sociologists were able to articulate an elaborate sociohistoric account of the origins of the Israeli polity which told the story of the colonizing community as an almost entirely self-made one, the Zionists being radically segregated from the Arabs, 'free' to develop their own stratification system, collective settlements, urban centers, and self-governing political institutions.

"Underpinning this interpretation," writes Zachary Lockman, "is an implicit or explicit representation of the Arab and Jewish communities in Palestine as essentially separate, coherent, and self-evidently cohesive entities that developed along entirely distinct paths ... The matrix of Arab–Jewish relationships and interactions in Palestine, and more broadly the local (largely Arab) environment in which the Yishuv and the Zionist project developed, are thereby defined a priori not as formative but as essentially marginal and limited in impact."[26] Still in the making, then, an emerging post-colonialist and post-Zionist research agenda aspires to replace the 'dual society' paradigm with a 'relational' approach which argues for a closer examination of the actual relations between Arabs and Jews and the way those relations have been shaped in the context of colonial rule. In fact, from this perspective, the framework of analysis is one that treats *both* Arabs and Jews as colonized people under British rule, a theme to which I shall come back later on.

Still, a 'second wave' of revision is called for, involving yet another missing link: the British colonial state in Palestine. Establishing this missing element is particularly urgent precisely in the light of attempts to conceptualize the Zionist project in terms of the comparative theory of colonialism. Gershon Shafir, for example, follows a typology of four types of colonial societies: an occupation colony, a mixed colony, a plantation colony, and a pure-settlement colony.[27] The first, the occupation colony, is distinct from the others in that it is exclusively concerned with military and administrative control over a strategically important territory, and not with extensive settlement. The other three relate to different types of social relations between colonizers and colonized, principally conceptualized in relation to the evolving nature of the labor market and the typical forms of land use. The Jewish settler community in Palestine is analyzed in light of these classifications and is eventually classified as a 'pure settlement colony;' that is, a colonizing society in which employers and employed belong to the same ethnic group, and one in which that ethnic group has effective control over the land in ways that enable it to extract and utilize its resources. Shafir uses this model in order to explain the origins of a split labor market in Palestine, essentially arguing that the Zionist colonization of Palestine was based on a dual strategy of ethnic exclusion: acquiring Arab-owned land (and nationalizing it in order to prevent a reversal of the process) and establishing a Hebrew Labor Union Federation that provided labor opportunities independent of the need to compete with cheaper Arab labor. Consequently, these strategies inhibited the development of Jewish–Arab workers' solidarity and preempted the future option of an integrated economy.

In passing, Shafir also refers to the role of Great Britain. First, he notes that from a British standpoint, Palestine was meant to be, and in fact had been, an occupation colony, not intended for settlement but for military utilization. Second, he writes that colonizing settlers elsewhere have been typically backed by the military and political might of colonial powers. Jewish settlers, however, "did not enjoy such protection. Conditions conducive to such Jewish settlement had been created at the inception of the British Mandate," he writes, "but did not last for long."[28] Ultimately, Shafir asks: "How did the Zionist movement manage to create a society, and later a state, in spite of the fact that it lacked the capitalist and military means available to the European colonial powers?" His answer (although he mentions briefly that British support did play some role in the process) mainly emphasizes the 'creative pragmatism' of the settlers themselves.[29] In this respect, the colonization model suggested by Shafir strengthens the hegemonic self-perception of Zionism as a story of settlers who took their fate into their own hands. In other words, Shafir also ends up with a principled distinction between Zionism and imperialist colonialism elsewhere, an approach not unlike that of more ardent Zionist writers.

A case in point is Ahronson's distinction between colonization and colonialism.[30] Ahronson argues that Zionism had been a *colonizing* movement, but not a *colonialist* one. This analytical distinction is remarkable in that it involves the naturalization and depoliticization of the first term and the statization of the second. Colonization is defined as "an essentially geographic phenomenon, consisting of immigration to another country and the establishment of new settlements in that country, different in their character from the local settlements:" while colonialism is defined as "a political and economic phenomenon whose primary properties are the takeover of territory and population by another state and their appropriation for the benefit of that state."[31] In the "land of Israel (i.e., Palestine)," Ahronson writes, "there had been a complete separation between the [colonial] rulers and Jewish colonization."[32] Ahronson thereby complements Horowitz and Lissak's "dual society" paradigm with yet another structural duality, this time between Jews and British. We may therefore see here the ideological outcomes of not taking the colonial state into account. For a Zionist historian, the analytic distinction between colonization and colonialism facilitates a process of moral cleansing, dissociating Zionist colonization – colonization having been defined in 'objective' (for example, 'geographical') terms – from the evils associated with, on the one hand, the backing of a colonial power, and, on the other hand, the colonialist legacy of excluding and oppressing local peoples.

Zionist historiography, then, consists of colonialism twice removed: first from Jewish–Arab relations and second from the Jewish–Arab colonialist structural bond. In bringing the colonial state back in, I propose to conceive of these latter relations through the concept of *dual colonialism*. While the British rulers of Palestine created a political and economic infrastructure, a functioning civil administration and a state-run legal system, the Zionist immigrants purchased lands, created mechanisms for drawing more immigrants, and developed self-governing institutions for the explicit purpose of a future takeover of the state apparatus.

It is interesting to see how this duality was perceived by the British. Commenting on Jewish immigration to Palestine – facilitated and regulated by the colonial Department of Migration – the 1937 Palestine Royal Commission Report to the Secretary of State for the Colonies (the Peel Report), stated that

> ... the Jewish population, which was reckoned at about 55,000 in 1918, had risen by March, 1925, to 108,000. This increase meant more than a difference in numbers: it meant a difference in character. There was more variety now not only in the provenance of the immigrants but in their type and outlook [modern and traditional, Western and oriental, educated and uneducated, workers and merchants, religious and secular, progressives and communists,

were some of the distinctions offered] ... Thus already the unique character of Jewish colonization in Palestine was plain. The colonies of the New World were mostly founded by settlers of a single nation, drawn mainly from the working or lower middle class and not of very varied occupations. The Jewish immigrants came from a variety of different countries, and represented all classes and activities. *Their settlement resembled that colonization by a complete society in miniature – a slice through all its strata – which the Colonial Reformers in England in the early nineteenth century dreamed of but never realized.* [emphasis added][33]

Horowitz and Lissak, in fact, came close to recognizing this dual model of colonialism when they asserted that "as a new society, the Yishuv did not experience the collapse of an indigenous political system following colonial conquest. On the contrary, British Mandatory rule, at least in its early stages, actually assisted the process of institution building in the Yishuv through formal recognition of the national institutions and cooperation with them."[34] Still, having granted that, they moved on to discuss the political institutions that were developed by the Jewish community and to treat those, and only those, as the foundation for the independent Jewish state to come.

Dual colonialism serves as a conceptual framework for understanding Palestine as both a Jewish settlers' colony and a British Crown colony. While the former population was active in the concrete material practices of colonization, the latter provided the political, legal, and administrative colonial umbrella. Yet this does not mean that the latter may be treated as a mere superstructure, reflecting or perhaps responding to practices at the base. It does not follow, moreover, that the two projects harmoniously complemented each other, combining to produce a functional division-of-colonization-labor. On the contrary, relations between the political and the social colonizers of Palestine fluctuated between cooperation and animosity, were marred by suspicion and hostility, and were, in general, ambivalent and conflictive.

This ambiguous relationship could be appreciated even at the most mundane level. The British did not quite know whether to treat the Jews as 'natives' and to couple them with the 'traditionally oriented Arabs', or to treat them as 'equals' who had acquired 'modern dispositions' in their European places of origin. An American journalist, traveling in Palestine in the late 1920s, offered the following telling observation:

> The English want to be just, and try to be just, in Palestine. But they feel at home with the Arabs as they do not, and probably never can, feel at home with the Jews. These Arabs are natives in the real sense of the word. They behave as the English have found

> natives behaving in other parts of the earth. They are indigenous to their own strange soil. Therefore the English know what to do with them and how to treat them. They can play their pipes as they have played them in a hundred lands.
>
> ... the English, as the governing authorities of Palestine, do not like the Jews as a subject population. In fact, they do not know what to make of them, as in all their imperial experience they have never had to deal with people of just this kind before. As comprising a part, and a large part, of the inhabitants of the country, the Jews must of course be classified as natives. But they do not seem like natives. They are acquainted with Western culture; they are themselves cultured, in the true English sense of the word; many of them speak the English language, and are familiar with English ways. What is more, these Jews do not act like natives. They are not submissive, and obedient, and grateful for benefits received ... The Jews are trouble-makers ... and thus are regarded by the English ... with the active dislike of a superior class for an inferior class which does not know and keep its place.[35]

A curious inversion occurs here. 'Home,' for English colonizers, had been that colony where clear cultural boundaries demarcated colonizers from colonized, in ways that allowed the East to be made "Europe's other, a land of exotic beings and exploitable riches that could service the economy and the imagination of the West."[36] Zionism, in that respect, prefigured in the English mind as a strange competitor, vying for the status of a colonizer while still subject to British colonial rule; at any rate one which disturbed the binary oppositions on the validity of which colonialism rested. Yet the fact that relations and attitudes had been ambiguous and tense had little to do with the structural reality in which British and Jews acted *on* Palestine – by different means – as colonizers.

Zionism's narrative of denial – in respect to the constitutive role the colonial state played in its own history – has been grounded precisely in these ambiguous relations between the two colonizing forces of Palestine. This narrative of denial is not simply a function of the desire to emphasize political independence as a crucial revolutionary moment which marks a radical break with an oppressive past (important as that is for asserting the new collective identity). This narrative of denial is also a product of the hybrid nature of the Zionist immigrants' cultural experience in Palestine. I am thinking of the hybridity bred of the experience of being situated as both colonizer and colonized. As colonizers, due to the nature of Jewish immigration to Palestine, they aimed at the eventual establishment of a 'National Home' for Jews through an alliance with a colonial power, resulting, eventually, in the displacement of the Arabs; and they experienced being the colonized in the *double* sense of living under colonial rulers who often treated them as 'natives,' regardless of Jewish 'credentials' to the contrary, and – most crucially – of belonging to a Hebrew nation that had been culturally and politically colonized for centuries. It is the assertion of the latter experience, in particular, which was of utmost importance to the existential and epistemological foundations of Zionism. In fact, the experience of being colonized, and its systematic articulation and circulation, has been a powerful tool for the very possibility of imagining the unity and coherence of a nation that had been subjected to the disarray of territorial dispersion. Thus the Zionist experience in Palestine was one in which the boundaries between a person's situation as a colonizer and a person's situation as colonized were blurred and confused both internally and externally. This experience, among other things, bred a refusal to situate the nation-building project within the context of the colonial state.

At the same time, the presence of the Arabs as the 'official' native population of Palestine (in both British and Zionist eyes), enhanced yet another type of overriding cultural experience. The Zionist national movement (with a few exceptions, which have been constantly marginalized to the point of utter silence) had been premised on a cultural alliance with the West, imagining itself as part of it, notwithstanding the fact that this West in itself had to be imagined (Zionism essentially being of Eastern European origins that had little to do with some of the core components associated with that West). Although some of the Zionist texts of the 1920s, premised as they were on an Orientalist discourse, treated the Arabs as exemplars of an authentic Eastern culture that would eventually overwhelm the exhausted and degenerate West, other Zionists by and large produced a 'Europe versus Asia' narrative in which the Zionists functioned as the vanguard for European nations who faced a primitive Asian East that had yet to be modernized and civilized.[37]

It was in 1914, when Palestine was still ruled by the Ottoman empire, that Weitzman – a Zionist leader – wrote, "Palestine is the natural extension of Egypt and the buffer zone that separates the Suez Canal from the Black Sea, and in any hostility … it can become Asian Belgium. Especially if it would be developed by the Jews."[38] In the years to follow, more and more Jews came to live in Palestine, and later in Israel, through the confusing experience of being in the 'Middle East' (a British colonialist geo-political perspective of the globe, to be sure), but acting as if they shared borders with the Netherlands – or Belgium, for that matter.

Both the people and the landscape of Palestine provided the contours for this cultural alliance. The land had been depicted as *vacuum domicilum* – an empty, barren and neglected space that was yet to be redeemed. And the Arab, accordingly, had been depicted as rootless, passive, primitive, and lacking in national character.[39]

David Malouf, in his novel *Remembering Babylon*, describes the experience of British settlers in early nineteenth-century Australia along lines that resonate strongly with what I have in mind. Malouf's powerful exposition confuses us by reversing roles and inverting sensations in ways that make us forget who rules whom and who is to fear whom. He describes the colonizing settlement as a ghetto within the bounds of which the colonizers live in perpetual fear of the surrounding outside. It is Gemmy, an English-turned-native person, who one day ventures out into their settlement, who disturbs the settlers' shaky sense of identity as distinct and superior. At the time Gemmy appeared:

> the country he had broken out of was all unknown to them. Even in full sunlight it was impenetrably dark ... and all around, before and behind, worse than weather and the deepest night, natives, tribes of wandering myalls who, in their traipsing this way and that all over the map, were forever encroaching on boundaries that could be insisted on by daylight – a good shotgun saw to that – but in the dark hours, when you no longer stood there as a living marker with all the glow of the white man's authority about you, reverted to being a creek-bed or ridge of granite like any other, and gave no indication that six hundred miles away, in the Lands Office in Brisbane, this bit of country had a name set against it on a numbered document, and a line drawn that was empowered with all the authority of the Law.[40]

And it is Mr Frazer, the humble amateur surveyor of the land, who, aided by Gemmy, is driven to write down the following confession in his field-book:

> We have been wrong to see this continent as hostile and infelicitous, so that only by the fiercest stoicism, a supreme resolution and force of will, and by felling, clearing, sowing with the seeds we have brought with us, and by importing sheep, cattle, rabbits, even the very birds of the air, can it be shaped and made habitable. It is habitable already. I think of our early settlers, starving on these shores in the midst of plenty they did not recognize, in a blessed nature of flesh, fowl, fruit that was all around them and which they could not, with their English eyes, perceive, since the very habit and faculty that makes apprehensible to us what is known and expected dulls out our sensitivity to other forms, even the most obvious. We must rub our eyes and look again, clear our minds of what we are looking for to see what is there. [41]

To the Zionist – regardless of what the British thought or did – the Arabs served as a constant reminder of difference and, moreover, as a reference point in relation to which the British were culturally and historically, almost geographically (in a metaphorical sense), in closer proximity to the Jews than the Arabs could ever be.

This dual colonialism, therefore, is a concept which captures not only the political but also the cultural dimension of the Zionist–English missing link. Amitav Ghosh, an Indian writer, writes about the experience of his father as a soldier in the British Army. At one point, he describes the shame and anger of Indian officers upon realizing that the army discriminated against them on account of their race. Ghosh then offers the following insight:

> The discovery of invisible barriers and ceilings disillusioned them with their immediate superiors, but it did not make them hostile to Western institutions. Rather, these encounters with racism served to convince them – as they had an entire generation of Westernized Indians – that the British colonial regime was not Western enough, not progressive enough. [they] ... held Gandhi in personal respect, but they generally had little patience with his critiques of Western science and economics. In this, as in so much else, they were closer to their European contemporaries than to their own compatriots.[42]

In trying to make sense of the 'colonial experience,' a distinction has to be drawn between Britain as a colonial power (an imagined cluster of potentially oppressive practices) and Britain as a representative of the 'West' (an imagined cluster of distinct values and institutions). I think there are some striking similarities with the Indian experience here. In Palestine, especially in the crucial first decade of British rule, England was experienced and viewed by Zionists not as a *colonialist*-repressive presence but as a *Western*-liberating presence, with which they could identify without having to compromise their identity as colonized people aspiring to liberation. Hence a second, overlapping 'narrative of denial' characteristic of Zionism, namely one which denied the colonialist nature of British rule itself.

Replacing the notoriously inefficient and corrupt Ottoman government, the British were seen as bearers of civilization who promised to turn Palestine from a neglected backward province into a modern state, not simply one with a modern infrastructure, a modern civil service, and functioning health and education systems, but also with certain cultural dispositions and 'civilities.'

In writing about Indian historiography, writers like Gyan Prakash and Partha Chatterjee have distinguished the orientalist phase from the nationalist one. The orientalist historiography, largely provided by British enthusiasts for the wonders of India, "created the spiritual and sensuous Indian as an opposite of the materialist and rational British," and portrayed an unchanging and passive Indian – standing outside history, so to speak – as a justification for British conquest.[43] Nationalist historiography, on the other hand, ushered in by Indian writers, challenged the orientalist representations by drawing on some Orientalists' findings concerning India's glorious past. These nationalists 'discovered' ancient India as providing the true origin of the nation-state. Thus, these historians thought in European terms about India's past in order to advance anti-colonial claims. On the one hand, "they thought of India ... as a cradle for reason, progress, and modernity. On the other hand, the assertion of nationhood demanded the projection of a distance from Europe."[44] In short, to use Chatterjee's terms,[45] Indian nationalism worked from within an Orientalist 'thematic:' the nationalists, while celebrating the authenticity of their cultural heritage, opposed colonialism in the name of reason, modernity, and other enlightenment concepts. They were, like Ghosh's father, more Western than their colonial rulers.

However, this was not the case in Palestine simply because Zionism had never been based on "the projection of a distance from Europe" and had never had to challenge colonial representations of its past and present. On the contrary, the Zionists largely shared the orientalist frame of reference, although with their own contradictions concerning the Jewish past. In the case of Jewish nationalism, the challenge had been that of establishing proximity to an ancient distant past while simultaneously creating a distance from the recent one. The distant past was to be imagined and celebrated as embodying all the essentials of a 'healthy' nation, namely, political sovereignty and cultural unity. The proximate past, the past of the present, so to speak – consisting of centuries of Jewish existence in numerous dispersed communities in exile – was to be rejected, denied, and despised as an 'uncivilized' and 'abnormal' form of living. It was the exilic Jew against which Zionism asserted the identity of the new Hebrew in Palestine. And the distance sought from this conceptual Jew-in-exile was based precisely on the fact that it was lacking in national spirit and an active and rational orientation to life, living, in short, as a rootless nomad outside history. In all this, the West – embodying the project of modernity and, most important, of nationalism – had always been a reference point for the future, while the ancient past, with its own unique forms of sovereignty, affirmed the nation's distinct authentic spirit.

Not distance from the West, but rather an asserted distance from the Jews' own past in the West, then, was to be the essential building-block of

Jewish nationalism. The new Hebrew nation, in this sense at least, was founded through a project of negation. Moreover, this project consisted of patterns of thinking about the Jews in Europe in terms of passivity, dependence, and even cultural decadence. The renewed Hebrew, the nationalistic Jew, escaped this imagined identity not simply by establishing a distance from the Jew-in-exile, but also through an act of transference in which the Arab was ascribed similar conceptual characteristics. In Zionist literary texts the Arab had become a mirror image of the Jew-in-exile, thus fusing the negation of the proximate past with the cultural distancing from the local native. In both cases, the West, concretely embodied in the presence of the British colonial state, had provided the magnetic pole against which Zionism could measure its ability to promote the constitution of the reinvigorated nation.[46]

In law, the identification with the West was directly expressed in the dominant attitude towards the newly established colonial system of justice. As we are yet to see in detail, English imported law and the legal ways of the British in general were perceived by most Jewish jurists in Palestine as the incarnation of a highly developed enlightened law. It was also through law, either by identifying with the legal traditions of the English or by rejecting the unified British legal umbrella as applicable to both Jewish and Arab 'natives,' that the distance from the culturally inferior Arab had been maintained.

So, let us come back now to the so-called second story, that which is told in law and by law, that which uncritically grounds Israeli law in the legacy of the colonial state. So, does all that I have expounded upon above mean that this second story is the one that 'got it right?' Again, I do not think it is a question of getting it right. But the law story is fascinating because it provides an opening for probing into the unstable and contradictory history of Jewish nationalism and because it does bring to the fore the dual-colonialism framework of Mandatory Palestine. Precisely because of their disciplinary innocence, numerous legalistic accounts of the impact of English law and the Mandatory legal system on Israeli law inadvertently narrate a counter-hegemonic tale. These accounts outline a history of state and society which, due to its adherence to the principles of continuity and stability in law, overrule the offcial Zionist version of rupture and revolution that marks the establishment of the state of Israel and, no less important, give utmost priority to the role played by the colonial state – through its law – in shaping the legal face of Israel.

Of course, it is not mere 'innocence' that accounts for this unexpected counter-hegemonic tale at the heart of a reputedly conservative scholarly discipline. In fact, it is precisely this conservatism that is inverted here to produce the counter-hegemonic narrative. Israeli legal history is positivistic through and through. It totally identifies the law with the notion of state-sovereignty and with the political–national identity of those who happen to rule over the apparatuses of the state at a given point in time. Practically every text and utterance about the history of Israeli law uncritically defines three evolutionary phases in its development: the Ottoman period, the British period and the Israeli period. This positivistic history (positivistic in the sense of reducing law to its basic appearance as the command of rulers) is also a linear one: each stage is linked to its predecessor through a number of formal rules of succession and is further backed by practical considerations and legal habits. The end result is that one can portray the history of law as an incrementally evolving process which is marked by institutional and intellectual continuity, checked by careful and non-dramatic innovations, and responding to the supposedly objective modernizing needs of market and society. In other words, it is the disciplinary cognitive loyalty to the state – as the provider of laws – which has led Israeli jurists to produce a body of knowledge which may be turned upside down, exposing the legacy of the colonial state that Zionist historiography has otherwise silently buried.

Yet the counter-hegemonic law story may be appreciated from another perspective as well, a perspective from which the two stories may be looked upon as complementary rather than as being at odds with each other. Zionist historiography marks 1948 as a crucial point, a moment of transition in which there is a shift from analyzing the development of the settlers' community to analyzing the career of the independent state of Israel. In other words, 1948 appears as a point in time that necessitates a paradigmatic shift from a society-centered to a state-centered focus. Yet it is interesting to note that this narrative as a whole is cast in state-centered terms, privileging the political history of the state over other possible types of historical periodization.[47] Moreover, even the presumably society-centered phase of pre-sovereign Israel is one in which researchers have mainly been preoccupied with recording state-formation processes, with looking at the creation of quasi-state institutions, and with analyzing the polity at large. Looked upon from this perspective, Zionist historiography in general and legal historiography in particular are embedded in a statist-oriented approach, in fact in line with the statist disposition adopted by dominant Zionism at least from the 1920s onwards. This latter aspect of Zionism, and its bearing upon the interplay of law and nationalism in Zionist history, will be explored in chapters to come. At any rate, the basic fact remains: by engaging in a state-guided analysis of law, Israeli jurists have brought back in the colonial state, thus rupturing the Zionist narrative of denial.

But it is only at this point that the irony truly begins. For it is not merely the legalistic story *on* law which turns out to be a counter-hegemonic one. It is also from *within* the law that yet another counter-hegemonic narrative has been produced and performed. It was from within the law, albeit from the margins of the dominant discourse, that some jurists called for national self-assertion in and through law. It was from within the law that some serious attempts at challenging the hegemony of British colonial law had been launched, and it was from within the law that Zionist jurists, mainly in the 1920s, tried to distance the nation-building process from too close an alliance with the colonial state, asserting the need to retain "independence from foreign rule and foreign nations." Thus, "They want to dress us in their fine (legal) clothes," wrote one, "yet select for that purpose an Arab–Turkish dress imported from other crown colonies or, at best, they measure us by London standards, yet we cannot accept this favor, we cannot wear clothes that are not made for us."[48]

At times, distance from the colonial state went as far as distance from the West in general. Consider the following vision, articulated by a Russian Jewish lawyer and published in Hebrew in 1910 in Berlin:

> Look to the shores of the Arabian sea and to the rivers of India! The great ancient people of the East are awakening from their generations-old sleep to fight for their freedom. A roaring sound of awakening vibrates through the halls of this ancient-culture universe, through the halls of the world of Babylon, a new enlightened society takes shape on the shores of Asia and in its laws of being and social manners, the spirit of religion is reflected in its pure Eastern form. The Law of the people of the East is rising, and as it gathers its life-force, it accepts the laws of the West only in order to overcome, for the time being, the chaos of these times of transition. The East craves and longs for the incarnation of an authentic and bold Eastern law, which feeds upon the roots of Eastern religion, and which inserts order into Eastern life. To this Eastern society, to the secret of nations, with whose spirit our soul is affiliated, with whose emotions ours are tied, we must introduce our advanced law, the law of the ancient Semitic people ... we must build an authentic Hebrew society on the basis of authentic Hebrew law.[49]

Another variant of a warning against too-enthusiastic an embrace of British traditions in law was voiced in the name of protesting a British legal framework which was not sensitive to the cultural differences between one class of 'natives' (high-cultured Jews) and 'another' (uncivilized Arabs):

> We should also say that the need for our own national courts and a distinct legal system may also be derived from the enormous developmental gap that exists between the two people of this country ... These deep differences between the two people, who are racially and geographically close to each other, prevent them from sharing one legal code that suits them both, and each shared law might lower the cultural level of the Jews and subject them to the more primitive ideas of the majority ... But there are many who kneel before the many ordinances issued by the Mandatory government, many who think that we better learn from the British nation, this daughter of high-civilization, and yet a true look at the legislative actions of the British rulers here shows that not all is right ... British policy is uneven: one law for the cultured people of the metropolis, and another law for the uncivilized people, the natives of the colonies, and it is for this reason that the government has blessed us with many laws which are inconceivable in England itself ... yet even if you find British laws to be perfect and flawless – still it is the absolute imperative of the revival movement – to return to our national juristic forms. To arrange our lives in this old-new mother-land according to our spirit, in line with our great past and in light of the ideals of the future that breathe life into us.[50]

We thus have two variants, the first recorded in Berlin in 1910, celebrating the national spirit by way of inclusion, the other recorded at Tel Aviv in 1926, celebrating the very same national spirit by way of exclusion. In both, albeit so different in tone and orientation to the Arab 'other,' the vision that had been articulated was that of creating a Hebrew national law distinct from that of the colonial state.

It is often by searching for the marginalized, the odd, and the silenced, that one can come to understand the taken-for-granted. It is by looking at unrealized options that one can, at times, problematize the given. It is by excavating thoughts and visions such as the above – so odd in their working against the grain – that one may create a clearing for appreciating the degree to which the Zionist national project was, ultimately, disposed toward the British colonialist state of Palestine and its representation of the West. This, I hope, may also tell us something about the character of Jewish nationalism and about the social relations that constitute Israeli society today.

In the early 1950s, soon after independence and for a handful of years to come, some voices still warned against becoming "a cultural dominion of the Anglo-Saxon family."[51] These voices have been ignored. They were going against the grain of Jewish nationalism: they disturbed an identity that distinguished itself from the Arab through euro-centric practices of cultural distancing based upon a self-image of belonging with the West. By the 1930s, the law of the British colonial state had already established itself as the uncontested law of the land. Earlier attempts to create (or 'to fabricate'[52]) Hebrew law, to speak of legal creativity as a constitutive part of the nation-building process, to think of law and to act upon law as if it were a central cultural arena in which a nation asserted its identity, had become obsolete.

In chapters to follow, I analyze these failed attempts as means of imagining lost alternatives and probe their potential sociological significance. I want to account for a process of self-censorship concerning the cultural aspects of law and for a practice of self-suppression with regard to the possibility of an 'authentic' national legal system. One thread has been suggested in this chapter by juxtaposing what I have termed the first and second stories: the national project was not a project of cultural distancing from 'the West,' but rather a project of asserting the right to sovereignty on the basis of 'Western' notions of liberation. Under such circumstances, the attempt by some Zionists to revive law as a distinct cultural creation – invoking notions of a distant 'Eastern' past of the Hebrew people or, alternatively, of exilic Jews clinging to their legal autonomy, or merely challenging the necessity of submitting to that colonial 'daughter of high-civilization' – undermined some of the basic premises of hegemonic Zionism.

Further, I show that a non-state, 'authentic,' culturally reflexive law, such as the one imagined by the voices quoted above, subverted the strong statist-oriented form of nationalism cultivated by the dominant forces of the Zionist movement. The idea of the state – with its centralist and bureaucratic apparatuses and its formal-rational positive law – and not the idea of community, was the guiding principle of the Zionist project; a concern with centralist institutions and the loyalty they demanded, and not a concern over the spiritual renewal of autonomous communities, was at the forefront of the national mission; and the idea of law as an effective instrument of control imposed from above, rather than a vision of law developing from below to reflect 'authentic' culture, has accordingly shaped the regulative discourse. In all this, the presence of a functioning colonial state served as a constant reference point for the future state of Israel and its future statist national character.

CHAPTER 2

WHOSE TRADITION? IMAGERIES OF THE PAST IN HEBREW LAW

A memorandum submitted to the British administration by the Zionist Palestine Office in 1919 summarized some essential properties of a non-state machinery of Jewish tribunals that had been operative in Palestine since 1909.

> The Jewish Court of Peace (*Beth Mishpat Hashalom*) has been founded by the Zionist Palestine Office 11 years ago. The well known lamentable state of the Turkish courts and a general want of the Jewish population to build up its own independent autonomous institutions, induced the Palestine Office to found the Jewish Courts of Peace, which have won the confidence of the Jewish population from the very moment of their establishment ...
> Immediately after the liberation of Palestine by the British Army the Jewish Courts of Peace were reopened and receiving fresh impetus, developed rapidly, particularly in the places containing a large Jewish population. The judges of these courts are elected in the colonies by the population and in the towns by the Jewish town committees. The members of the Supreme Court in Jaffa which have the supervision of all courts in the whole of Palestine, are elected by the *Va'ad Leumi* (National Council).
> The Jewish Courts of Peace are based on a system of three instances, the local tribunal deals with cases involving values up to 100 Pounds (and that of the 2nd instance deals with cases above 100 Pounds) and decides on appeals against judgments passed by courts of the 1st instance. The courts of 2nd instance are called District Courts. The Supreme Tribunal Court decides affairs of public interest and character, such as cases between

public organizations, institutions and colonies, and deals with all appeals that arise against judgments of courts of the 2nd instance. [Statistics follow, indicating the number of cases resolved and pending, Nov. 1918 to Aug. 1919.]

The great number of cases dealt with by the Jewish Courts of Peace proves evidently that these courts fulfill a real need of the Jewish population. And indeed these courts have great advantages for the Community. The judges, elected from all classes of the population, are well versed in the conditions of the litigants and know their situation. The proceedings are conducted without lengthy formalities and suits are brought to an end as soon as possible, thus obviating the services of a solicitor. The judges fulfill their duties with great conscientiousness and devotedness. These circumstances explain the confidence of the population in the courts and judges.

...

The Jewish Courts of Peace are courts of arbitration i.e. the court has no power to force anybody to appear before the court, nor have they the indirect power to enforce the execution of their judgments. But when a sentence has been passed, the proper procedure having been observed, the ordinary Court of Justice extends its help to enforce the execution of their judgments ... We may thus conclude that the Jewish Courts of Peace fulfill a very important function in Jewish life in Palestine; the value of this work is confirmed both by the confidence of the population and of the British authorities.[1]

There are many issues that this conciliatory memorandum – seeking to ground the legitimacy of the system by framing it as an arbitration forum dependent upon British approval – fails to mention. One of those missing issues has to do with the fact that there were other Jewish courts in Palestine at the time, in fact 'more Jewish' than the above, at least in the sense that they were run by orthodox rabbis who followed the strict dictates of what they considered the true Jewish law. As a matter of fact, it is curious that the report referred to the *Jewish* Courts of Peace, rather than to the *Hebrew* Courts of Peace, the name by which they were known to the Jewish public: Hebrew, not Jewish, thereby emphasizing the national, rather than the religious, disposition of these courts. Perhaps this was due to the fact that the author of the memorandum did not yet make this fine distinction between Hebrew and Jewish, or at least thought that it did not matter as far as the British were concerned. Or perhaps this choice reflected a deliberate attempt to soften the nationalistic character that this system of courts assumed after the war, a character that is understated throughout the memorandum, the only timid reference being to "the general want of the Jewish population to build up its own independent autonomous institutions."

At any rate, the creation of the Hebrew Courts of Peace corresponded to the major social division in the Jewish community of Palestine before the First World War, namely that between the so-called 'old' Yishuv, comprising mostly religious Jews who emigrated to Palestine and lived there without necessarily being affiliated with Zionism, and the 'new' Yishuv, namely the colonizing settlers who came to Palestine in the name of Zionism. It was not only the religious outlook of the 'old' community but also their general orientation to the desired forms of life as settlers that led the two communities to engage in some bitter confrontations.

A letter sent to Rabbi Kook, one of the most important rabbinical figures in Palestine, in response to a decision he rendered in a 1910 dispute over which he had presided, illustrates a growing sense of animosity between these two social groups:

> Last year, when the young among us had a dispute with our elders, we resolved to assign a tribunal of arbitrators to resolve the matter. We elected you to preside over this tribunal, although we were aware of the fact that we thus assigned an orthodox rabbi whose opinions must be closer to those of the elders ... still we believed in you and in your love for the settlers' community.

Yet the rabbi's decision had not been to the liking of the letter-writer, leading him to warn Kook that "you should know that our new generation of settlers will not allow itself to be ruled by Jesuits. A new generation is rising, a free one, and should you fail to make the Torah and its laws agreeable to and likeable with this generation, it would then be your fault when this generation would set it all aside and pave new roads for itself."[2] An important impetus for creating the Hebrew Courts of Peace thus involved a self-conscious attempt to provide secular Jews with an alternative to the old rabbinical courts that operated in Palestine; the latter were considered to be outdated and incapable of responding to the needs and expectations, both cultural and commercial, of the new settlers' community.[3]

The Hebrew Courts of Peace purported to be much more than a friendly arbitration forum. They were embarked upon by enthusiastic and entrepreneurial Zionist jurists who thought they had identified in these forums the nucleus of a national and secular legal system and a potential foundation for the creation of an authentic autonomous Hebrew law. "We should create a secular Hebrew Law relieved of religious chains," wrote one, "We should create the secular law precisely as we created the secular Hebrew school."[4] Paltiel Dickstein, a Russian-born Zionist jurist who settled in Palestine in 1921 and became the leading spokesperson for the Hebrew Law of Peace, articulated the guiding principle:

> The Law is a substantial part of a people's spiritual life and an inseparable part of its culture. A resurrected nation must seek to revive and renew not only its artistic and cultural and literary forms, but also its Law, where its political, moral, economic, and social views are expressed, and in whose symbols and external features the spirit of the nation is preserved ... We resist imitation in the arts of poetry, music, painting, building, literature, etc., and we therefore must resist imitation in Law, we must not adjust ourselves to the juridical forms of the Turks, or even to those of the British ... We know not of any other cultural craft in which the self-development and the self-determination of a people is so important as it is in Law ... We already fully recognize that there will be no full revival without a land, a language, a culture, and agriculture, but we have not yet realized that there cannot be a national revival without national courts and national Law. The history of nations clearly shows that the Law is a primary element in the process of asserting the liberation of oppressed peoples.[5]

The above statement aimed to locate law within a cultural domain and to legitimize the Hebrew Law of Peace by reference to the cultural aspects of the nation-building project. This law-as-culture orientation drew inspiration from the development of a Jewish cultural center in Palestine during the 1920s. In this formative decade, writes Cordova, "local buds" of the social organization of the cultural sphere developed alongside the political one. This sphere, he writes, was dominated by intellectual elites who had already formed a center of Hebrew culture in Odessa (Russia) and Warsaw (Poland). Most of these intellectuals were well versed in the teachings of Ahad Ha'Am, who prioritized the cultural–spiritual aspect of national revival over the political–territorial one, and in their personal backgrounds they epitomized bourgeois respectability and did not perceive themselves as socialists.[6]

The promoters of the Hebrew Law of Peace were remarkably similar in orientation and background to the members of the intellectual circles who originated in Odessa and Warsaw. But while the latter were legitimated as 'official' revivers of Hebrew culture and language precisely because their sphere of activity had been perceived to have no political implications, the advocates of the Hebrew Law of Peace operated in a sphere of activity that forever transgressed into the 'political.'

Unlike literary practices, the establishment of an operative system of courts and the claim to practice the actual shaping of social relations among individuals and between individuals and institutions could not be contained within a distinct cultural sphere. The transgression into the domain of power and politics, in turn, alarmed other Zionist groups and circles. Primary among those were orthodox Zionists who perceived the cultural claims of the Hebrew Law of Peace as threatening their own version of Jewish tradition.

Throughout the 1920s, the career of the Hebrew Courts of Peace had been cloaked in a strong nationalistic rhetoric that aimed simultaneously, and, as we shall see, often in contradictory ways, to construct a distance from both the colonial state and its laws and from religious Judaism and its application of Jewish law. Distinction on both fronts, however, involved recourse to the Jewish past in general and to the acclaimed Jewish legal tradition in particular.

This tradition, as it had been expounded in scholarly and legalistic texts, described the law of the Jews – specifically that part that concerned civil matters – as that body of knowledge which was contained in the texts, compilations and codifications that have been arranged and incrementally revised in the course of three thousand years of Jewish history: from the biblical era, through the editing of the *Mishna* by Rabbi Yehouda Ha-Nassi in the second century, the post-Talmudic era of the *Geonim*, when Jews followed the dictates of the academies of Sura and Pumbedita in Babylon, to the medieval rabbinical period in which foundational compilations were sealed (for example, from the twelfth-century Maimonides to the sixteenth-century *Set Table (Shulhan Arukh)* by Yosef Caro).[7]

The thrust of this exposition of tradition was that the loss of political sovereignty with the fall of the Second Temple in the first century C.E. did not result in the abrogation of Jewish juridical autonomy and legal creativity. The Jews managed to enjoy a considerable degree of legal autonomy, were able to develop a *Halakhah* – the fully fledged legal system of the Jews-in-exile – and to retain a living system of courts and judges who ruled on the basis of this living Jewish law: "During its long and wide dispersion throughout the world," writes Elon, "the Jewish people carried with it its own law and its own courts, diligently preserving their prerogatives by charters obtained from governmental authorities and by the imposition of strict internal discipline."[8] Therefore, the legal autonomy of Jews was often referred to as the most visible and concrete manifestation of Jewish national unity in exile, in fact a living proof of their being a nation.

The general contours of this Jewish tradition of law – as told and re-told by orthodox scholars and rabbinical authorities – have been largely accepted by the advocates of the Hebrew Law of Peace. The adoption of this traditional story-line served highly useful purposes. First, the emphasis on the legal autonomy of Jewish communities in exile had been of crucial importance in the effort to justify the existence of non-state tribunals alongside the courts of the newly established colonial state. On the face of it, and as some opponents fiercely argued, this attempt to recreate an autonomous system of non-state courts amounted to a redundant, if not subversive and risky, attempt to create "a state within a state."[9] To counter this argument, the proponents of the Hebrew law project developed an anti-positivist and non-statist view of law, relying on the readily available examples of Jewish rights of 'legal self-determination' in the Diaspora.

Second, reliance on this asserted tradition helped to 'prove' the feasibility of creating a reinvigorated national Hebrew law and provided an anchor to the nationalistic present. It allowed the proponents of the Hebrew law to activate that principle of continuity typically required for the construction of national unity and for establishing a sense of shared collective memories in which to ground the national future. Third, the reliance on a glorious past of legal creativity provided the foundation for asserting a *secular* national identity, in contra-distinction to the religiously based sense of unity:

> The novelty here is this establishment's secularism. The Hebrew people preserved their legal autonomy through thousand of years in exile, but all the time the basic form of their self-determination had been religious, and now come the times of renewal and the desire to adopt national forms without the religious flavor. In this respect also our establishment builds on prior experiences, like the establishment of courts in Mantova and other Italian cities in the seventeenth century or the arrangement of a court in Moscow, and much more.[10]

It is this latter aspect of distinction that interests me here.

The advocates of the nationally distinct Hebrew law saw themselves as direct heirs to a glorious Jewish tradition of legal creativity. This self-image, however, collided with an orthodox view which considered religious courts, presided over by rabbis, to be the authentic upholders of this very same tradition. The advocates of the Hebrew Law of Peace and the obviously threatened rabbinical custodians of Jewish law soon engaged in fierce competition, not merely over who was offering a 'true' interpretation of Jewish law, but over the very meaning of tradition in general, each side trying to discredit the other, often resorting to bitter rhetoric.

Two somewhat overlapping arguments were developed by the advocates of the secular and national Hebrew Law of Peace in their effort to establish their legitimacy and to win over the hearts and minds of the settler community in Palestine. First, they argued that Hebrew law had been monopolized by the rabbinical establishment of late medieval Europe and that under the authority of rabbis, this law had become 'fossilized:' a captive of rigid formalism that had fixed the creative spirit of the law into dead letters and complex rhetorical structures. Accordingly, the advocates of the Hebrew Law of Peace declared their principled commitment to a "true traditional Hebrew law which aspires for justice and equity, grace and truth in human relations without binding them to the chains of religion."[11] The advocates of Hebrew law thus pledged allegiance to age-old Jewish texts and compilations while emphasizing their resolve to "uphold the traditional Hebrew law in its general spirit only," and to follow it only as "a guide to adjudication in light of the spirit and needs of contemporary times," "not simply following the formal rule of the *Set Table*, but by reaching into its inner spirit."[12]

Second, and contrary to the way Jewish tradition was ordinarily portrayed, they argued that the main living spirit of Hebrew law was embodied neither in texts nor in rabbinical authoritative dictates, but rather in the fact that it had been developed, shaped, and carried by the community as a whole. "The tradition is based on a democratic and popular idea: The people are the makers of their laws," wrote Eisenstadt. Most of the products of this legal creativity were either not recorded or simply lost, he argued, but the spirit still persisted, embodied in the recognized practice of oral law which had always been the real foundation of Hebrew law. In short, Jewish legal traditions were based on the democratic, popular idea that "the people is the creator of its laws."[13] Thus, not unlike the pre-Doomsday legal ways of England, when "a community's customs would be known to its own members who, insofar as they knew their customs, would have no need to write them down," the vision of a Hebrew law had been grounded in an oral tradition that licensed similar contemporary re-creations.[14]

In other words, the 'secular' approach to Jewish law was linked with the idea of law as a community-centered project. The carriers of the Hebrew Law of Peace promoted the idea of law as a popular communal product which had retained a considerable degree of flexibility and which had been laid down by a sporadic configuration of lay tribunals and other types of popular forums. Judges, according to this evolving view, reflected the preferences of the community and had to rely on common sense and substantive notions of justice as much as on the written law. The advocates of the Hebrew Law of Peace thus developed a particular way of imagining the communal Jewish past. The thrust of this newly offered imagery of communal life was that Jewish legal autonomy should not have been conceived of in religious terms but rather in cultural terms; that the laws of the Jews were developed and constantly re-shaped in accordance with the mundane affairs of the community and that it was this particular legal creation that begged to be enlivened. It is this mundanity-of-law vision, this particular imagination of communal past and legal autonomy, on which I would like to elaborate.

Abraham B. Yehoshua's novel, *Voyage to the End of the Millennium*,[15] will serve here as a literary blueprint for probing the ambiguities involved in trying to imagine the Jewish community in exile as the source of a Hebrew 'indigenous law,' at a place and time where no indigenous culture was readily available as a source of inspiration for a national, let alone anti-colonial, project.

Yehoshua sets his story at the turn of the first millennium, when Abulafia, a North African Jew, nephew and business partner of Ben-Atar, settles in Paris and marries a European Jew. When Abulafia's wife, Ms Esther-Mina, discovers that his uncle, Ben-Atar, has two wives, she is appalled[16] and asks her husband to sever all ties with him. Deeply concerned at the influence of this "savage" Jew (Ben-Atar), she demands that her husband spurn him.[17] She then engages the help of Rabbi Kalonymos ben-Kalonymos, a relative of her late husband, who will certainly see to it that any man contemplating a second (or third) wife is not merely spurned but excommunicated.

So Ben-Atar, deeply offended, sails from Tangiers to France with his two wives and Rabbi Elbaz to plead his case before the European Jews: "We have come to assert empyreal law against you and against your spurning," he says, "and we therefore brought a wise Rabbi from Seville with us."[18] Ms Esther-Mina and her relatives are only too eager to have the case heard before the court, as they are convinced that the ordinance will stand.[19]

The parties decide to litigate in a nearby village inhabited by a small community of Jews, where there is a winery owned by a Jew. Yehoshua portrays the community justice tribunal which is set up and the intense local curiosity about the case: there is not only to be a rabbi from Andalusia, but the "sweetness of the issue" and the fact that the two women (Ben-Atar's wives) will themselves be there. Local Christians, too, appear to witness the proceedings. With a throng which finally overflows the small synagogue, the court is transferred to the open cellar of the winery.

Rabbi Elbaz is deeply worried about the identity of those who are about to adjudicate the case. "*Who would the judges be?*" he keeps asking everyone. "*Who will select the judges?*" "*Were the judges appointed already?*"

"*Yet how were the judges appointed?*" And he gets his answer when "three slender people" are ushered in:

> [They are] wearing dusty black caftans, carrying with them a papyrus scroll and a small greenish tableau. These are quickhand scribes, copiers of Bible books, Tefillin and Mezuzahs, who were brought from nearby towns to serve as Judges of the court. Quickhand scribes? The Andalusian sage [Elbaz] disappointedly mutters as he sees these persons who try to make sense of texts by copying them over and over again. But Mr. Lewinas thinks highly of them. They will know to pass judgment according to the books. But which books? And why books? Rabbi Elbaz protests. Would it have occurred to him to leave his town and cross the ocean waves were such matters explicitly inscribed in one of the books? Would he have allowed Ben-Atar to put his wives at risk for something which had already been inscribed?[20]

He demands loudly that the judges be replaced and Abulafia in turn quietly begs his wife to intercede on behalf of Ben-Atar to this end. Then it is up to the rabbi:

> Elbaz duly calms the upset litigants by asserting his readiness to be satisfied with the spirit of the ancient ancestors, which is the true spirit, the spirit that may turn, for example, this simple, good congregation into a community of peacemakers and guardians which may resolve the dispute, whether for plaintiffs or for defendants, as had been said in the Book of Names, *aharei rabbim le-hattot* [follow the majority].[21]

Yes, he affirms, these judges will include the workers; also the women – why not? And, finally it is agreed,

> in accordance with the ancient spirit, seven judges will suffice, as forming *Shiv'at Tovei Ha'ir* [the seven best persons of the town]; but since this is not a town and the foreign travelers still do not know the best among these people, a lottery is called for ...
>
> And now everything is ready. And even if those who are now present on the small platform are not *Shiv'at Tovei Ha'ir*, as the scripture demands, but simply a random seven, it is only because there has been no Jewish town for nearly one thousand years now, only small dispersed communities ...[22]

Yehoshua's story is loosely set against the background of an ordinance banning plural marriages, backed by the sanction of excommunication; it touches upon one of the most central aspects of every community's social structure. The exact timing of the ordinance, the identity of its promulgators, and the intended scope of the ordinance, are all matters that are still debated among Jewish scholars.²³ Yehoshua exploits these ambiguities in order to consider the cross-cultural tensions that they may have brought about.

In this case, we encounter a rabbi who challenges the validity of an ordinance not by merely relying on the force of scholarly arguments but by appealing to the common-sense justice of the community's lay members. Yehoshua thus masterfully blurs the lines between various possible sources of authority in Jewish tradition and in fact re-opens for debate the very meaning and content of that tradition to new imaginative perspectives. The story of the "trial," in short, invokes what Zerubavel calls "countermemory,"²⁴ using the law as a central site for the invention of tradition; the law being a particularly effective site for such purposes because an authorized and inscribed decision by a court has the potency of transforming an asserted custom or memory into an official verdict on truth.²⁵

The advocates of the Hebrew Law of Peace never went as far as challenging the prerogatives of rabbinical courts in personal-status matters. Nonetheless, the relations between the two systems of justice were strained precisely on this issue of *who will select the judges?*; on what should be the appropriate composition and nature of the tribunals that render justice for the Jewish, now designated Hebrew, community of Palestine.

In their efforts to maneuver between state law on the one hand and religious law on the other, the jurisdiction of the Hebrew Courts of Peace did not purport to include personal-status and criminal matters, deferring the former to rabbinical courts and the latter to the colonial administration.

Furthermore, wishing to appease the rabbinical establishment, advocates of the Law of Peace repeatedly acknowledged the legitimate jurisdiction of the rabbinical courts in other matters as well, provided that the litigants consented.

Nonetheless, the rabbinical establishment waged war on the Hebrew Law of Peace by exerting political pressure on Zionist institutions to avoid these tribunals and by publicly labeling the Hebrew Law activists as "simple-minded ignorant laymen" who "know neither law nor religion."²⁶ The executive committee of *Ha'Mizrachi* – the central political organ of orthodox nationalist Jews – expressed "its fierce objection to the attempt to constitute secular courts [Hebrew Law of Peace] which are not based on the Law of the Holy Bible and have no roots in Hebrew tradition, and demands of the Hebrew community and its institutions to bring their cases only before Israeli Judges who pass judgment on the basis of the Laws of the Bible and Israel."²⁷ The thrust of the argument against the Hebrew Law of Peace had been straightforward: "The revival of Hebrew Law and a National Court is doubtless an essential part of national revival, but we say that the *revival* of Hebrew Law is part of national revival, and not the *creation* of Hebrew Law" (emphasis added), thereby accusing the advocates of the Hebrew Law of Peace of fabrication, if not outright forgery and usurpation.[28]

In other words, the advocates of the Hebrew Law of Peace were not the only ones claiming exclusive rights of ownership over the term 'Hebrew law,' or one's identity as Hebrew, for that matter. According to Elon, a contemporary scholarly voice of the orthodox version, Hebrew law is roughly that part of Jewish law that encompasses civil matters, in contrast to religious matters; a definition that enables him to embrace the term by situating Hebrew law in a direct and unbroken continuation of the established practices of rabbinical authorities, while at the same time dismissing the relevance of the Hebrew Law of Peace to that history. This tactic is crucial because Elon does acknowledge that "the use of the term *Ivri* (Hebrew) in connection with the 'legal' portion of the *Halakhah* originated at the beginning of the twentieth century, with the awakening of the Jewish national (Zionist) movement."[29]

Similarly, the orthodox guardians of Jewish tradition in the 1920s naturalized Hebrew law as simply interchangeable with Jewish law, 'Hebrew' thereby transformed into a taken-for-granted generic term designating the Jews as a nation. And since there was nothing new about being a Hebrew, they could dismiss the Hebrew Law of Peace as a mere fabrication: "Hebrew Law cannot and should not be born and created, in the same way that the Hebrew people cannot and should not be born and created. The Hebrew people, the most ancient people to exist, never lived a moment without a national law;" therefore, the Hebrew Law of Peace "has no ties whatsoever to our original national life, that is the national life which is truly authentic, grounded in the spontaneous life of the nation – originating neither in auto-emancipation nor in the State of the Jews – that stretches thousands of years into the past."[30]

It was no coincidence that the advocates of the Hebrew Law of Peace and the self-appointed guardians of Jewish laws and traditions invoked identical terms and insisted on coining and adhering to similar expressions, specifically those retaining the Hebrew law designation. The rabbinical establishment understood only too well what was at stake: not merely a jurisdictional conflict and not merely a jurisprudential competition with the Hebrew Law of Peace, but a struggle over the very meaning of Jewish identity at its nationalist moment in history. The Palestinian Jewish orthodoxy, as much as the Palestinian secular Zionists, cast their ambitions and aspirations in the nationalist rhetoric of the times, each trying to project the conceivably 'valid and authentic nature' of Jewish nationalism while fiercely discrediting the version of the other. Fighting over the same cultural turf and for the same territory, they developed conflicting images of the Jewish past. While the religious orthodoxy naturalized the nationalist project by treating the nation and its religion as inseparable entities, the secular advocates of the Hebrew Law of Peace sought to distinguish between the religious and cultural elements of Jewish collective history. The latter, for them, was where the spirit of the nation resided, religion providing only the outer layer – tentative if not superficial – of shared cultural traditions.

As so often happens, the debate was cast in such embittered tones precisely because the parties had so much in common. Assaf Likhovski, a legal historian, challenges the Hebrew law narrative-of-continuity which Elon outlined by looking at the use of the term by the advocates of the Hebrew Law of Peace (in the course of their activities in a Hebrew Law Society which they established). He problematizes the term, Hebrew law, by arguing that it was a fabrication of secular Zionists. Hebrew law, he argues, represented not "a continuation of the Jewish past, but a break with it, not so much the 'restoration' of an old tradition, as the invention of a new one. Secular Zionists sought to create a new 'Hebrew' person who will be the anti-thesis of the old Exilic Jew," and "Hebrew Law, like the rest of Zionist culture, was constructed by its early advocates ... as a reflection of Zionist ideology and identity needs."[31]

Yet Likhovski's counter-reading of the history of Hebrew law only holds to the extent that the advocates of the Hebrew Law of Peace wanted to reinvigorate and renew what they thought of as the old traditional ways of making and declaring the law. (This creative aspect of the Hebrew Law of Peace project, which involves the anti-formalistic interpretive techniques and free-law-making dispositions of its advocates, will be discussed in another chapter.) Yet this reading overlooks the fact that Hebrew law was a contested concept. It overlooks that aspect of the Hebrew Law of Peace which was premised on notions of continuity with both ancient (sovereign) and exilic past as much as the religious narrative was. In short, it seems to me that the war waged in religious circles would not have been so fierce had it not been for the fact that at stake were not merely tradition versus anti-tradition/continuity versus change tensions but, rather, a struggle over the very meaning of tradition and the adequate conception of law within it. We are faced here with two conflicting inventions of a Jewish past, rather than with the single fabricated story that Likhovski outlines in countering the orthodox narrative of continuity.

The crucial point here is that the advocates of the Hebrew Law of Peace, as much as their religious adversaries, did not abruptly break away from the concept of the exilic Jew. On the contrary, in their efforts to legitimize the autonomous national Hebrew legal system they seemed to be celebrating the legal past of the Jews-in-exile as one which served as a model for the practices of the present. In this sense, the advocates of the Hebrew Law of Peace, ardent Zionists as they were, subverted the hegemonic Zionist agenda and offered a culturally disposed and a community-based nationalist version which was at odds with the dominant version. They deviated, however inadvertently, from mainstream Zionism, which indeed sought to distance itself from the Jews-in-exile and from the cultural forms they represented because exilic times were portrayed as times of deprivation, degeneration and passivity, times between a glorious past of national sovereignty and a near future of renewed organic links with the land. In this particular sense as well, the secular advocates of Hebrew Law were not unlike their orthodox adversaries in not sharing the Zionist agenda of a radical break from the proximate past (antiquity having been celebrated by all nationalists as a glorious sovereign existence).

It is precisely because the advocates of the Hebrew Law of Peace ventured to offer a different reading of Jewish traditions that the religious establishment became so alarmed. First, the Hebrew Law of Peace threatened the rabbinical monopoly of Jewish texts not by dismissing or avoiding these texts but rather by arguing that they were also in a position to read and interpret them. Second, at least some advocates of the Hebrew Law of Peace depicted a very threatening picture – from an orthodox point of view – of the traditional law-making practices of Jewish communities in exile, a picture that substantially undermined and challenged the rabbinical view; a threat, in short, that corresponded with our theme of *Who will select the judges?*

The thrust of the position articulated by the advocates of the Hebrew Law of Peace was that Hebrew law should be grounded in and sought for in the actual practices of the *community*, and not only in formal texts and codificatory literature. This community-centered and culturally based version of law was corroborated by historical reference to the fact that the Jews always developed all kinds of popular tribunals, that Jewish courts of law were often presided over by one scholar and two lay persons, and that oral law – which had become the *captive of a narrow and restrictive Halakhah* – had always been a central pillar of Jewish self-regulation. In particular, the advocates of the Hebrew Law of Peace alluded to the fact that Jews often held trials in which the rabbinical authority had not been the ultimate arbiter.

One writer invoked traditional notions of Jewish lay justice by arguing for the important principle of majority opinion, also taking the opportunity to assert the distinct character of Hebrew law vis-a-vis

English law. Unlike English law, where a single judge was allowed to sit in judgment and where minority opinions were routinely published, he wrote, Hebrew law forbade a trial by a single judge and suppressed minority opinions when there was more than one judge. These contrasting customs, he wrote, told a whole story of difference between the national spirit of the British nation, which celebrated the individual, and the Hebrew spirit – not necessarily as religion but as a communal form of life – which did not rely on single opinions and adhered to the voice of the majority and to the principle of a shared collective responsibility. Further, "it is precisely in the age-old Hebrew Law," he wrote, "that the common way of rendering justice had been based on a judicial tribunal composed of 'one expert and two lay-persons'."[32]

This community-centered emphasis resonated with that part of Jewish tradition in law that had been acknowledged, and often hotly debated, within the rabbinical establishment itself. Elon refers in his study of Jewish law to various such communal legal practices. For example, it is evident that communal enactments (*Takanot Ha'kahal*), either by assembly or through elected representatives, "started to become a major creative force from the tenth century c.e., as the Jewish communities in the various Diasporas began to flourish. Communal enactments were the product of wide-ranging and fruitful legislative activity by Jewish communities over many centuries in numerous and broad areas of civil and criminal law."[33]

Another important institution was the one referred to above in *Voyage to the End of the Millennium*: *Shiv'at Tovei Ha'ir* (the seven best people of town), the practice of appointing or electing people who enjoyed high social and moral standing in the community for enacting rules in vital matters and for adjudicating internal disputes. The practices of the judges in the Hebrew Courts of Peace, argued its advocates, were reminiscent of this spirit. Accordingly, the report cited at the beginning of this chapter spoke of the fact that "the judges elected from all classes of the population are well versed in the conditions of the litigants and know their situation," that these "judges fulfill their duties with great conscientiousness and devotedness," and that this explained "the confidence of the population in the courts and judges," thus involving memories of a traditional judicial institution. Further, the advocates of the Hebrew Law of Peace repeatedly emphasized the nature of this non-juristic adjudication. The judges, they argued, "in line with the age-old traditions of Hebrew Law," based judgments on their common-sense, good will, and notions of equity and justice, thus exhibiting "a true traditional Hebrew Law which aspires for grace and truth in human relations without binding them to the chains of religion."[34]

Indeed, rabbinical sources refer to the fact that it had been a common practice among Jews to appoint such community leaders as both judges and law-givers and acknowledge that these community leaders sometimes issued judgments and enactments not in line with the strict dictates of the *Halakhah*. Hence, many Halakhic sources engage in debates concerning the appropriate powers of such community leaders and the ways they should be treated by religious authorities.[35]

In fact, it seems that relations between the law-making institutions of self-governing communities and Jewish rabbinical authorities have often been a source of concern for the latter. Consequently, available sources reflect the tendency of rabbinical authorities to recognize and validate the legal creations of such popular forums *ex post factum* in order not to lose their grip over the community. Elon provides a striking example in citing a seventeenth-century European scholar who wrote:

> There are towns without persons who know the *Torah* [Bible], and in order to preclude resort to non-Jewish judges it was permitted to establish a Jewish court even though its members do not know the law. The practice has persisted over time, throughout many generations, until judging according to the Torah has been forgotten; and even where there are those who know the law, ignorant leaders are chosen as judges in order to pay them honor; and they decide cases according to their own whim and desire ... On the same facts, sometimes they find liability, and sometimes they do not ... Even those who have mastered the Torah and are well versed in the law, when they sit together with the communal leaders, judge as they wish, contrary to the law of the Torah, and do not hesitate to act as advocates rather than as judges.[36]

Keeping in mind the particular concerns of the writer, it is nonetheless quite tempting to read between the lines about practices of widely accepted and widespread communal law-making and law-dispensing institutions which assert jurisdiction over the community in ways that overwhelm a rabbinical authority that reluctantly complies. Read in this light, the complaints of this seventeenth-century writer about the uncertainty and unpredictability of these tribunals are reminiscent of the rhetorical strategies typically employed by legal professions who wish to de-legitimize competitors and of the standard legalistic logic in the name of which positivistic state law tends to label popular tribunals as 'non-law'. I shall come back to the above complaint, therefore, in a later chapter, where I discuss the hostile response of the Jewish legal profession in Palestine to the Hebrew Law of Peace project.

Here, the crucial point is that the idea that the sources and origins of Hebrew law were not necessarily – and certainly not exclusively – found in the teachings and ordinances of rabbinical authorities allowed the advocates of the Hebrew Law of Peace to defend themselves against the charge that they were not versed enough in Jewish legal traditions. Furthermore, by imagining the law to be the cultural product of the community, the advocates of the Hebrew Law of Peace vindicated their own courts: the rabbinical court had been depicted as an outdated forum unable to satisfy the expectations of the community, while the Hebrew Court of Peace, based as it was on lay judges, embedded in the community and relying on their common-sense, communal responsibility, and natural sense of justice, was the truly authentic reincarnation of a glorious communal Jewish legal past.

Voyage to the End of the Millennium opens up original ways in which to imagine the community life and law-making practices of the Jews-in-exile. It has done so by literary means. The advocates of the Hebrew Law of Peace, seventy years earlier, had done so by institutional means, establishing a network of courts all over Palestine; a network which processed, throughout the 1920s, hundreds of cases a year, covering almost every conceivable aspect of civil law. Through their very actions, let alone the elaborate justifications and explanations that accompanied those actions, the meaning of Jewish tradition and the place of law within that tradition were re-negotiated and re-conceptualized: to what extent had Jewish communities in the past indeed been dominated by strict rabbinical dictates? What was the place of formal biblical law in the life of the community? Had it been hegemonic or had it been often overwhelmed by the mere pull of everyday life? 'History' could not resolve the issue because history was that which had been contested, because at the heart of the matter stood attempts to stir up the national imagination and to set it loose from the official history articulated under the supervision of rabbinical monopoly.

The Hebrew Law of Peace, in sum, had been a modern invention that involved a reformed articulation of the nature of Jewish tradition. In the absence of a living indigenous law upon which one could have drawn in asserting distinction from the colonial rulers, and themselves being colonizers, the advocates of a Hebrew Law of Peace had to search for and imagine their own particular brand of indigenous law in the communities-in-exile of the past. (These 'communities' had certainly been moribund since the Enlightenment of the eighteenth century and the 'in-exile' addition, of course, suggested a nationalist construction of the past.) By opening up the question of tradition, however, the Hebrew Law of Peace represented a clear threat to the 'established' tradition, as this had been imagined and articulated by its orthodox, self-appointed guardians, in fact threatening to open to re-negotiation the very power structure of the Jewish community of the past, and, by the sheer force of analogy, the power structure of the Jewish national community of Palestine. The Zionist orthodoxy vehemently fought the Hebrew Law of Peace precisely because it challenged its hegemonic version of 'tradition.' This orthodox backlash, in fact, corresponded to orthodoxy's treatment of Zionism in general. From the early days of the Zionist movement orthodox Jewry had been hostile to the cultural version of Zionism – which insisted that the national 'problem' was a spiritual one – while it quite comfortably accommodated the political–instrumental version that dominated the World Zionist Organization.[37] The reason should be obvious: the latter form of Zionism, interested and invested in achieving political sovereignty, did not pose a threatening alternative to the orthodox historic narration of the nation.

The promoters of the Hebrew Law of Peace understood only too well the threat they represented. Their status and standing still precarious, they tried not to provoke the religious establishment to exert more pressure on Zionist institutions to stay clear of Hebrew Courts of Peace. On the one hand, they insisted on their legitimacy, directly confronting the rabbinical establishment: "Some say that Jews are forbidden to litigate in lay tribunals (and that is how they think of us) as much as they are forbidden to litigate in gentile courts," wrote Dickstein in reply to orthodox pressure; "this view utterly contradicts the needs of our people and is further disproved by well-known and explicit scholars of the *Halakha.*"[38] On the other hand, the advocates of the Hebrew Law of Peace refrained from any action that might have been conceived as a jurisdictional transgression. A striking example of this strategic self-censorship is illustrated in the response of the High Hebrew Court of Peace to the opportunity it had to assert its jurisdiction vis-a-vis that of rabbinical courts.

In 1926, Ben-Zion Ben-Aharon, a Jerusalem lawyer, petitioned the High Hebrew Court of Peace in a matter concerning the judicial activities of the rabbinical courts. The petition was directed against the Town Committees of Jerusalem, Tel Aviv and Haifa, the two Chief Rabbis, Yaakov Meir and A. I. Ha-Cohen Kook, and other judges (*Dayanim*) of the High Rabbinical Court. The petition stated that in 1921 the Town Committees elected the other respondents to serve as judges in the rabbinical court. The petitioner argued that these elections were not prescribed by law and in any case were only in effect for three years. Regardless, the judges still held office and routinely pronounced judgments, thereby "subjecting the general public to their abused powers." The High Hebrew Court of Peace was asked to order the judges to cease all their judicial activities in the rabbinical court until a final resolution.

Two special meetings of the judges and activists of the High Hebrew Court of Peace were subsequently convened in order to decide whether to hear the petition.[39] The debates that followed reflected divided opinions. Some were of the opinion that the petition provided an excellent opportunity for the Hebrew Court of Peace to expand its jurisdiction and to establish a public law prerogative over the internal affairs of the Jewish community of Palestine:

> It is a common rule of law that every citizen has the right to advance claims in public matters ... In England, every judge is authorized to handle administrative matters. The idea behind establishing a Hebrew Court of Peace is to discourage Jews from turning to the courts of the government. Unless there are special reasons compelling us to restrict our jurisdiction, all cases are within our jurisdiction. In all cases when a possibility exists to utilize a Jewish court, turning to government courts is against the spirit of this institution and against Hebrew Law.[40]

"We refer to those who address the courts of the government as traitors and criminals," warned another, "and shying away from this business will encourage the petitioner to address these courts."[41]

Others were less confident and pointed out that the regulations of the Hebrew Courts of Peace did not authorize the courts to rule over matters concerning the powers of rabbinical courts or indeed of any other administrative or judicial institution for that matter. This formalistic argument was countered by others who said that the Hebrew courts must not submit to the "dead letter of the regulations" and that the Hebrew courts' jurisdiction may be established by setting precedents. Still, the second meeting saw some shifting of opinions as more of those present argued that there were compelling strategic and political reasons not to hear the petition: "We must not interfere with matters that fall under the authority of the Chief Rabbinate and we have no jurisdiction to issue opinions concerning institutions that enjoy the same status and authority as we do," said one, expressing the opinions of those who thought that the Hebrew Courts of Peace and the Rabbinical courts were corollary institutions and that attempts to tamper with this balance of power would only "upset the government and the religious circles" and damage the long-range interests of the Hebrew Law of Peace.[42]

The wish to avoid confrontation with the rabbinical establishment combined with practical concerns. "What shall we do if they will refuse to appear before us, or demand that we apply *Din-Torah* [literally: biblical law]? The matter smells of propaganda, not of law," said one; he was seconded by others who warned that the rabbinical court would not comply with a decision rendered by the Hebrew court, thereby undermining the prestige and honor of the Hebrew court.[43]

A face-saving solution was suggested by Paltiel Dickstein, officially the Secretary of the Hebrew Courts of Peace and practically the most visible and vocal speaker on behalf of the Hebrew Law of Peace: "We cannot sit as judges over the Chief Rabbinate. The issue should be resolved by a special tribunal, to be composed by the National Council, which will include representatives of both parties as well as neutral judges."[44] This suggestion became the official resolution of the meeting. Yet the conscious and deliberate effort to avoid confrontation – even at the price of restricting its jurisdiction over matters that were deemed highly important if the Hebrew Law of Peace was ever to establish itself as a central national institution[45] – did not absolve it from coming under ferocious attacks by the rabbinical establishment.

This is what *Ha'tor*, the journal of *Ha'Mizrachi*, had to say about the petition that had been submitted to the High Court of Peace in the matter of the Chief Rabbinate:

> Nobody knows who gave birth to the Hebrew Law of Peace, high and low, and no one understands the legal foundation upon which it rests its authority. This so-called 'Hebrew Law of Peace' has neither a basis in Hebrew tradition nor powers derived from the Hebrew public ... The 'Hebrew Law of Peace' is a foreign branch in the vineyard of Israel. Foreign as it is to the spirit of Judaism, it must not assist in the proper establishment of Israel's Chief Rabbinate.[46]

Indeed, it was none other than the colonial state itself that assisted "in the proper establishment of Israel's Chief Rabbinate," in securing a state-granted monopoly for rabbinical courts over personal–status matters (thereby establishing the state–religion alliance that is part of Israel's political structure to this day) and in facilitating, albeit indirectly, the demise of the Hebrew Courts of Peace.[47]

These latter developments, in the context of bringing the colonial state back into the discussion of law and nationalism in Palestine, will be dealt with in the next chapter. Preceding that, a short interregnum and preview recapitulating the idea of an imagined community-centered law serves as a bridge between this theme and the next.

INTERREGNUM

In Barry Unsworth's novel *Morality Play*,[1] set in fourteenth-century England, the narrator is a renegade priest who joins a traveling group on its way to Durham where they are scheduled to perform their set of Mystery (religious) plays: the Play of Adam and the Play of Christ's Nativity, and the Play of Noah, the Rage of Herod, and the Dream of Pilate's Wife. Hungry, cold and penniless, they stop at a small rural town in the hope of performing and earning some money. But they soon find out that recently a boy, Thomas Wells, has been murdered in the town, robbed of his money, and a young woman locked away as the culprit. A series of events then leads the traveling company to break from the strict tradition of enacting the established truths of the past and to venture into the present, playing out the story of the murder and its moral lessons.

The group, encouraged by its leader, Martin, begins to deliberate on how to give a truthful representation of the murder. Yet as the facts unfold, the players have to delve into inconsistencies, uncertainties, and indeterminacy. This is an occasion for speculation, novelty, creativity, and yet also one of fearing the unknown, dreading something which is yet to be granted the official stamp of truth. The players discuss the issues:

> "It is madness," [Straw] said. "How can men play a thing that is only done once? *Where are the words for it?*" ... "The woman who did it is still living," Margaret said. "If she is still living, *she is in the part herself, it is hers, no one else can have it.*"

Martin insists that the murder of Abel by Cain was something that happened only once, yet the group could enact the story, and indeed did so regularly; so why should the murder in this town be any different? "There is not authority for it," says another player. "*It is not written anywhere.* Cain and Abel are in the bible," and the narrator continues:

> "(B)ut in this one there is no common acceptance, God has not given us this story to use, he has not revealed to us the meaning of it. So it has no meaning, it is only a death. Players are like other men, they must use God's meanings, they cannot make meanings of their own, that is heresy, it is the source of all our woes, it is the reason our first parents were cast out." But already, looking round at their faces, I knew that my argument would fail. They were in some fear perhaps, but it was not fear of offending God, *it was fear of the freedom Martin was holding out, the license to play anything in the world.* Such license brings power ... yes, he offered us the world, he played Lucifer to us there in the cramped space of the barn ... "We can do it as a Morality Play," he said.[2]
>
> He looked at me steadily. "It has been in my mind for years now that we can make plays from stories that happen in our lives. I believe this is the way that plays will be made in the times to come."[3] (emphasis added)

The company finally decides on a version and makes its first attempt at enacting it in public. As the drama unfolds, the play is interrupted. The mother of the murdered Thomas, sitting in the audience, disputes the interpretation presented in the play; her protest encourages more shouts from the audience and, subsequently, the drama collapses.

The players realize that they must have overlooked some essential facts or interpreted them falsely, so they decide to try again, to launch further inquiries, and ultimately to produce the true version. Finally, they offer a play in which the facts do not point to the accused woman, who has been locked up by order of the local Sheriff's court.

It transpires that the play has also been watched by a Justice of the King, who apparently had come to oversee the justice dispensed by this Sheriff's court. At the end of the performance, he falls into conversation with one of the players, and tells him about the true purpose of his visit, which concerns Richard de Guise, one of the most powerful barons in the north, who is perceived as challenging the power of the King.

> "Do you think I would leave his [the King's] business in York and come these weary miles in this weather, to this wretched inn where I am served food not fit for the swill tub, for the sake of a dead serf and a dumb goatgirl?" ... "You thought I was one of your company, one of the players, somewhat belated, come to put on the mask of

Justitia in your True Play of Thomas Wells ... But I am in a different play ... we have had trouble with this stiff-necked de Guise ... *He takes the law into his hands.* Only royal commissioners have the power to try cases of felony in the shires, and all fines and expropriations should go to the royal exchequer, yet *this lord arrogates such powers of trial to his sheriff's court and all the moneys go into his coffers.*"

... "And now you will bring him to justice and serve the King's cause at the same time."

... "Do you think he would meekly consent to be tried? Justice is less easily applied to the strong than to the defenseless ... you will wait for us now some little while. Then we will take a ride together, and I promise you enlightenment at the end."[4] (emphasis added)

Morality Play is all about a paradigmatic revolution; the excitement and the horror that come in that moment of rupture where representations are set loose. Michel Foucault, in his "Discourse on Language", talks about "disciplines" and "commentaries" as two distinct ways of approaching a text.[5] The treatment of a text as a basis for further elaboration is the organizing principle of "disciplinary discourse." "What is supposed at the point of departure is not some meaning which must be rediscovered, nor an identity to be reiterated; it is that which is required for the construction of new statements. For a discipline to exist, there must be the possibility of formulating – and of doing so ad infinitum – fresh propositions." This, in contrast to the principle of commentary which allows only that discourse which retains a special type of relationship to the original text: "... whatever the techniques employed, commentary's role is to say finally, what has silently been articulated deep down ... it gives us the opportunity to say something other than the text itself, but on condition that it is the text itself which is uttered and, in some ways, finalized ... The novelty lies no longer in what is said, but in its reappearance."[6]

It is this new sense of power and responsibility that haunts the actors in Unsworth's novel, as they defy the rules of representation dictated by the traditional religious drama and yet are still gradually steered towards a new form of representation: an inquiry into the truth of empirical facts. A struggle over meaning and interpretation ensues. The liberty to invent engages with the chains of authenticity to produce justice in action, justice from below – popular justice, if you will. The process of investigating and acting becomes a drama in which the actors and the audience interact to become an embedded community of juries, peers, and judges who ultimately pronounce the law. In so doing, they defy the local Sheriff's court. Moreover, they assume this active role while the King's Justice is restricted to a position of mere spectator. "Looking toward the rooms above," the narrator comments, "I saw open casements and faces watching us, one of them a white face with a black cap fitting close and it came to me that this might be the Justice."[7] No – more than that, invited to watch and to grant, at the end of the play, his official recognition.

In this sense, *Morality Play* is also about jurisdictions, about the never-ending struggle over the right to say what the law is; a struggle that positivist state law – in its struggles with local forms of justice which it tends to suppress, but at times to embrace – often denies, as if there were only one valid law.

Whenever we discuss community-based law, then, we are at once compelled to consider these two related aspects: its relation with state law, namely the tension between a community-based law and the law which is authoritatively declared as such by state officials, and the problem of interpretation, namely the ability to pronounce and configure law in the (relative) absence of compelling texts or without being able to assume these texts contain hidden meanings that need to be uncovered. I shall address both these aspects, turning now to the former before considering the second in chapter 4.

CHAPTER 3

STATE LAW AND COMMUNAL JUSTICE

One of Foucault's most central polemics against the discourse of modernity was that 'in political thought and analysis we still have not cut off the head of the king' – that is, the theory of power is still organized around the centrality of the state, the question of sovereignty, and the right to rule. Accordingly, a major theoretical effort of Foucault has been to shift the analytic gaze to sites of power which were less visible; bio-power, the disciplines, normalization techniques, and so on.

Subversive and enlightening as this call has been, it seems that Foucault did not apply it to his own discussions of law. Foucault mainly spoke of law as a manifestation of the Sword; as the representation of the power to take life. He thought of law as both a symbol of and a concretization of sovereignty, and of legal discourse as part of the discourse on state power. Arguing that modern power is not embodied in the power to take life but rather in the power to normalize, regulate and govern life, Foucault tended to underestimate the importance of law for understanding modern forms of power. In this respect, his focus, highly valuable as it has been for a critique of state law, seems to have been itself grounded in the view that essentially (con)fuses law and sovereignty and treats the former as a system of official commands and prohibitions. But is it not possible and, further, necessary, to cut off the head of the king in legal analysis as well? In other words, is it not necessary to expand our vision of law to include not only state legal forms but also other, less majestic, sometimes more discrete laws and legal systems, and analyze them in their relation to state law?

Equipped with a Western state law bias, a whole tradition in the social sciences builds upon the distinction between law and custom. In this concept natives, primitives, and indigenous people have custom but no law. The latter is defined as a set of abstract rules originating from a political community, while custom is a set of practices presumed to be known by everyone. The distinction between law and custom, useful as it was for justifying colonialist regimes of order, was not only applied to colonized people. Rather, it has been a powerful epistemological–political tool for privileging state power, sovereignty, and the right to rule as the leading discourse on power since the Enlightenment, thereby subjecting local communities to the centralizing forces of the day. In either case, the organizing paradigm has been positivist; a paradigm that identifies law with those rules and norms which are officially stamped and authoritatively recognized and defined as law by king or state, relegating all other normative forms to the domain of the quasi-legal, non-legal or pre-legal.

Marianne Constable, in *The Law of the Other*, succinctly unsettles this positivist paradigm by probing precisely into the heartland of 'Western law,' namely the common law.[1] She first offers the crucial distinction between "personal" and "territorial" law: "Under a principle of 'personal law,' the law of the community to which a person belongs determined the law applied to the person and his or her transactions; this is distinguished from a principle of 'territoriality' in which the laws or customs of a place govern all those who reside there."[2] Constable then invokes the distinction in her exploration of the English legal institution known as the 'mixed jury,' a forum that was used when persons from two communities with different laws were involved in a dispute, ensuring that representative members from both communities would address the matter at stake.[3]

Constable argues that throughout the eleventh century and possibly as late as the fourteenth century, the mixed jury institution was premised on notions of personal law, that is, on the idea that a "judgment of a person must be according to the law or customs of that person's community; such judgment must be by those with knowledge of those customs or – what amounts to the same thing – by those who share in those customs and belong to the same community."[4] Constable shows, in short, that the mixed jury was based on recognizing and respecting "the law of an other." Yet she also shows that historians and jurists have often dismissed or ignored actual personal-law practices in their analyses of the history of the mixed jury. In a key passage, she offers the following explanation for this:

> That historians and writers concerned with conflict of laws and with the mixed jury have seemingly dismissed the community-based and personal-law implications of the practice of mixed juries raises questions about their understanding of law, an understanding that grounds law in the strength of a unifying

> territorial power. What has led students of Anglo-American law to neglect the practice of the mixed jury and even to ignore the presence of mixed juries before the fourteenth century? ... [T]he answers to these questions lie not so much in the history of the mixed jury as in the legal positivism of its modern interpreters. That is, modern texts about juries ... reveal a particular understanding of law as doctrine and as official behavior, which denies to practice or custom the status of law ... For them, law begins, as Hart puts it, with 'the mere reduction to writing of hitherto unwritten rules,' and the crucial step 'from the pre-legal to the legal' is 'the acknowledgment of reference to the writing or inscription as *authoritative*, that is, as the *proper* way of disposing of doubts as to the existence of the rule.'[5] (emphasis in original)

In sum, Constable shows that "the positivist understanding of law precludes the possibility of any law other than positive law."[6] At the moment of recognition, when the state validated the mixed jury as a legal institution, it also designated all that antedated it as 'pre-legal.' It was at that moment that "the *history* of the official *doctrine* of the mixed jury, as distinct from the *tradition* of its *practice*, began"[7] (emphasis added). In this chapter I look at two 'histories,' two distinct trajectories of community-based legal practices, in their relation to state law. I begin with the Hebrew Law of Peace and then move to consider the case of rabbinical courts.

In 1925, defending the Hebrew Law of Peace against accusations that it strove to create a state within a state, Paltiel Dickstein retorted:

> How is it possible to maintain within one state and within one territory two systems of law ? How can a national Hebrew law exist among the waves of the Anglo–Arab legal sea? ... *The puzzlement with this phenomenon is only a product of those legalistic views which are grounded in the premises and principles determined by eighteenth and nineteenth centuries science.* Yet in medieval times, the coexistence of legal systems and the functioning of one legal system within another one had been common. Different laws applied for different classes, various strata kept to their own courts of law and their own legal customs, and various distinct laws applied in the same town and in the same state. In early medieval times, the citizens of Rome in the Germanic states retained their own Roman law. It is also well-known that the Jews enjoyed self-determination in law in their various countries of residence, especially in Babylon, Spain and Poland.[8] (emphasis added)

Dickstein's formulation, articulated in the 1920s in the context of projecting a Hebrew community-centered form of law, anticipated a post-colonial reading of those colonialist-era studies of the so-called folkways of colonized populations; in fact it anticipated that whole sociolegal discourse on legal pluralism that, as Merry points out, is essentially premised on a non-statist conception of law.[9]

To be sure, the Hebrew Law of Peace imagined itself as the nucleus of a future legal system of a sovereign state. Yet it refused to privilege the state – a colonial or an independent one for that matter – as the authoritative source of law.[10] Recorded memories of Jewish self-government in law facilitated the Hebrew Law of Peace advocates' ability to articulate a community-centered conception of law which was at once non-statist and nationalist: "Our unique legal institutions are not a new creation and they were not established as a mere protest against the courts of the state. Our religious courts exist for thousands of years," wrote Dickstein, "and the roots of the secular court as well – our Hebrew Law of Peace – are deeply implanted in our past traditions."[11]

Indeed, given Constable's project of unsettling the positivist conception of law and history, it is not surprising that she also refers to the Jews as a strong case of respect for the law of others. Jewish courts of law, she writes, exercised exclusive jurisdiction over the internal affairs of Jewish communities. "In about 1200," Constable writes, "confirming even earlier privileges, King John declared that 'excesses which may arise among them except those which belong to our crown and justice, as homicide, mayhem, premeditated assault, burglary, rape, theft, arson, and treasure-trove, shall be brought before them according to their law and remedied, and they shall do justice thereon among themselves'."[12]

The British Crown's treatment of Jews was not unique. Jews elsewhere enjoyed similar privileges, so extensive in scope as to allow them to formally ban Jewish litigants from non-Jewish courts (*Arka'ot Shel Goyim*). Elon, for example, cites the twelfth-century Maimonides: "Anyone who litigates before non-Jewish judges or in their courts, even though their law is the same as Jewish law, is an evildoer, as if he has reviled, blasphemed, and raised his hand against the Torah of Moses ..."[13] Constable, following Jacobs, cites a French Synod of Rabbis who at about the same time excommunicated "every man or woman, far or near, who summon his neighbor before a Gentile tribunal."[14]

While such bans were predicated on the idea that Jewish laws antedated state law and should have been privileged as such, the ability to uphold such bans over time was by and large dependent on the approval of the sovereign. In other words, the ban against appealing to the courts of the sovereign had been premised on an anti-statist principle which was sustained by the protective approval of this very same state. We are dealing here, then, not with a mere opposition between state and community law, but with an interplay, with an ongoing tension, with competing jurisdictions and with the contingencies of state treatments of non-state law. In short, we are dealing here with the dis-unity of law, with "*a plurality of legal forms over which state law persistently, but never with complete success, seeks to impose a unity.*"[15] In the remainder of this chapter, I shall consider two distinct ways in which the colonial state law "imposed its unity" over the aspiring community-based Hebrew law projects of Palestine; one applied to the Hebrew Law of Peace, the other to the orthodox version of dispensing justice to the Jews.

The extant literature on law and community reveals the degree to which litigation is often perceived as disruptive to community life, a perception held by community members who thereby simultaneously invent their membership in a closed community and idealize the harmonious character of that community's social fabric. Resort to litigation is thus constructed as a sign of distance from the community and as a way of creating differences among social participants.[16] The Hebrew Law of Peace, in its attempts to discourage resort to the courts of the state, was predicated upon such sentiments. In this respect at least, the Hebrew Law of Peace contributed its share to the very invention of the community as distinct from the colonial state on the one hand and the non-Jewish majority population on the other. At the same time, the Hebrew Law of Peace had a stake in constituting itself as a formal arena in which the members of the invented community were invited to litigate, however user-friendly the system purported to be. This practical necessity, upon which the very existence of the system depended, bred an attempt to activate the system on the basis of voluntary consent alone, without resort to the sanctioning powers of the state on the one hand and without resort to internal mechanisms of violence on the other hand. The challenge, in short, was to create a non-disruptive mechanism that would nonetheless be both effective and symbolically assertive of the community's vitality.

Still, the Hebrew Law of Peace cannot be properly understood without taking account of the colonial state law in the shadow of which it functioned. This is most evident when we look at the sanctions that the system garnered in order to assert its authority over recalcitrant 'members' of the community. Lacking state powers, maintaining the Hebrew Law of Peace depended on the Jewish community's voluntary readiness to submit to the authority of the courts and to comply with their decisions. This essentially depended on persuasion: on appeals to communal solidarity and national responsibility.[17]

The primary sanction against those who refused to litigate in the Hebrew Courts of Peace was to publicly denounce them as *shirkers* (*mishtamet*), a *shirker* being one who displayed poor citizenship in respect to the community in general and the national project in particular. The name of the shirker would be published in the press and periodically the Hebrew Courts of Peace would also publish a list of shirkers and send it to various Zionist institutions, to Jewish settlements, and to town councils.[18] Occasionally town councils refused to issue various necessary documents to persons who were listed as shirkers, thus adding more force to the sanction.[19]

It is hard to determine how effective this sanction was.[20] It certainly worked well in small rural settlements where the force of public opinion strongly affected 'legal' and 'non-legal' matters alike. The deterrent effect of the sanction in larger settlements such as Tel Aviv (or in towns with an Arab majority like Haifa and Jerusalem) seemed to have been weaker.[21] It seems that open defiance of the Hebrew Court became more prevalent from the mid-1920s onwards, when a wave of new immigrants – with a high proportion of urban middle-class settlers – changed the social composition of the settler community and accelerated its transformation into a society of strangers. The more this happened, the more vocal became the advocates of the Hebrew Law of Peace in their cries over the decline of the national spirit and the lack of communal responsibility among the settlers: "Old exilic habits," complained Dickstein, "implanted in us a submissive character and a sense of admiration for foreign external powers. We seem to prefer the kiss of a foreign whip and subservience to a shining button over voluntary self-discipline and obedience to the Jewish public's own authorities."[22]

It is also noteworthy that in their efforts to develop a voluntary community-centered legal system, advocates of the Hebrew Law of Peace were not particularly eager to embrace venues that tied them to the colonial state law even when it offered them the option of state enforcement of their rulings under existing arbitration laws. A letter sent from the Hebrew Court of Peace in Jaffa to the Hebrew Court of Peace in one of the smaller Jewish settlements instructed thus:

> As far as *shirkers* are concerned, it is advisable not to employ the coercive powers of the government. Our goal is to educate the public to settle disputes without using state courts, and it is therefore not advisable to appeal to it for help. The settlement committee should employ all necessary means and it has sufficient power and it is not necessary to turn to the government.[23]

The official regulations of the Hebrew Court of Peace also advised courts "to use all possible means to coerce the shirker to obey the court."[24] But what exactly would such "all necessary means" entail above and beyond the official designation of someone as a shirker?

Excommunication, a long-standing Jewish practice in exilic communities and a valid recognizable sanction in Jewish law, is perhaps the ultimate communal sanction. Every form of punishment is a societal act of distancing, designed to constitute the offender as an outsider, whether at the physical, emotional or symbolic level. Yet while the designation of shirker aims primarily at the symbolic, excommunication aims at the material severing of all social ties and at creating an aura of utter silence around a person's existence. In short, it is a social death-sentence.

A case brought before the Hebrew Court of Peace of Tel Aviv in 1925 concerned a case of excommunication. The following is something of an illustrative digression; readers interested in strictly linear narrative may proceed directly to the end of this excerpt.

> 8.2.1925
> Plaintiff: Dr Haya Fogel
> Defendant: Town Council of Kfar-Sava
> Re: Honor
> *Counsel for Plaintiff:* Plaintiff works as a private physician in the settlement of Kfar-Sava. She recently received a letter as follows: "The Honorable Council resolved in its last meeting to notify Her Honor that since she misbehaved lately and had been involved in certain scandals, she must leave our settlement within the next three days." The same day the Council addressed Mr Goderstein, in whose place plaintiff resided, and told him that he should vacate her room and must not rent it to her any more. All the settlers of Kfar-Sava were similarly notified that they must not let her any residence (these two letters are attached herewith). A similar letter has been sent to the baker where she bought her bread, and in general she was sort of excommunicated. This sanction was imposed on plaintiff without providing her the opportunity to defend herself. Plaintiff, through her attorney-at-law, therefore asks the court to recognize that charges are illegal and contradict the basic premises of a civilized public, and to commit the Council to compensate her for the insult and to publish the judgment at its own expense.
> *Counsel for Defendant:* The settlement previously had to decide whether to accept plaintiff as the settlement's public physician at a monthly salary of three Pounds or whether to ask Hadassah (a Zionist medical institution) to provide the settlement with health care for the monthly cost of five Pounds. Two votes were taken,

one at a regular meeting, and a second at a polling station that had been available for a whole day, and the majority voted to seek medical aid from Hadassah. But the settlement in effect could not find the means to subsidize the enterprise and the physician that settled in Kfar-Sava left it. By that time plaintiff saw an opportunity to retaliate and refused to offer the settlers medical assistance and to sell them various common medicines and Mr Moller, owner of the pharmacy, had to steal them from her and to sell them to the settlers. All this upset the settlers and the Council resolved, under pressure from many settlers who came to the Council meeting and raised their voices in protest, to notify her that she had to leave Kfar-Sava within three days and also resolved to make it publicly known that she should not be allowed residence and goods in the settlement. It was not excommunication, but a response to one, a protest of the settlers against the boycott of the physician, but truth is that it was not implemented and she stayed in the settlement and shops sold her goods and my wife sold her a coconut.

Judgment: Looking at the materials before us, we were not convinced that the charges were well-founded. At any rate, the actions of the Council of Kfar-Sava, which turned to illegal means that contradict civilized life, which used insulting expressions in its letter in a way that could badly hurt the honor of the plaintiff, and all this publicly deserve the harshest reprimand.

Therefore, the Council should publish this judgment at its own expense in *Ha'Aretz* and *Doar HaYom* [two daily Hebrew newspapers] and should pay the plaintiff for the expenses she bore in this trial at the sum of 0.77 Pounds.

Both parties have the right to appeal to the High Hebrew Court of Peace. [25]

Rumors that excommunication had been applied to *shirkers* were alluded to in a letter in which a Hebrew Law of Peace activist, Daniel Auster, reported on a conversation he had with Norman Bentwich, the senior legal adviser of the colonial government. "Bentwich wanted to know," he wrote "whether it was true that recalcitrant litigants were subjected to excommunication."[26] Shortly afterward, a Zionist representative body (*Vaad HaZirim*) informed the Hebrew Courts of Peace that

> the High Commissioner asked us to exert our influence on you and to ask you to allow full liberty to those who want to litigate in the courts of the government. Litigants in the Hebrew Courts

may only be those who choose so out of their own free will, without any external pressure. We, at any rate, already notified the government that as far as we know no pressure is exerted on those who address the courts of the government. We hope our said notification would not be contradicted by the facts.[27]

The attitude of Zionist institutions towards the Hebrew Law of Peace, and further attempts of the Hebrew Law of Peace to assert its jurisdiction through the assistance of these institutions, are discussed in detail in chapter 7. The important point for present purposes is that, as the above exchange indicates, the Hebrew Law of Peace could not ignore the expectations and general directives of the sheltering colonial state. As much as it tried to establish itself as a community-centered system, distinct from state law and state institutions, the Hebrew Law of Peace had been dependent upon and concerned with colonial state law for recognition and protection.

"I was very badly impressed with this conversation," wrote Auster about his meeting with Bentwich, "[i]t is now clear to me that the government does not approve of our courts. They consider them as competitors, as a display of mistrust in the courts of the state, and as a government within a government. Naturally they do not like it. We must anticipate difficulties."[28]

As far as the colonial government was concerned, the Hebrew Courts of Peace could be accommodated under existing legal provisions allowing for arbitration forums. Judgments issued by Hebrew Courts of Peace could be ratified by state courts and executed by the state machinery had a party declined to comply with such judgment or appealed to a state court for reconsideration.

In 1920, the colonial Chief Judicial Clerk had issued a notice in which the Hebrew Courts of Peace were officially recognized as valid arbitration forums and which simplified the existing Ottoman procedures concerning ratification of such judgments.[29] Nonetheless, the advocates of the Hebrew Law of Peace argued that the ratification proceedings of the state law were too cumbersome, allowed parties to evade compliance, and therefore diminished the attractiveness of the Hebrew Courts.[30]

In March 1926, a new Arbitration Ordinance came into effect. This Ordinance reflected some of the direct interests of the Hebrew Courts of Peace, allowing for simpler, more expedient and more accessible ratification procedures.[31] However, promoters of the Hebrew Law of Peace argued that the new Ordinance had not sufficiently simplified these procedures, thereby still steering litigants away from the Hebrew Courts of Peace. They therefore submitted a memorandum to the colonial

Chief Justice, asking for amendments to be made that would further accommodate the needs of litigants.[32]

Although such procedural difficulties could be interpreted as an indirect attempt by the colonial government to undermine the Hebrew Courts of Peace, there is strong evidence that suggests otherwise. While the Hebrew Courts processed an average of twelve hundred cases a year, only a handful were overruled by state courts. In 1926, a colonial district state court nullified a judgment of a Hebrew Court of Peace on the grounds that it overstepped its authority by referring the parties, for purposes of appeal, to a Hebrew Court of Appeal. Using particularly harsh language, the state court ruled that it would not tolerate tribunals which inappropriately ascribed themselves titles which belonged exclusively to the courts of the government of Palestine.

This judgment was a matter of considerable concern among the advocates of the Hebrew Law of Peace and it was therefore with considerable relief that they greeted the decision of the colonial Court of Appeals which overturned that decision and reaffirmed that "the Hebrew Courts of Peace are permanent arbitration tribunals whose nature and existence had been previously substantiated in the judgments of this court."[33]

Thus, in spite of the concerns expressed by activists of the Hebrew Law of Peace, the colonial government did not treat the Hebrew Courts as subversive competitors. Norman Bentwich himself became quite an enthusiastic supporter of the Hebrew Law of Peace and praised it as "one of the most tremendous expressions of Jewish self-rule," explicitly expressing the hope that this "legal authority which is based on voluntary consent will become a legal authority which is based on the moral consciousness of the whole public; and a court which has neither coercive powers nor a legislative role will nonetheless create a law acceptable to the people."[34] In general, the colonial state never tried to seriously undermine the Hebrew Courts of Peace. This form of non-intervention and remote-control supervision, in fact, had been in line with colonial policies elsewhere, typically based on imposing structural unity 'from above.'[35]

To sum up the argument so far, then, it may be seen that while at the practical and operational level the Hebrew Law of Peace was in fact dependent on the coercive powers of the colonial state, and while its advocates invested considerable effort in securing its legitimacy in state law as a valid arbitration forum, its community-centered ideology – as well as its sanctioning, shame-oriented practices – were based on the idea that the Hebrew courts provided much more than this: real, 'living authentic' law, which flourished and developed independently of state-backing; fulfilling crucial nation-constitutive functions under structural conditions that dictated distinct trajectories for the colonial state on the one hand and the national community on the other hand. While the Hebrew Courts of Peace, like popular judicial forums elsewhere, often resembled in their symbols and actual procedures those of state courts, and while they faced the apparently inescapable paradox of depending on a state law from which they tried to distance themselves, it may fairly be said that these courts were offering in earnest a potential venue for the avoidance of state law and, moreover, a symbolic venue for asserting the possibility of law without a state.

It was not the colonial state and its legal officers, but rather forces from within the Jewish colonizing community of Palestine, that ultimately brought about the demise of the Hebrew Law of Peace. Conceiving of law in terms of a communal product ushered in a nationalist version which collided, as we are yet to see in detail, with the dominant Zionist effort to consolidate the national idea around sovereignty, state and state-like institutions.

The conception of law suggested by the advocates of the Hebrew Law of Peace, thinking of it not in terms of instrumental rules for maintaining social order but rather in terms of a creative process responsive to values and collective memory, represented a *cultural*, as distinct from a *political* (or 'scientific') approach to law. This approach corresponded to a broader nationalist orientation that emphasized the *cultural*, rather than the *political*, aspects of the national project precisely at a time when the latter form of nationalism – investing in the institution-building 'practicalities' of national revival – became the dominant orientation of the Zionist movement.

It is in this context that we should evaluate the entirely different relational form that developed between the colonial state and the orthodox version of Hebrew law. In a nutshell, a strong state-oriented disposition had been displayed by no other than the orthodox nationalists. On the face of it, as we have seen in the previous chapter, the orthodox historical narrative had been similarly based on a non-statist conception of law (with different ideas, of course, as to how the Jewish community had been regulated and how justice was dispensed in the past). This principled ideological stance notwithstanding, the historical fact is that the orthodox nationalists of Palestine developed an unabashed and uncompromised statist orientation: seeking the protection of the state for their courts, imposing their jurisdiction by means of state law coercion, and in effect encouraging the public at large to use the colonial state's courts. It is here, in short, that the colonial state returns to our story with a vengeance.

Religious courts which dealt with matters of personal status for various religious communities (including the Jewish one) were recognized under the Ottoman system. Yet the authority and prestige of the rather loose and disorganized Jewish rabbinical tribunals which operated prior to the British occupation of Palestine deteriorated immediately afterwards. Secular Zionists perceived these courts as ill-suited to their modern needs and expectations and moderate orthodox Jews sought to assert their own spiritual leadership in religious matters. Both groups advocated reform. Accordingly, the orthodoxy engaged in various efforts to centralize rabbinical authority throughout Palestine and to reassert the jurisdiction of rabbinical courts by organizational means. Yet the Jewish population of Palestine – divided as it was between Zionists and non-Zionists, secular and religious communities, Ashkenazi and Sephardic Jews, orthodox and ultra-orthodox groups – could not agree on an appropriate, or even desirable, religious representative body. Guidelines for reform, ultimately, were left in the hands of the British.

The British colonial administration, typically reluctant to interfere with local legal practices of a 'customary nature,' nonetheless had to respond to an all-too-real situation of disarray and to pressures from various Jewish constituencies to reorganize the religious-based system of rabbinical courts. A British commission of inquiry established in early 1920 proposed various procedural reforms for the system as a whole. A follow-up commission, headed by Norman Bentwich, was specifically assigned the task of proposing an administrative solution to the question of rabbinical authority and courts. The Bentwich commission, after hearing evidence from all the sectors of the Jewish population, recommended the creation of a Chief Rabbinate; this body was to be be invested with the powers to establish a system of state-backed religious courts with jurisdictional monopoly over matters of personal status for Jews.[36]

For the British, the deployment of such courts under their auspices merely served administrative purposes, in line with the colonial interest in asserting centralized forms of unity and order while keeping away from the internal religious affairs of native communities. The very term Chief Rabbinate, in fact, seems to have originated with British legal tradition, which recognized such an institution as the official leader of the Jews of England and the colonies.[37] The British solution, therefore, as promulgated by the Bentwich commission, had little to do with any particular "evolution of the Zionist idea or with the structure of the settlers' society of Palestine in 1921."[38] The British initiative had been practically ignored by ultra-orthodox circles, who maintained their own courts and refused to submit to the authority of orthodox nationalists anyway. But the secular community of Palestine reluctantly complied, thinking the matter to be of lesser priority than other national issues.[39] However, *Ha'Mizrachi* – the political organ of the nationalist orthodox community – enthusiastically embraced that initiative and became its ardent defender and promoter.[40]

Why did the orthodox nationalists so eagerly embrace the colonial creation? It seems that the statist route for establishing authority by legal and official means substituted for their lack of spiritual and cultural leadership. The social and communal authority of rabbis deteriorated and became significantly dispersed after the colonization of Palestine by the British and the social and demographic changes it brought about. The orthodox nationalists understood only too well that the institution of the Chief Rabbinate and its affiliated courts would be subjected to their de facto control simply by default; the ultra-orthodox refusing to cooperate and secular Jews lacking the intellectual means (and probably the will) to have a voice in Jewish law, at least that part of it that applied to personal-status matters.

In fact, in spite of the war they waged against the Hebrew Law of Peace, the orthodox nationalists never tried in earnest to assert a spiritual and moral leadership in law. The disarrayed rabbinical courts that existed prior to the British initiative did not (and probably could not) make any serious efforts to establish themselves as wide-ranging tribunals, did not try to adjust to the needs and expectations of the settler community in Palestine, and did not attempt to base their authority on the force of public opinion and the fear of public shame like the Hebrew Courts of Peace did. Rather, the orthodox leadership was primarily interested in asserting a monopoly over one particular area of the law, namely personal-status matters. For that purpose, state-backed coercion was certainly the most effective way of asserting its jurisdiction.

The strong and, for all practical purposes, the sole interest in asserting a monopoly over personal-status matters reflected the orthodoxy's distinct understanding of 'the community' and of 'the nation'. At the heart of the nation, according to this conception, stood the family. States come and go and territorial political sovereignty has been historically contingent, but the family always remained the basic reproductive mechanism that ensured the purity and authenticity of the Jewish nation. The identity of an individual as a Jew, as well as the identity of the community as Jewish, had to be secured through the strict regulation of marital bonds and the subsequent close supervision of the question of who was a Jew (only someone born to a Jewish mother, or someone who became such under the strict supervision of rabbinical authorities). Thus, under the conditions prevailing in Palestine, where the secular nationalist settlers considered rabbinical authority to be outdated and irrelevant, the orthodox enthusiastically embraced the British 'solution,' thereby simultaneously ensuring their monopoly over personal-status matters and relieving them of the need to reform their laws in order to appeal to the secular population in other matters as well.

In this sense, the newly established rabbinical courts, in fact the whole machinery which I refer to as the rabbinical establishment, were brain-children of the colonial British state. These rabbinical courts were not continuing a Jewish tradition of the past any more than were the Hebrew Courts of Peace. Rather, the orthodox were now in a position to fix and impose – by statist means – their version of tradition, their version of Jewish law, and their ideas concerning the desired composition and nature of Jewish tribunals. The ability to impose these versions was particularly salient given the challenge represented by the Hebrew Law of Peace. As we have seen, one of the greatest of these challenges was the very bold attempt to rethink Jewish traditions in law and to thereby transform tradition into a contested terrain. Under these circumstances, seeking state protection and in fact advancing a statist-oriented approach to law, was a brilliant move.

Not only was the British state embraced for securing the jurisdiction of rabbinical courts, but also for providing a 'neutral' forum in which to litigate other matters of the law. The orthodox nationalists had been unequivocal on this point: "Either Hebrew Law [i.e., religious, rabbinical courts] or the Law of the King" but never the Hebrew Law of Peace.[41] In other words, in all other areas of the law, save that of personal status, the law of the colonial state had been explicitly preferred by the orthodox nationalists over the secular Hebrew Law of Peace. And quite understandably so: the law of the colonial state did not pose a threat precisely because it had no national pretensions and did not claim to represent the spirit and tradition of the Jews. Colonial law, looked at from this perspective, was deemed 'neutral,' in fact precisely as colonialists (and positivist jurists) always wanted it to look. Thus, while the Hebrew Courts of Peace had certainly been an invention of some secular nationalist minds, based on an imagined past of Jewish self-government in law, those rabbinical courts which purported to merely continue the unbroken chain of Jewish tradition had been in fact a formal administrative invention of the colonial state.

The 1921 colonial legal framework that created the state-protected Chief Rabbinate and rabbinical courts still determines the state-religion binding structure of present-day Israel. A 1996 decision of Israel's High Court of Justice may be rather telling in this respect. The case which had been reviewed by the court involved the powers of the state-protected rabbinical courts *to sanction excommunication* to parties who refused to litigate and be tried by them (in matters other than personal-status, when the voluntary consent of the two parties needs to be secured prior to litigation).[42]

The opinion of the majority was that rabbinical courts could not apply such sanctions because the state law that defined their jurisdiction and regulated their scope did not invest them with such powers:

> A Rabbinical court is established on the basis of law and its authority is grounded in law. It is financed by the state's treasury, and its judges are paid just like other state servants, the rabbinical judge passes judgment while the state emblem is behind his back and he writes his decisions on official state stationery ... the Rabbinical court has no authority other than the one granted it by law.[43]

In other words, the majority opinion was based on the view that rabbinical courts, their uniqueness notwithstanding, were state institutions which could not exceed the powers granted them by the state law that also constituted and authorized them.

The minority opinion in that case was handed down by an orthodox judge. He applied quite a different narrative: "Courts which pass judgment on the basis of the law of the Torah have been in operation since time immemorial," wrote Justice Tal. The present-day Rabbinical court is but another element in a long chain of tribunals which had been applying the Law of the Torah since the days of Moses; "In contrast to what may be inferred from the opinions of this court," he wrote, "it is not the state of Israel that established the Rabbinical court. The Rabbinical court has been there prior to the constitution of the State of Israel." According to this line of reasoning, therefore, the Rabbinical court, in issuing the sanction of excommunication, did not operate in its capacity as a state court – admittedly limited by state law – but rather in its capacity as a Jewish community-based court with inherent powers to apply the law of the Torah, regardless of the state law purporting to have created it.

Neither the majority nor the minority in this case were innocent of fabrication. The majority opinion was based on that strict positivist conception of law according to which history always begins, as Constable has shown us, with authoritative declarations of state officials. Ignoring, or unable to perceive actual communal practices as a valid form of law, the majority judges assumed that rabbinical courts could not *but* be a creation of the state, forever *ultra vires* when applying rules other than those prescribed by state law.

It is the minority opinion, however, which is invested with an irony within an irony. An orthodox judge had to resort to a non-statist and a non-positivist reasoning in order to defend the jurisdiction of rabbinical courts which were created by the positive law of the former colonial state (regardless of the history of *other* Jewish courts in the absence of such a state). Whereas the majority opinion was premised on a positivist fabrication, the minority opinion was premised on a metahistorical one, smoothly establishing an uninterrupted continuity between Moses and the colonial-era rabbinical court.[44] Moreover, the minority opinion sought to ground the legitimacy of the rabbinical courts' power to exert the ultimate communal sanction, that of excommunication, while these courts never tried in earnest to base their authority, like the Hebrew Courts of Peace did, on the voluntary consent of community members who share in an experience of common destiny and purpose. In short, while the Hebrew Court of Peace, focused as it was on community-oriented law, had considered excommunication to "contradict civilized life" seventy years earlier, a 1996 state-oriented court embraced this sanction as a prerogative accorded in the name of communal authority.

But I think that more is at stake here than simply establishing the 'right' historical perspective or musing on ironies. The point, rather, is that the majority opinion – expressing both anger and frustration with the rabbinical court's practices – and the minority opinion – seeking to defend those practices – jointly tell us something about orthodox nationalism on the one hand and the nature of Israeli 'secularism' on the other.

In law, orthodox nationalism comfortably accommodates two contradictory positions: seeking the protection and backing of the state while at the same time articulating a supra-state and non-positivist conception of law. In political thought and practice, just like in law, orthodox nationalism exploits the state's resources and its capacity to exert so-called legitimate violence, but in situations of conflict, when the dictates of the state seem to collide with what are perceived to be religious principles, the orthodox nationalist will quickly resort to a transcendental supra-state reasoning. Of course, it is plausible to argue that this tendency attests to nothing more than an instrumental orientation to the state (in fact, one may even find such a conception to be quite sobering compared with the sanctification of the state by 'secular' Zionism). But still there is more to it.

First, what we have here is a dialectical master-trick in which state-protected control over the laws regulating personal status allows for a non-statist definition of the nation. Dependence upon the law of the state sustains the force of non-statist law; and this configuration, in turn, breeds a process which constantly undermines state sovereignty under the auspices of this very same state.[45] Second, and most urgent in the context of this discussion, is the fact that the rabbinical alliance with the state, British-ruled and Jewish-ruled alike, enabled the orthodox version of Jewish tradition and Jewish law to monopolize the national imagination.

The institutionalization of rabbinical courts as formal state apparatuses (complemented by a whole set of statutes and legal rules) is a visible symbol of the firm grip that this particular version of Jewish tradition retains over the national imagination, even when it often seems to alienate secular groups in society. The ability of orthodox nationalism to capture the national imagination in this particular way owes much to two typical dispositions of so-called secular Zionism. First, is the tendency to situate nationalism within the domain of a state ideology, that is, to organize the national reconstruction around the prospects of attaining an independent state and to treat the latter as both an organizing and a legitimizing principle of the national project as a whole. Second, and most important for our immediate purpose, is the fact that "even the most severe Zionist critics of exile did not advocate a total rupture with it;"[46] unable to do so simply because this would have undermined the national narrative of historical antiquity and continuity.

Indeed, the establishment of the Chief Rabbinate by the British served the interests of the Zionist leadership as well. Seeking religious legitimacy for the national home project, and manifestly shunning debate on the meaning of Judaism and developing a viable alternative to the orthodox view, the Zionist leadership embraced the orthodox nationalists as the ones who had exclusive rights of representation over what constituted Judaism in general and Jewish law in particular.[47]

A curious paradox followed. In Zionist thought, the period of exile was strongly linked with a 'religious' form of national life, in fact a form that kept the nation alive in the absence of an organic connection to the land and in the absence of political sovereignty. Exilic conditions and religious practices were wedded in what Zerubavel calls the "master commemorative narrative" of Zionism.[48] Yet while granting the validity of that historical wedding, ardent secular Zionists based the project of national revival on the repudiation of that form of life. However, from a sociological standpoint, one should distinguish between the repudiation of a certain tradition as, say, outdated, and the rejection of a certain tradition because it is not perceived as historically 'correct.' It is only the former type of repudiation which characterizes the so-called secularists. The irrelevance of religious practices to modern life, the outdated doctrines of Jewish law, or the evils of rabbinical clericalism may have been reiterated by secularists, but the very idea that Jewish life in exile was indeed exclusively shaped by rabbinical authority and that the orthodox nationalists are the true heirs to that tradition is seldom challenged. Thus, as such 'outdated' forms as those embodied in the practices and doctrines of the rabbinical courts have eventually found their way into the state apparatus, in itself the strongest symbol of national reconstruction, the result has been a consolidation of the orthodox version of Jewish tradition and Jewish law as the hegemonic one, albeit in an often 'rejected' form.

In sum, one of the products of the early alliance of the orthodox nationalists with the colonial state has been the casting away of alternative community-centered notions of law and, by extension, alternative national imaginations. The effectiveness of this casting aside may be demonstrated by an anecdotal fact: Anita Shapira, a prominent Israeli historian, misleadingly concluded her analysis of the early alliance between the colonial state and the orthodox nationalists by saying that "with the establishment of the Chief Rabbinate came an end to the Hebrew Courts of Peace;" these courts, in fact, only began to gather strength at that time (their impending decline following only in the late 1920s).[49] At any rate, to ask what would have been the trajectory of Jewish religion in Palestine without that British imposition, or whether a state–religion structure would not have become the national trademark, or whether the version developed by the Hebrew Law of Peace would have had a better chance of prevailing, is now, as one writer observes, purely a matter of speculation on history.[50]

CHAPTER 4

CELEBRATING AUTHENTICITY AND PRACTICING HYBRIDITY

Shmuel Eisenstadt and Paltiel Dickstein were the two primary 'theoreticians' of the Hebrew Law of Peace. They met for the first time immediately after the revolution, in Moscow,[1] where they ventured to establish a Hebrew Law Society that would revive Hebrew law in line with Zionist national aspirations. The project was to be carried out by the joint efforts of orthodox Zionist rabbis and secular nationalist jurists.[2] Describing his vocation in no less romantic than scientific terms, Eisenstadt wrote in his private diary:

> A day will come when the Society for Hebrew Law will redeem my soul and relieve the burden of daily life that tears my soul to thousands of splinters and takes me away from my spiritual world. I can envision a noble universe: All day, save for the hours spent in the Rumiantzov library, I shall research, inquire and write, I shall delve into details, into the secrets of Hebrew law, and shall perform my studies in those hours which are neither day nor night, after a day of trouble and after running from one lesson to another ... I shall enrich myself ... and I shall give the science of Hebrew law my creative powers, now bursting and thirsty for revelation after years of collecting materials and teaching in Odessa. I am so thirsty to see my work completed. I shall rejoice with my family and only then shall I know that it was not in vain that I lived and that I shall perhaps leave a mark behind me, because these are the founding blocks for a national regime of law that our work molds today.[3]

Eisenstadt, a Russian-born legal scholar, received his legal education in Switzerland, where he was exposed to the works of the German historical and comparative schools in jurisprudence and familiarized himself with the intellectual debates in and around law in the German-speaking world. It was this 'scientific' orientation to law that he wedded passionately to the dream of national legal revival. This dream, in its purely academic version, consisted of laborious studies and interpretations of Jewish texts in order to equip the nationalists with systematic compendiums of legal postulates adjusted to modernity.

Yet while Eisenstadt, still in Moscow, continued to orient himself toward an academic kind of legal work, thinking of Hebrew law in 'scientific' terms, Dickstein, upon arriving in Palestine in 1921, found a different reality of law-in-action. The Palestinian Hebrew Courts of Peace, already providing a concrete foundation upon which to develop and constitute a living Hebrew law, displayed little 'scientific' orientation. The overwhelming majority of the judges who served on the tribunals of the Hebrew Law of Peace were not jurists, let alone experts on Jewish law. While a few advocates and enthusiasts, like Paltiel Dickstein and Shmuel Eisenstadt, wove the dream of reconstructing Hebrew law (and later re-establishing the Hebrew Law Society in Palestine), others who served in the Hebrew courts dealt with the mundane and often tedious business of having to reconcile claims, calculate and award damages to parties, to the chagrin of their adversaries in numerous petty affairs: broken promises, insults, neighbors' disputes, unpaid debts, damaged goods, labor lay-offs and numerous other commercial, residential and monetary matters. While a handful of jurists wrote manifestos and learned articles about Hebrew law, lay judges were busy producing it. And often they did so without any reference to Jewish legal principles.

Most decisions at the lower local and district courts had no 'legal' flavor at all, that is to say legal in the narrow sense of grounding judgments in abstract rules. Judges spelled out factual findings and made rather common-sense judgments on the basis of these facts. In hundreds of such cases, there was hardly a trace of any explicitly articulated legal principle, let alone of attempts to elaborate on Jewish legal doctrines and rules. In that, of course, the Hebrew Courts of Peace were not much different from what present-day scholars designate as community justice and popular justice tribunals, or from the lower-tier courts of the state, where the 'legal' is often not much more than an abstract and remote source of legitimacy. The routine practice of rendering justice, so to speak, is invested in the mundanity of sorting out competing narratives rather than in a jurisprudential universe of abstract rules; a fact that corresponded well with the basic claim of the Hebrew Courts of Peace that they were the appropriate forums for handling such tasks (the 'legal' in lower-tier courts, however, is often revealed in procedures and rules of evidence, requiring the need for professionals with the technical know-how required to sort out competing narratives. I shall return to this issue below, where I discuss the Hebrew Law of Peace in terms of a 'professional project').

The picture was somewhat different in the High Hebrew Court of Peace.[4] In principle, the judges and advocates of the Hebrew Law of Peace owed allegiance to Jewish law and were committed to legal interpretations of some agreed-upon fundamental Jewish texts: the learned treatises of Maimonides, *Mishnah-Torah* (*Yad Ha-Hazakah*) (1180), Jacob Ben Asher's *Sefer-HaTurim* (1340), and Josef Karo's *Shulchan Aruch*, a most comprehensive legal compendium which was completed in the sixteenth century and became an authoritative source that "replaced the authority of (early) Talmudic responses."[5] In particular, Hebrew Law of Peace jurists turned to Hoshen Mishpat, "one of the four principal divisions of *Sefer-HaTurim* and the *Shulchan Aruch*, dealing mainly with matters of Hebrew Law."[6] Asserting that these Jewish texts became lifeless over the years, the theoreticians of the Hebrew Law of Peace argued that they were in a position to offer fresh interpretations of these texts and to adjust them to the needs of modernity.

Decisions rendered by the High Court occasionally cited Jewish law, mainly referring to the rules and provisions of Hoshen Mishpat. In a handful of cases, the citation was complemented by some elaboration and by some attempts to accommodate the legal principle to other legal and extra-legal considerations. Consider the following example of law-making in action:

> January 22, 1923
> In the Matter of Aharon Shochat vs. Zeev Gluskin
> Re: A conflict between a written binding contract and undocumented oral promises.
> Judgment: The lower District Hebrew Court of Peace ruled on the basis of *Hoshen Mishpat* in favor of Gluskin. Appellant, a contractor for building Gluskin's house, argued that unwritten promises overrode the binding contract and that the case should have been decided according to the Jewish law of fraud. Respondent argued that according to Jewish law, the law of fraud applied only to movable property and not to real estate. The District Court found that a formal contract bound the parties, yet awarded partial remedies under the law of fraud. The High Court rules that:
> a. The Hebrew Law of Peace is not compelled to follow all the intricacies of the law of fraud in the same detailed form that this law assumes in the *Talmud*. Therefore, it does not find the present case to be outside the scope of the law of fraud due to the 'no fraud in real-property' rule. The moral foundation of

the law of fraud also includes this case of a contractor building a house.

b. The protection of contracts has great value for maintaining proper negotiations between parties. It is a world-redeeming issue. And still, when we find that in making the contract a fundamental mistake has been made, or that it involves fraud, our internal sentiment rebels against the wrong that would follow from strict adherence to the contract – and thus we rely on the law of fraud and nullify the contract.[7]

As in the case cited above, references to Jewish law were sometimes accompanied by bold attempts at innovation and creative interpretation. In most such cases, however, the thrust of decisions was not based on thorough interpretative techniques. Although judges at the High Court of Peace genuinely tried to cite Jewish law, it was hardly ever legal interpretation per se that they offered (in the sense of Foucault's paradigmatic shift from commentary to discipline – see Interregnum), but rather an interpretive mood in which Jewish texts played a background role while appeals to common sense, to the imperatives of modernity, and to abstract moral obligations provided the immediate rationale for decisions. Thus, while references to Jewish texts were quite common, it would be a gross exaggeration to suggest that the picture at the High Hebrew Court of Peace was fundamentally different from the lay-justice one employed at the lower-tier local and district Hebrew Courts of Peace. In these forums as well, most decisions were fact-oriented, displaying a strong nominalist tendency to focus on the case and not on abstract rules. Again, this was not surprising given the social background of most judges: secular, unprofessional peace-makers, whose judicial roles reflected their social standing in the community and not their embeddedness in Jewish legal scholarship.[8]

This seeming contradiction between praxis and ideology, between practicalities and capacities on the one hand and projections and theoretical intentions on the other hand, was the unstable and ambiguous foundation upon which the Hebrew law project took shape. In fact, the project consisted of a complex series of such apparent contradictions. Depending on speakers, audiences and circumstances, one could extract a variety of statements and practices that often looked mutually exclusive: Hebrew law as a product of spontaneous present-day judicial activities versus Hebrew law as a scholarly-inspired continuation of the past; Hebrew courts as friendly informal forums versus formal and rule-bound Hebrew courts; litigation as an outreach for compromise versus litigation as rational competition for entitlements; law without lawyers versus emphasis on lawyers' contributions; and Hebrew law as a non-statist (even anti-statist) law versus Hebrew law as the nucleus of a future state law.

The Hebrew Law of Peace, in short, should be read as a pastiche; as an amalgam of incoherent, contradictory, and unstable notions, dreams, practices, aspirations, and formulations that changed over time and context. My intention, however, is neither to try and settle these contradictions, nor to celebrate them, and certainly not to bemoan the confusion and ambiguity they entailed. Rather, this unstable amalgam of contradictory (yet sometimes also mutually constitutive and affirmative) practices and ideas, should allow us to probe into the social conditions that eventually shaped the trajectory of the project. As a surplus, such probing may also allow us to say something about the trajectory of Jewish nationalism in general.

A concrete manifestation of the above ambiguities was played out in the ambivalent attitude of the advocates of Hebrew law (many of them lawyers) towards the embryonic Jewish legal profession in Palestine. In fact, the project was such an amalgam of ideas and practices because it wedded an operating system of courts which relied on lay persons and user-friendly methods with a group of jurists who tried to turn these courts into a non-state, yet fully legalized, system of law. In some respects, these Hebrew law jurists acted as agents who did not wish to alter the rules of the professional game but, rather, to adjust them to the particularities of the Hebrew courts and mainly to the idea that professionalization was possible without adherence to state law and state apparatuses. In this sense, the story of the Hebrew Law of Peace is a story of an internal struggle among jurists and lawyers concerning the appropriate ways to produce law under colonial and nation-building conditions. On the other hand, the Hebrew Courts of Peace, in their origins and, mainly, in their actual operational mode, were made up of non-jurists and relied on non-professional ways of settling disputes. In this sense, the Hebrew law project at least had the potential to become a cultural site for imagining alternatives to the law–state–profession hegemonic configuration of justice to which we ordinarily submit. As we shall see, the attempt to reconcile these incompatibilities led to an unstable mode of operation and, moreover, to reliance on an open-ended jurisprudence which would have served as the theoretical foundation of the project.

Thus, on the one hand, lawyers were often described by the advocates of the Hebrew Law of Peace as instrumentally oriented professionals who used their craft only for furthering their own material wellbeing. Moreover, lawyers were criticized for lacking a sense of national commitment. For example, their unreflective adherence – if not enthusiasm – to the colonial state law was seen as a form of promoting assimilation into the culture and politics of the British colonial rulers (see Salle d'Attente).

On the other hand, the advocates of Hebrew law were acutely aware of their dependence on the ability of lawyers to steer prospective litigants away from the state courts and into the Hebrew Courts of Peace. Thus, concurring with the critique of the lawyers, the advocates of Hebrew Law of Peace made serious attempts to convince lawyers that the Hebrew courts were efficient and law-governed juridical arenas which were conducive to strict lawyerly habits and expectations, thus hoping to incorporate them into more active roles at the service of the Hebrew tribunals. For example, the Hebrew law activists resolved to allow the Lawyers' Association, "to the extent that it was willing to establish permanent connections with the institution," to elect and nominate two representatives who would have served on the Law of Peace's executive committee. Moreover, the revised 1925 Regulations of the Hebrew Courts of Peace established that "to the extent possible, each [Hebrew] district court shall admit a lawyer proficient in Hebrew and modern law as an office manager of the court," responsible, among other things, for drafting the reasoned judgments (ch. C, art. 8). Another regulation stipulated that at least half the judges at the High Hebrew Court of Peace would have formal legal education (ch. D, art. 3) and another chapter discussed the establishment of an "experts and lawyers council," to be composed of representatives elected by the general body of lawyers and by lawyers who served as judges of the Hebrew Law of Peace (ch. E). A particular effort was made to recruit lawyers as "expert" judges and hence to establish firmly the institutional ties of lawyers to the Hebrew Law of Peace.[9]

The ambivalent attitude towards lawyers, however, was only an outward manifestation of a deeper ambiguity. The Hebrew law project explicitly celebrated itself as a form of popular justice, "in contrast to professionalism, expertise, and legal education."[10] The Hebrew courts were portrayed as informal community-centered tribunals that catered directly to the needs and expectations of lay persons. The typical description of the ideal judge in the Hebrew Court of Peace emphasized traits which were portrayed as the exact opposite of a legalist-professional approach to dispute resolution. The ideal judge was one whose legitimacy and authority derived precisely from his or her embeddedness in the community and familiarity with the everyday life experiences of the litigants and who shared an equal social standing with them: "The judges," stated a report of the Hebrew Law of Peace, "are well versed in the conditions of the litigants and know their situation. The proceedings are conducted without lengthy formalities and suits are brought to an end as soon as possible. Thus obviating the services of a solicitor." Further, the legality displayed by the Hebrew Courts of Peace was explicitly one that had to be situated and contextualized: "In order to properly fulfill the role of the judge," wrote Dickstein, "one need not simply master professional legal knowledge, but rather a knowledge of life and an understanding of life, one needs the perspective of the lay-person ... without the barriers erected by scholastic and legalistic concepts, formulas and rules."[11]

However, on the other hand the Hebrew law project gradually also developed an unabashed commitment to rules, formalities, and legal expertise, in fact launching a fully fledged professional project. The High Hebrew Courts of Peace, in particular, tended to be quite strict in adherence to procedures, routinely upholding or reversing decisions of lower courts strictly on the basis of formal considerations.[12] At the operational level, the professional project consisted of attempts to educate and discipline judges to orderly professional norms, of revised procedural regulations that minutely detailed the formal ways to initiate and handle litigation,[13] and a growing emphasis on the production of written reasoned decisions. At the same time, a major effort was made to cloak the Hebrew Law of Peace in a scientific aura; its advocates were closely affiliated with two newly published law journals, *Ha'Mishpat* (*The Law*) and *Ha'Mishpat Ha'Ivri* (*Hebrew Law*), which ran articles by many of the Hebrew law activists, published bibliographical references to relevant legal works, and where the precedents of the Hebrew courts were routinely published alongside procedural innovations and statistical reports. Moreover, in an attempt to demonstrate the scientific-legalistic character of the Hebrew courts, the Hebrew law promoters revived the Hebrew Law Society, dedicated – at least implicitly — not simply to the development of Hebrew law but also to provide legitimacy to the Hebrew courts on the ground.[14] The celebratory statement of Mordechai Eliash and Paltiel Dickstein, which opened the first volume of *Ha'Mishpat Ha'Ivri* (*Hebrew Law*), which the Hebrew Law Society published, follows:

> Law Societies exist in many countries and their general purposes are quite well known; But we have an especially difficult task ... in proportion to the magnitude of our cultural-legal past, which begs for inquiry and study, and in proportion to the task of constructing and reviving our people. The enormous and plural legal material is spread in an ocean of literature, in the bible, in the Talmud, in compendiums and codifications, in community regulations, in archives and in collections of inquiries, and no other people faces such an ocean which on a qualitative level can only be compared to Roman law. And all this requires our Society

> to collect and arrange the material in a form that would allow legal scholars to process it, that would free them from the task of collecting raw materials and would allow them to study it and to find within it the inner spirit of our law, its light, the logic and the line of development which are unique to our people, to find the direction that would enable it to develop and improve ... The revival movement of our people imposes new and harder duties upon us. Life posits new questions and problems daily and we cannot settle for a cold scientific analysis of the material and treat it as mere archeologists; we must insert life into it, to locate the seeds that will guide us further, to identify the foundation of the logic that will enable continuity ... The Hebrew Law Society, whose task is to bridge the past and the future, cannot but consider every possible element which may complement the historical and abstract picture of Hebrew Law.[15]

In short, the Hebrew law project constantly swung between lay justice and disciplinary justice (professional, quasi-state law), between common sense and legalistic reason, and between the notion of legality as practices of the present and the notion of law as a scholarly reconstruction of the past. The most fundamental expression of this swing may be found in the juridic-scientific foundation carved for the Hebrew Law of Peace by its theoreticians. In the following pages, I shall argue that the search for an authentic spirit of Hebrew law and the promise to extract the logic of its future development, were in themselves grounded in a 'foreign' tradition, namely a German jurisprudential context, and even in respect to this context the advocates of the Hebrew Law of Peace managed to wed two distinct and unrelated German jurisprudential traditions, thus providing us with a truly hybrid project: writing in 1922 on the judicial process in the Hebrew Courts of Peace, Dickstein argued that there was no need to decide between judicial reliance on *Hoshen Mishpat* and reliance on the Swiss legal code. Let us probe a little into this confident juxtaposition of a modern European codification with a major source of Jewish law.

In his *Economy and Society*, parts of which were published in Germany in the early 1920s, Max Weber analyzed the sociohistorical conditions leading to the emergence of what he termed formal-rational law. Weber articulated a sociology of jurisprudence, linking the history of various jurisprudential schools of thought with the social formation of the bureaucratic state, with the rise of the capitalist global market, and with the strategies of an emergent legal profession. Weber, fascinated with the process of occidental rationalization, considered the law to be one of its more explicit manifestations: "Present day legal science," he wrote, "proceeds from the following five postulates:"

first, that every concrete legal decision be the 'application' of an abstract legal proposition to a concrete 'fact situation'; second, that it must be possible in every concrete case to derive the decision from abstract legal propositions by means of legal logic; third, that the law must actually or virtually constitute a 'gapless' system of legal propositions, or must, at least, be treated as if it were such a gapless system; fourth, that whatever could not be 'construed' rationally in legal terms is also legally irrelevant; and, fifth, that every social action of human beings must always be visualized as either an 'application' or 'execution' of legal propositions, or as an 'infringement' thereof, since 'the gaplessness' of the legal system must result in a gapless 'legal ordering' of all social conduct.[16]

Weber, for all practical purposes, thought of a positive legal system, backed by the coercive powers of the state on the one hand and intellectual legal imperialism on the other hand, seeking to impose a comprehensive, loophole-free system of unitary laws upon a given population in a given territory. Through the concept of formal-rational law, he looked at the triumph of legal positivism, that continental jurisprudence which was premised on the axiom of the "logical 'closedness'" of the positive law as stated by Bentham and implemented as a primary instrument for the regimentation of populations and the organization of the sovereign state.[17]

In a few short paragraphs, however, Weber also commented on a backlash, observable among jurists who became discontented with the intellectual consequences of the dominant axiom:

> Being confined to the interpretation of statutes and contracts, like a slot machine into which one just drops the facts (plus the fee) in order to have it spew out the decision (plus opinion), appears to the modern lawyer as beneath his dignity; and the more universal the codified formal statute law has become, the more unattractive has this notion come to be. The present demand is for 'judicial creativeness', at least where the statute is silent. The school of 'free law' has undertaken to prove that such silence is the inevitable fate of every statute in view of the irrationality of the facts of life; that in countless instances the application of the statutes as 'interpreted' is a delusion, and that the decision is, and ought to be, made in the light of concrete evaluations rather than in accordance with formal norms.[18]

The dissenting free-law jurists, Weber continued, looked to the Swiss code for inspiration: "For the case where the statute fails to provide a clear rule, the well-known Article 1 of the Swiss Civil Code orders the judge to decide according to that rule which he himself would promulgate if he were the legislator."[19] This interpretive option, at the heart of a rigid code which was based on the notion of law's systemic coherence, provided an opening. In fact such a wide opening that Weber himself was skeptical of its logical results: the free-law campaign, he argued, not only aspired to recognize as fiction the coherence and gaplessness of law, but also asserted that the judicial process "never consisted, or, at any rate never should consist, in the 'application' of general norms to a concrete case, just as no utterance in language should be regarded as an application of the rules of grammar." This, Weber argued, could lead not only to non-formal but also to "irrational law finding."[20]

Weber's writing was deeply influenced by the German experience of the late nineteenth and early twentieth century, when state law had been perfected to a level such that in comparison to it the English common law looked like nothing more than a tentative collection of incoherent precedents. On 1 January, 1900, the German *Burgerliches Gesetzbuch* (*BGB*) – a general code of civil law for a unified Germany – took effect. The *BGB* was the culmination of a collective effort – undertaken by German jurists – to reinforce the political unification of imperial Germany under Bismarck in 1870 with legal uniformity as well. The *BGB* was the model legal code that Weber had in mind when he outlined the triumph of positivism in his formal-rational terms and when he commented on the slot-machine character of its *modus operandi*: "Everything a judge needed to know about the civil law," write Herget and Wallace, "was contained in the *BGB* or could be deduced from it directly:"

> ... The law was autonomous, deductive, authoritative, positive, and, through its organic unity, provided the answer to every possible case that could come before a judge. In short, the law – broadly conceived as an interrelated system of concepts, principles, and rules – was a logically closed system.[21]

Furthermore, the *BGB* project brought together two heretofore opposing jurisprudential schools: positivism and historicism. In the second half of the nineteenth century German legal thinkers could be classified according to three jurisprudential trends as positivists, historicists or advocates of natural law. The polemic central to these trends concerned the question of law's gaplessness. Natural law – a collective term for norms which "owe their legitimacy not to their origin from a legitimate law giver, but to their immanent and teleological qualities"[22] – grounded the normative validity of law in a theological morality which was superior to any positive law and to which one turned in order to fill gaps. For the historicists, on the other hand, grounded as they were in

German romanticism, a true law was that which reflected the organic growth of the nation, and one which embodied the customs, traditions, experiences and, in general, the spirit, or *Zeitgeist*, of the people. Gaps would be bridged, according to the historicist view, by tracing the overall 'organic' meaning of the law.

Both natural-law adherents and historicists, therefore, anticipated situations in which the judge would have to transcend the positive dictates of the law in order to solve a legal problem. Both schools, moreover, were premised on the idea that the 'dignity' of positive law derived precisely from the fact that it could be legitimized on grounds external to the law; that the binding force of positive law was derived from its having been founded either in sacred law or in the spirit of the nation.

Legal positivism, grounding the validity of law in the dictates of the sovereign and considering these dictates to be the 'true' beginning of law, freed itself from these transcendental anchors, thereby divorcing morality from the field of law. The principled positivist approach to the problem of gaps was to assert the gaplessness of law, arguing that codified law (in Germany or France) or even the age-old pool of precedents (in England) provided the expert jurist with all the materials needed in order to fill anything that might seem like a 'gap' from within the system itself.

It is noteworthy, however, that while the doctrine of natural law gradually lost its appeal, the *BGB* represented an achievement agreeable to both positivists and historicists. "To the positivists," write Herget and Wallace,

> the code represented the great opportunity to systematize in logical and consistent form what had been a hodge-podge of legal sources. Codification also placed the unequivocal stamp of authority on the entire body of civil law. Law and morality could no longer be confused, and natural law would die a natural death. To the historicists ... it represented the opportunity to purify German law, to restate that law in terms that were true to the organic growth of the German legal tradition ... The historicists did not regard the *BGB* as essentially new law but as a mature statement of the old ...[23]

The fusion between the positivists and the historicists, in other words, took place at the practical level. The historicists did not give up the idea of law as an organic product, yet adopted the practice of the rational organization of the law by 'legal scientists' who systematized the cultural and historical properties of the law within a codified structure.

It was in reaction to these developments that the German free-law (*Freirecht*) movement asserted itself. According to Herget and Wallace – who studied the influence of the free-law movement on Roscoe Pound and the American legal realists – the term 'free-law' was first used by Hermann Kantorowicz in 1906; yet Herget and Wallace also pointed out that Francois Geny in France and Eugen Ehrlich in Germany had been using similar terms even earlier. Early conceptual seeds were planted in the mid-nineteenth century, when scholars like Kirschmann and Bulow launched their attack on conceptual jurisprudence in general and on the positivist denial of gaps in particular.

The free-law movement was a kind of a lawyerly response to the slot-machine qualities of the law which were described by Weber. The skepticism these jurists exhibited towards the edifice of the *BGB* and its foundation in legal conceptualism was essentially based on the idea that judges did not find or discover the law but were routinely making it, simply because even the most precise statutory text still employed vague concepts and ambiguous terms which were forever open to shifting interpretations. Therefore, they argued that courts should give up the fiction of gaplessness and instead engage in a process of free and creative law-making, responsive to social needs and to the substantive expectations of parties.

A practicing attorney like Ernst Fuchs lashed out at positivism from the point of view of practical experience, in fact anticipating American legal realism's distinction between law in the books and law in action. The "true essence of law," Fuchs argued, was grounded in experience and one could not but feel "a real disgust – the expression is not too strong," seeing "our whole civil-law justice system time and time again stumbling around in a philological and dialectical maze."[24]

Yet the movement also relied on the solid theoretical foundations provided by prominent German law professors like Josef Kohler (writing in 1886 about expanded interpretive techniques), Eugen Ehrlich, who provided the historical and sociological basis, and Rudolph von Jehring, who began to emphasize the role of law as a means to obtain utilitarian social and economic ends.[25] The free-law movement, in short, had been founded on the emerging idea that "the true foundation of the law is entirely 'sociological'."[26]

The work of Josef Kohler provides a particularly appealing link between German scholarship and the Hebrew law enterprise. Not only did Kohler entertain 'free-law' ideas concerning the economic and social purposes of the law and their relevance to legal interpretation, but he also later achieved scholarly prominence in his comparative studies of Jewish law. Eisenstadt and Dickstein, who were familiar with the German jurisprudential scene, were well aware of Kohler's work.[27] When Kohler died, Dickstein paid him tribute, reminding his listeners not to forget "those important scholars whose work has been invaluable in reviving Hebrew Law," and among them, principally," the Christian law professor Josef Kohler, whose comparative law journal provided a major impetus for the study and research of Hebrew Law by scientific methods and by using the European scientific platform."[28]

Kohler's intellectual proximity to the idea of law-as-culture, in the general German context of a historicist approach to law, corresponded well with the nationalist sentiments of the Hebrew Law of Peace advocates. His work on Jewish law turned it into a legitimate object of scientific study and intellectual inquiry, providing some 'European' intellectual legitimacy to the Hebrew law project. Yet inscribing a national character into law could not have sufficed for establishing a legitimate jurisdiction. Images of a community-based law and reconstructed memories of legal autonomy, backed by appeals to people's nationalist sentiments, still did not make up for real substance.

No less important was the fact that Kohler, like other notable legal scholars in Germany, displayed remarkable 'free-law' tendencies. This theoretically grounded approach to legal interpretation ushered in yet another type of scientific legitimacy for the Hebrew law; not only in terms of scholarly inquiry, but of the forms and methods of the judicial process itself. In other words, the free-law approach provided a 'scientific' basis for an anti-positivist and anti-formalist conception of judicial reasoning.

It was in this spirit that Dickstein juxtaposed the Swiss code with *Hoshen Mishpat*. It was no coincidence. It was Article 1 of that code that attracted his scholarly imagination – not unlike the free-law adherents. "What is the essence of the problem?" he asked in 1925,

> Should the judge be subjected in all his actions and decisions to fixed and particular laws, facing nothing but the factual grounds of the dispute and the correct applicable rule, and after having logically solved these problems applies the law in a mechanical fashion? Or should the judge apply his own discretion, relying on what he actually witnesses, deciding according to his inner consciousness and his deeply rooted sentiments for justice and equity ... ? This problem, known as the question of 'free law' has been hotly debated among European scholars in the past few decades ... thus, for example Ehrlich declares that "we still do not know what exactly German law means by 'abuse of right' ... because the law does not elaborate on such matters. We will only know what it means when the courts, in the course of the next hundred years, will interpret the term." Article 1 of the Swiss civil code stipulates that where a statute fails to provide a clear rule, the judge should consider customs, and in the absence of a custom, he should decide according to that rule which he himself would

promulgate if he were the legislator ... The free-law movement is but a result of the excessive servitude to the letters of the law which prevails in Europe.[29]

Thus, the Hebrew law advocates aspired to develop an authentic national law, yet based their claims to authenticity, and validity, on a distinctly European experience. On the one hand, colonial law was despised and rejected as a "mere mechanical mixture of Moslem-Arab, Ottoman-Turkish, French, Italian and British elements – mostly a mixture of these various nations' cultural refuse, often distorted by ignorant cultural pimps," whereas the true vocation was to revive a pure and authentic Hebrew law. On the other hand, the basic postulate that "the law is a substantial part of a people's spiritual life and an inseparable part of its culture," was directly borrowed from the German historical school. The idea of law as a popular creation, reflecting particular customs and traditions and a specific national culture, was articulated by Karl von Savigny's Hegelian theory of law and came of age under the aegis of German nationalism. It was embraced intact by the proponents of the Hebrew Law of Peace in their own search for the legitimizing principles that would have allowed for the rejection of colonial positivist state law (with its universalistic pretensions) and the simultaneous invention of an unbroken Jewish legal past. "The rejection of foreign influence," writes Likhovski, "always existed in revival thought side by side with the recognition that revival would mean the acceptance of foreign legal influence, and that Hebrew Law would have to be a 'synthesis of eastern and Western law,' a mixture of 'traditional law and the legal notions ... brought from Europe.'"[30]

The biographies of the Hebrew law advocates, and the imagined history of a Hebrew nation, combined to produce a hybrid intellectual product. Many of the activists and judges of the Hebrew Courts of Peace were Russian-born Zionists with a strong orientation towards the cultural aspects of national revival. Most of these people came to Palestine in the early 1920s, as part of what was called the 'third wave' of immigration. Middle-class in background, many of them were educated in major academic institutions. Those who were trained in law became the inner circle of the Hebrew Courts of Peace and mainly served at the High Hebrew Court. A substantial number of this hardcore group of activists received their education in law schools that were under the influence of German jurisprudence. Paltiel Dickstein and Zvi Belkovski studied at the University of Odessa (specializing in Roman Law), Daniel Auster and Haim Shmeterling studied at the University of Vienna, Shimshon Rosenboim studied at the University of Odessa and later at Vienna, Haim Rosenthal studied at the University of Warsaw, Eliahu Berlin at the University of Moscow, Ya'acov Klebanoff studied in St Petersburg and later in Germany and Switzerland, Mordechay Gorodiski studied at the University of Paris, Yossef Keizerman and Shmuel Eisenstadt studied in Switzerland, and Avraham Weinshel studied in Switzerland and Germany. I think it is safe to say that the alleged unique Hebrewness of the Hebrew Law of Peace was predicated on German legal thought. On their way to conceiving an authentic national Hebrew law, these European-trained jurists fused ideas borrowed from the German historical school with those from the German free-law movement, each providing them with a much sought-after 'European scientific rationale:' the former by linking law and culture (affirming the search for the 'spirit' of Hebrew law) and the latter by licensing judicial creativity (affirming the need to develop and improve Hebrew law).

The free-law approach supplied the theoretical foundation (complementing the community-centered vision) for asserting that "in order to properly fulfill the role of the judge, one need not simply master professional legal knowledge, but rather a knowledge of life and an understanding of life, one needs the perspective of the lay-person ... without the barriers erected by scholastic and legalistic concepts, formulas and rules."[31] Moreover, the free-law approach to legal interpretation was also wedded in the minds of the Hebrew law advocates to their experience with Russian law after the revolution. If reliance on the free-law movement did not suffice, the civil code of the Soviet Socialist Republic – like the Swiss code – served as another point of reference. "The drafters of the Russian code," wrote Dickstein, "established the law on the following foundation: The law should allow for a wide judicial discretion. It is only by using such discretion that the judge would be able to order the relations between litigants according to just principles."[32] And if all that was not enough, one could always turn to the legal traditions of the colonizers themselves. Thus, when one lawyer lashed the Hebrew Law of Peace for its pretentious attempts to modify "general rules of law" and to subvert the "objective laws" of the land through vague referral to equity, conscience, and discretion, he was rebuked for his subservience to the colonial formalistic 'golden calf': in order to develop an autonomous Hebrew law, one had to privilege common sense over 'objective laws' and '*ratio scripta*' over '*jus scriptum*.' Even the history of the English common law was recruited to the service of legal creativity: "Let us mention," wrote one defender of the Hebrew Law of Peace, "that England managed itself rather well without a legal code, that the English were not ardent followers of codifications but rather opted for an accumulative legal growth from below and an equity which thought little of the distinction between codified and uncodified law."[33]

The German free-law movement, as well as the Russian license for judicial discretion, offered a platform from which to target not only the 'frozen' formalistic Jewish law of the rabbinical courts, but also British colonial law and the structure of opportunities it created for legalistically minded lawyers who lacked 'national consciousness.' Time and again, the Hebrew law jurists emphasized the tension between formalistic legalese – a source of power and authority for lawyers and judges – and the ability to attain substantive justice. The judge who actually created law, the judge who was guided by substantive principles of 'justice and equity,' had been portrayed and celebrated as the ideal judicial figure. Thus, while an imagined Jewish past provided the historical depth, the actual conditions of the present provided the stage upon which the idea of Hebrew law as a spontaneous cultural creation took shape. Judges, according to this emergent conception, were licensed to draw on their own experiences with the community, on their moral notions and common sense, and to develop the law on a case-by-case basis, not unlike, wrote Eisenstadt, the English common law tradition and the Jewish tradition of oral law.[34] Further, the ideal judge made law not only by reiterating rules of law but also by bringing disputing parties together, providing a friendly forum for conciliation.

A case in point is the way the Hebrew Law of Peace managed the idea of compromise in litigation and judicial decision-making. In general, the Hebrew Courts of Peace emphasized their commitment to the 'principle of friendly compromises between litigants' already under Ottoman rule, treating this principle as having its own independent communal value. (In the next chapter, we shall see that this commitment was perceived by the critics of the Hebrew law system as proof of the system's non-legal character.) The defenders of the Hebrew court insisted on the importance of a compromising judge, not least because they considered it to soften the tension between legal form and legal substance: the artisan-jurist, they argued, should bring together the "weighty law and the conscience of the heart" and create "a bridge between formal law and equity of free-law."[35]

Such sentiments against rule-bound judges deciding between two contesting parties was somewhat reminiscent of the attitude that some American legal realists displayed toward the judicial process. "Trial by Combat and the New Deal," was written by Thurman Arnold and published by the *Harvard Law Review* in 1934. Arnold, a Yale Law Professor, challenged the competitive nature of the formal judicial process and the romantic technique of battle employed by American courts:

> If one were compelled to summarize the assumptions underlying the ideal of a law-making body, which never speaks except to

settle a combat properly brought before it, the result would be somewhat as follows: Every trial should be a contest over issues presented by the parties and not an investigation of what the facts were which created the necessity of the suit ... These assumptions are reconciled with practical efficiency by the notion that courts are more apt to formulate or apply rules soundly if the opposite sides are prevented from sitting around a table together in friendly conference. Mutual exaggeration is supposed to create lack of exaggeration. Bitter partisanship in opposite directions is supposed to bring out the truth. Of course no rational human being would apply such a theory to his own affairs nor to other departments of the government ... Yet in spite of this most obvious fact, the ordinary teacher of law will insist (1) that combat makes for clarity, (2) that heated arguments bring out the truth, and (3) that anyone who doesn't believe this is a loose thinker. The explanation of this attitude lies in the realm of social anthropology.[36]

The courts, Arnold argued, functioned as theaters, providing a hungry public with the thrill of drama, employing nonsensical, irrational, and socially irresponsible methods for finding out the 'truth.' Arnold, therefore, envisioned friendly forums, whose *modus operandi* depended on cooperation rather than competition, as did other legal realists of his time, in the search for administrative regulatory forums that would operate alongside courts.

The ideal of informal law that would be creative and yet still be conducive to the needs of the community, appealed to the advocates of the Hebrew law because it also coexisted with the imagination of the Jewish communal past. In one case, a major Zionist institution refused to subject itself to the jurisdiction of the Hebrew court, on grounds that the case required the judges to apply more than "equity principles and mere notions of justice." The decision of this Zionist institution was backed and also explained by a lawyer who published an article on the issue in the daily, *Davar*. Another lawyer, defending the Hebrew court, responded in another article:

The major argument of [the critic] is that 'compromise is no law.' We concede, indeed, that the Hebrew Law of Peace consists of many compromises ... and that this is often the case when the judge does not wish to issue a verdict because the law does not coincide with his conscience, and he then urges the litigants to compromise. But a compromise is not a jurisprudential monster: '*Lo Harva Yerusal'iim, ela mipnei she'e'emidu ba ha'kol al ha'din*' [Jerusalem would not have been destroyed but for the practice of

> deciding everything on the basis of (formal) law]. It is only a uniquely virtuous judge who knows how to reestablish peaceful relations between litigants rather than filling their hearts with relentless hate and hostility and with legal ambitions that only burden them with heavy costs which often impoverish both parties by the time their dispute moves along the heavy apparatus of all judicial instances ...[37]

In sum, above and beyond images of a communal past which served as an overall legitimizing principle, the advocates of the Hebrew Law of Peace imported from Germany, *mutatis mutandis,* a 'scientific' basis for the 'authentic' law-without-science they practiced in Palestine. They thereby created, I believe, a work of bricolage.

Still, and concurrently with the theoretical formulations which were designed to legitimate judicial creativity, there had been clear signs that the Hebrew Law project was incrementally distancing itself from its former community-based orientation. Apparently responding to growing pressure from lawyers and Zionist institutions, Paltiel Dickstein wrote in 1927: "It was not a principled policy which led us to select unprofessional judges ... but conditions and circumstances. Seventeen years ago, when the Hebrew Courts were formed, there were hardly any people in our community who had been socialized into a high legal culture. Yet over time we try to absorb persons educated in law." Similarly, he distanced the Hebrew Law of Peace from the community-based commitment to facilitate compromises: "In the early years of [British] occupation, when the colonizing community lacked adequate legal forces, the [Hebrew] court had been composed of mere lay persons and displayed a natural tendency to compromises based on pity. But it is for several years now that the [Hebrew Law] Institution distances itself from compromises and pity and tries to create a legal culture which is based on traditional Hebrew law, and self-made permanent regulations ... it makes every effort it can to establish legality, consistency and stability in its judgments."[38] Not unlike processes recorded in other national settings, the Hebrew Law of Peace had, over time, adopted not only the forms and symbols of state law, but had also placed a growing emphasis on state law's source of legitimacy, namely its affiliation with notions of scientific expertise and a coherent body of abstract theoretical knowledge.

"There is in all nationally defined cultures, I believe, an aspiration to sovereignty, to sway, and to dominance," writes Edward Said in his *Culture and Imperialism*:

> In this, French and British, Indian and Japanese cultures concur. At the same time, paradoxically, we have never been as aware as we

now are of how oddly hybrid historical and cultural experiences are, of how they partake of many often contradictory experiences and domains, cross national boundaries, defy the police action of simple dogma and loud patriotism. Far from being unitary or monolithic, or autonomous things, cultures actually assume more 'foreign' elements, alterities, differences, than they consciously exclude. Who in India or Algeria today can confidently separate out the British or French component of the past from present actualities, and who in Britain or France can draw a clear circle around British London or French Paris that would exclude the impact of India and Algeria upon those two imperial cities?[39]

The Hebrew Law of Peace was a hybrid creation par excellence. The Russian jurists who immigrated to Palestine – entertaining the nationalist project of legal revival and encountering local Hebrew courts in the search for identity and legitimacy – brought together a number of distinctly European influences. They fused German free-law ideas with a German historical approach to law for the purpose of re-establishing an authentic Hebrew law, contemporary and yet one that purported to continue a long Jewish tradition.

However, I do not mean to suggest that there was an unbridgeable gap between the public ideology of the Hebrew Law of Peace and its actual performance, or that we should be content with identifying a project infused with incoherent contradictions. Rather, my point is that the ideas and rhetoric surrounding the Hebrew Law of Peace and the ideological efforts to ground it 'scientifically' could not be separated from the actual practices of the courts and their ever-present need for legitimacy. The law, after all, is about conflicts, interests, and competing expectations. It is about confrontation, agonies, pains and frustrations, about unresolved disputes and about setting out at least some of the rules of the social game. In short, the Hebrew Law of Peace was not only an idea, but a practice, a daily show at courts all over Palestine. The fundamental problem facing the Hebrew Law of Peace – however community-centered it purported to be – was to establish a legitimate jurisdiction; a project that necessarily involved the task of convincing relevant constituencies (the general public, lawyers, institutions, politicians, etc.) – no matter how committed to national revival – that the Hebrew courts were actually able to solve problems and that they were equipped with at least some form of technical expertise, that justified authoritative position in the community. The impending questions were straightforward: how was the judicial process supposed to function in resolving real-life conflicts? How was the Hebrew judge to decide what the law was?

There were many answers to these questions, depending on context, audiences and speakers. In the last instance, they were articulated from within the experience of practicing the idea of national, autonomous, and secular legality. The very meaning of the term 'Hebrew law' was shaped by the necessities of practice, leading to the notion that Hebrew law was but a cluster of experiences that grew out of the actual performance of the Hebrew courts and which produced, over time, a distinct body of knowledge. When such an answer fell short of satisfying demands for certainty and consistency, it was possible to imagine Hebrew law as a modern continuation of the norms of Jewish law and of past communal practices. Hebrew law, in short, became a 'present-tense' concept, assuming a meaning which corresponded to the necessities of practice and to the varying expectations of various audiences. Hebrew law, like the vision and trajectory of national revival which it sought to reflect, had been shaped in action and acquired meaning through experience and by responding to the imperatives of practice. By necessity, it was a project that carved itself a space *in* contradiction. Thus, the Hebrew Law of Peace defies all attempts to classify it as a definite form of justice.

Consider, for example, Merry's classification of systems of popular justice: Reformist, Socialist, Communitarian and Anarchic. The reformist and the socialist types, she argues, tend to "promote institutions of popular justice closely connected to and controlled by state law." The latter two, by contrast, promote institutions "more closely connected to and controlled by indigenous ordering."[40] Of course, one may argue that the Hebrew Law of Peace was created as a form of "indigenous ordering" but eventually evolved into one more closely associated, directly and indirectly, with state law. This, I think, misses the point. Rather, the Hebrew Law of Peace, from its inception, was grounded in a non-statist approach to law and yet at the same time conceived of itself as a nucleus of a future state law. Similarly, the Hebrew Law of Peace oriented itself to a colonizing community, but from a very early point in time conceived of this community in the abstract terms of the nation. Thus, while at some point, and for some audiences, the Hebrew Law of Peace tailored itself as a project based on substantive notions of justice, on voluntary submission and compliance, on compromises, spontaneity and local modes of ordering, on the popular, on common sense, and on situational and contextual forms of justice – it also displayed, simultaneously, a distinct taste for order, hierarchy, rules, formality, and affinity to the symbols, if not content, of state law.

It is only in retrospect that national movements, in law, in politics, and in culture, try to ascribe to themselves a sense of coherence, of orderly development and movement, casting aside contradictions, confusions, and instability. In the case of the Hebrew Law of Peace, this had been performed with a vengeance. The history of Israeli law is organized around a repressive hypothesis against which the enlightened and liberated present is celebrated. A fundamental conceptual change, so the story goes, took place at the Supreme Court of Israel in the course of the 1980s. Traditionally conceiving of its judicial duties as primarily involving the resolution of concrete disputes in light of 'law-finding' formalistic practices, the court has begun to articulate a policy-making role and to depict judges as active social actors who may and should employ wide discretionary powers. Chief Justice Barak, the (almost) undisputed intellectual leader of the court, has been portrayed as the architect of this conceptual revolution, advocating the role of the judge as a social engineer. Menacham Mautner writes:

> The critical process taking place in judicial activity during the 1980s is the decline of a whole world-view concerning the guiding norms of the court and concerning the role the court should play within the state. The declining world-view has been formalistic. Instead, a non-formalisitc world-view has ascended, emphasizing values and substantive justice considerations, and highlighting the social role of the court.[41]

Some variations notwithstanding, there seems to be a firm scholarly consensus that the origin of the court's formalism has to be sought in the legacy of British Mandatory law and its wholesale adoption by Israeli jurists. It is against this historical background of a 'self-repressed judiciary' that the new practices – discretionary powers, liberal interpretive techniques, and a general civil responsibility posture – are celebrated.

In this chapter, I have tried to unsettle this 'repressive hypothesis' by suggesting that the Hebrew Law of Peace displayed some of the above attributes seventy years earlier, at least some of the time and at least for some purposes: positing judges as makers of law and celebrating their discretionary powers, shunning formalism and situating the law in a social, political and economic context. In this respect, this chapter offers another angle from which to consider the fact that the Hebrew Law of Peace has left no trace. The reasons for this oblivion lie not so much in the history of the Hebrew Law of Peace as in the positivism of Israeli scholarly interpreters. For all practical purposes, the history of the law of Israel begins with the colonial state. Non-statist options became obsolete in the narration of law as well as in the narration of the nation.

CHAPTER 5

NATIONALISM AS A DISCIPLINARY REGIME

Nationalism is a disciplinary regime. It is a rhetorical resource. It is a call, a buzz-word for interpellation, commanding one to say *I am within* and to respond to expectations of action and non-action. It is a call for certain practices and for the avoidance of other practices. Yet to discuss nationalism from this vantage point, one must always ask who speaks on behalf of nationalism and to whom? We cannot assume that there is one singular authoritative voice which articulates an inventory of national practices and designates other practices as non-national or not national enough. Rather, a national project, or a nation-building atmosphere, is constructed in numerous sites of cultural-political production, by an indefinite number of groups speaking in the name of nationalism in efforts to advance this or that cause, and by a multitude of institutions invoking nationalism as a regimentation device. What is national and what is not national, what serves the national cause and what does not, therefore, is not a given, but rather an unstable product of ongoing negotiations and persuasion efforts by various social forces.

There were as many ways to betray the national cause as there were forces able to impose their view of nationalism on the Jewish community in Palestine of the 1920s. For instance, a person's reputation as being not loyal enough to the national cause was often a cause for legal action. In fact, a substantial part of the workload of the Hebrew Courts of Peace comprised such 'honor' cases, cases in which parties often claimed that their reputation as committed nationalist members of the community had been compromised. In such honor disputes, regardless of the substantive cause of action, convicted parties were obliged to pay compensation to the Jewish National Fund (acquiring land for Zionist colonization) rather than to the winning party. This practice in itself symbolized the fact that such cases, while fought in the name of individual honor, were not grounded in selfish motivations but rather in communal-educational ones. These cases, of which only a handful are mentioned here, provide a rich source of data from which to learn about everyday life in the colonizing community. Further, in rendering judgments over these cases, the Hebrew courts actively drew the contours of 'national' or 'anti-national' forms of action. At times, the 'national' aspect of cases was only implicitly suggested:

> Donkelblum vs. Shenkar
>
> Donkelblum, a lawyer, claimed his Honor from Arie Shenkar, owner of a textile factory. Plaintiff argued that defendant cursed him in the Russian language and accused him of embezzlement. Defendant, in counter-claim, argued that "Donkelblum compared me to De Han, a national traitor who lives with a non-Jew,[1] and that I am a materialist; one deserves a slap on the face for such words. I became sick for a fortnight. One should lock the mouths of lawyers and limits should be placed on their freedom of expression." Donkelblum, replying: "I did not say that Shenkar was like De Han because this is not a matter of national betrayal ... I only wanted to portray the character of Shenkar who thinks himself to be the only honest person while all his opponents are villains."
>
> The court found that in comparing Shenkar to De Han, Donkelblum did not mean to suggest that the former was of equal status with the latter in his attitude to the nation. The implication was that had such meaning been attributable, Donkelblum would have been convicted on this count. Eventually, the court found Shenkar guilty of hurting the honor of Donkelblum simply because he used improper language.[2]

As the next example will demonstrate, improper language in itself was sometimes deemed to run against what was judged to be the national ethos.

> Mann vs. Agronski
>
> Plaintiff was assigned as a guard to the back entrance of a Gymnasium in Tel Aviv upon the visit of Lord Balfour in 1925. Plaintiff argued that the defendant and his party insisted on entering the hall in violation of the orders that he had received to prevent entry to the compound after Lord Balfour's arrival. Defendant refused to comply and tried to prevent him fulfilling his duties. Having been granted entry at a later point, "the defendant turned and said to others who were standing around that we were idiots. I seek to punish him accordingly." Defendant argued

that he was the press officer of the Zionist Executive and that he was accompanied by foreign journalists. "This unpleasant and ridiculous situation could have led me to use expressions far more insulting than the one I have used." The court ruled that "the defendant, a public official, an educated and civilized person, had a duty to suppress his feelings and to set an example of courtesy for public educational purposes." Defendant was convicted.[3]

Other cases recorded the shame involved in not speaking the Hebrew language. In one case, a Hebrew Court of Peace convicted a person who, while delivering a speech, accused a certain voluntary association of using "jargon" (i.e., not Hebrew) in its meetings, without having solid evidence to substantiate the accusation. In another case, dealt with by a Comrades' Law Court of the Jewish Federation of Labor, a defendant explained that he disrupted a Workers' Committee meeting because some speakers were not speaking in Hebrew. The real issue in this trial, he argued, was "the continuous disregard for the rule that forbids anyone who is over two years in the country to deliver a speech in a foreign language."[4]

Another form of 'un-national' action concerned private or even public profit from land transactions. In the mid-1920s, speculation in land seemed to have gotten out of hand and to be seriously threatening the colonization effort, as prices kept rising beyond the reach of most Jewish settlers. The idea that one made a profit through successful speculation, therefore, while in fact a widespread practice, was publicly denounced as national betrayal. Thus, a Hebrew court in Tel Aviv heard a plaintiff who argued that one of his acquaintances told "dozens of people" that he, the plaintiff, speculated in real estate. "The rumor," he complained, "even reached Jerusalem and now many of my friends avoid greeting me on the street and I must therefore defend my honor."[5]

In another case, the Municipal Council of Tel Aviv sued the Association of Home Owners when the latter accused the former of having profited through speculation. This case, in which many lawyers on both sides took part, provided a public opportunity to look at the details of the council's land acquisitions and to debate the very meaning of terms such as 'speculation' and 'easy profits,' and their relation to the national duties of public servants.

Of special importance, in this context, was the articulation of appropriate ways to resolve internal disputes. In fact, the very concept of 'internal dispute' suggested and affirmed the existence of a real bounded community, and thus appeals to a third party who resided outside this community could be construed as a form of betrayal and desertion. This had been obvious in small communities, perhaps not so much because of explicit 'national' notions as for the imagined notion of intimacy. Narrating a tale about a 'founding father,' an early Zionist pioneer who wished to be buried in his own yard and not with other settlers at the community's designated cemetery, Shalev writes:

> He knew that no one would dare to uproot him from his land, because the village had never let its scandals out. We solved our problems alone. The police would be called only in terrible and grave matters. But we never had rape or murder; and stealing, assaults and other deviances were taken care of by our institutions and with the loyal assistance of social pressure and the village bulletin.[6]

This general rule of not handing over disputes to third, 'external,' parties, held true, or at least seemed to, not only in small rural communities but in urban settings as well. One case on record from the Comrades' Law Court concerned two groups of Jewish workers who fought over the right to work in a particular area. One group, named Sid, summoned the other, named Rushmia, to trial on the grounds that the latter involved the police in that 'internal' dispute. Rushmia responded: "Sid promised not to work at a certain area before settling its dispute with us. But they broke their promise and we therefore called the police. We recognize that we were wrong; it was an action prompted by our great and unusual anger. We are ready to accept a fair punishment." The court found that in summoning the police Rushmia performed "the lowest form of demoralization of Hebrew organized labor" and punished the group accordingly.[7] I think that this case was not only about workers' solidarity, but also about national solidarity. At any rate, it was precisely this notion – keeping the forces of the state away from internal disputes – that the Hebrew Law of Peace utilized as a jurisdictional and disciplinary resource. In its efforts to secure a solid jurisdiction and to attract litigants to its forums, the Hebrew Law of Peace engaged in an ongoing effort to persuade relevant constituencies that avoiding it amounted to national betrayal. However, the idea that Hebrew courts constituted an essential part of the national project, and the notion that by litigating in the Hebrew Courts of Peace one was enacting a national duty, was not obvious. These ideas depended on steady work of persuasion, threats, appeals, and practical moves.

In chapter 3, I mentioned how Hebrew courts tried to discipline those who evaded their authority by publicly labeling them as *shirkers*. In the absence of state power, they had to resort public opinion as a deterrent. Evidently a disciplinary measure whose force lies in the fear of public shaming – substituting for the coercive powers of the state – is inherently dependent upon the concrete social relations characteristic of a given community. Usually, attempts to secure the force of law by relying on such sanctions presuppose a high level of collective solidarity or at least a densely interactive community in which people know each other *in person*. While the coercive powers of state law presuppose an abstract *society*, a community-centered law is premised on the *personal*. (In the latter case, judges are elected because they are known to the members of the community and respected as such; compromise and conciliation are valued more than rules and confrontational tactics, sanctions are premised on the strong desire to avoid shame and embarrassment, and so on.) It is a law premised on the inter-human aspect of social life, conceiving of society not in terms of abstract individuals, but rather in terms of human networks in flux, constantly shaped and reshaped by face-to-face interactions. Under such conditions, what other people think becomes a crucial existential question because a person's reputation is often directly linked to their being able to access a whole range of social, political and economic resources.

Reflecting on Gluckman's "Gossip and Scandal," Merry shows the power of public opinion (transmitted and dispensed through gossiping) not only in 'simple' societies and among rural villagers, but also in urban social settings – provided that group members are interdependent "for economic aid, jobs, political protection, and social support" – where there is a normative group consensus concerning what types of behavior merit ridicule, shame, or loss of face.[8] The practice of naming people as *shirkers* was designed to create a scandalous effect not unlike the one produced when gossip was turned into a public affair. Accusing someone of having shirked their duty to adhere to the community-based law, when effective, became a powerful instrument for establishing a person's social standing in the group; at the same time it reproduced the community as a whole, in the sense that it allowed the group to imagine itself as such. Like gossip and scandal, in short, this sanction shaped – or at least had been premised on its potential to shape – the community's "cognitive maps of social identities and reputations."[9]

The ability to maintain a legal system on the basis of this sanction, however, seems to be a factor of the actual size of the population and its forms of organization in space. Community-centered law, considered from this perspective, is a privilege (or a burden) of the "local." (For instance, in rural areas, one occasionally encounters filling-stations or stores with signs saying: 'Do Not Accept Personal Cheques from The Following …,' naming persons whose cheques have bounced at this or that particular establishment. Rarely, if at all, does one encounter such a measure in the city.) Anthropological research, as Merry shows, suggests that "with increasing social complexity, informal social controls diminish in significance and are replaced by formal mechanisms of social control."[10] Yet it seems that strong nets of interdependencies – characteristic of a face-to-face communal setting where 'informal social controls' are said to be effective – are extremely important in a colonial setting as well. The existential position of the colonizer is precisely that of relative isolation from the larger social environment and of dependence upon the political, economic and moral support and protection of fellow colonizers. This fact, it seems, enables that type of sanctioning that we ordinarily expect to find in a face-to-face social context. A colonizing society, in principle at least, is conducive to the possibility of transforming a 'local' sanction into a more generally applicable one.[11]

Indeed, the Hebrew Law of Peace was distinct in that it tried to discipline the community on the basis of nationalism, 'overcoming' the problem of size by substituting symbolic proximity for a physical one. Furthermore, naming a *shirker* was not reserved to individuals alone. Zionist institutions were also expected to litigate in the Hebrew Courts of Peace and were subjected to the same public-shaming sanction if they shirked that duty. To borrow from Giddens' terms, the Hebrew Law of Peace shifted the application of the sanction from circumstances of co-presence (based on 'local involvements') to the abstract 'interaction across distance' (connecting presence and absence). Ordinarily, this is precisely the shift underwriting the hegemony of state law. Here, the abstraction focused on the dream of a revived nation. The issue, in other words, was transformed from being concerned with a person's belonging to an inter-human-constituted community to that of a person's role in the nation-building process.[12] Appeals to the 'official' law of the state, under these circumstances, were supposed to generate sanctions that would mark individuals as outsiders and stigmatize institutions as irresponsible.[13]

Further, litigation in the Hebrew Courts of Peace was framed not only as a symbol of commitment to the national project, but as an actual national *praxis*, a demonstration of one's readiness to apply and actualize words, opinions, and ideas.[14] Establishing one's standing as a *shirker* presupposed an inter-human community engaged in the process of imagining itself as a *nation*; the Hebrew Law of Peace in effect asserting itself as a constitutive element in this process: *shirkers* were often blamed not only for damaging the national project as a whole but, more specifically, for hurting the 'honor' of the Hebrew Law of Peace itself.[15] Thus, the Hebrew Law of Peace simultaneously engaged the double task of harnessing the public to the national project and convincing it that a functioning and operative system of autonomous Hebrew law was in fact an essential part of that project.[16]

A major effort in persuasion by the Hebrew Law of Peace was directed at the embryonic Jewish legal profession in Palestine and at Zionist political and economic institutions. These two social forces were critical to the ability of the Hebrew Law of Peace to establish a firm jurisdiction. Lawyers' support was crucial because they were in a position to steer individual and institutional clients towards or away from the Hebrew courts (that is to say, a gate-keeping position); and Zionist institutions were crucial because they were in a position not only to fund and to provide legal work to the Hebrew courts but also to create an overall sense of national importance and legitimacy for Hebrew law.

The advocates of the Hebrew Law of Peace were well aware of their dependence on these social forces. As far as institutions were concerned, they tried various methods of mobilization. For example, they tried to enlist institutions to insert a compulsory arbitration clause in their various contracts with individuals and other institutions, assigning the Hebrew courts as the exclusive arena for dispute resolution. These attempts were almost exclusively based on the argument that the development of Hebrew law and the jurisdiction of the Hebrew court were matters of prime national importance. The same rhetoric was invoked in those cases where institutions showed signs of evading the Hebrew courts, mixing appeals to the national cause with threats to designate whole institutions, or individuals thereof, as *shirkers*. In one case, the Palestine Zionist Executive (PZE) refused to submit to the jurisdiction of the Hebrew court in a case involving a dispute over wage compensation with one of its former employees. "We have never realized that such a possibility even existed," wrote Dickstein, "that the PZE would even consider a refusal to litigate in a National Jewish Court and would openly prefer a foreign court." His letter appealed to the national sentiments and duties of Zionist officials:

> We do not think it possible that the P. Z. E, afraid to lose a few scores of Pounds in a Hebrew Court of Peace because its judges tend to be more liberal in matters of job security and compensation to workers (a unsubstantiated fear in itself) would undermine the national legal institution, whose whole existence is based on public moral recognition. One may understand an individual who fears for his money and scarifies national matters for greed, but we cannot comprehend how a public institution whose funding is derived from the national idea and from the desire for national revival would so act.[17]

Similar appeals were addressed to lawyers. Aware of their dependence upon the gate-keeping functions of lawyers, the advocates of the Hebrew Law of Peace tried to persuade lawyers that the national mission should guide their professional practice. The 1927 National Convention of the Judges of the Hebrew Courts of Peace addressed "the Jewish lawyers in the land" with the expectation that they would "spread the idea of national law in their professional work and ... instruct their clients to prefer national discipline over the state courts."[18] In 1928, addressing the first convention of the Jewish Lawyers Association, Dickstein implored:

> The convention cannot ignore questions concerning our juristic revival and the approach that should be taken in regard to our national law and our national courts. It should finally recognize and declare that the building of a national home is impossible without self-made law and national courts. The lawyers must not accept the debasing and disrespect which some of them display towards institutions which are foundational for the national revival.[19]

Attempts were also made to discipline recalcitrant lawyers who opted for state courts. Three brief examples follow:

> File 183, January 1923: A Hebrew disciplinary tribunal convened to address a complaint against Adv. Gershman who asked a government court to intervene in a dispute that had been pending at a Hebrew Court of Peace. Gershman explained that he could not resist his client's wish to litigate at the government court and that he thought that the proceedings had been conducted as an ordinary arbitration unrelated to the Hebrew Law of Peace. He also declared that he held the Hebrew Law of Peace in "the highest respect." The tribunal excused Gershman, but rebuked him for "displaying a lack of confidence in the Hebrew forum."[20]
>
> File 214, February 1924: A disciplinary tribunal addressed a complaint against Adv. Feinstein who represented a client at a lower instance and, after losing the case, succeeded in nullifying the decision at a government court. Feinstein refused to appear before the tribunal. He wrote a letter stating that "every reasonable person knows that lawyers cannot be held responsible for such actions because these are undertaken on behalf of their clients." The Hebrew Court found him guilty of "undermining the Hebrew Law of Peace" and removed him from the list of persons entitled to serve as judges in the local Court of Peace.[21]
>
> File 244, February 1925: A Hebrew disciplinary tribunal convened to address a complaint against Adv. Gershman who, while representing a party at a Hebrew Court of Peace, declared that since "everyone seems to be addressing the government's

courts these days, there is no reason why I should not do likewise." Gershman explained that he had made this remark only in order to please his client. Gershman was reprimanded for failing "to protect the honor of an institution that has a great national value."[22]

Verdicts such as the above were intended to create a deterrent effect similar to that produced by declaring ordinary individuals *shirkers* (see chapter 3). In all the above cases, nationalism was used as a resource, as a disciplinary measure designed to simultaneously guide actual practices, shape the boundaries of the national community, invest particular institutions with national value and, ultimately, lend the term 'nationalism' substance.[23] But once we understand nationalism as a resource, we should expect ongoing competition and negotiation over its practical implications for action. What constitutes a national practice for one may be dismissed as irrelevant to the national cause by another. Further, such negotiations do not take place in a vacuum. Rather, the nature of nationalism, so to speak, is shaped and articulated in accordance with interests, experiences, habits, needs and expectations that are grounded in actual situations. Hence, we shall see that the national appeal of the Hebrew Law of Peace was less and less effective as competing notions of nationalism in law emerged and were developed by other social forces, namely the embryonic Jewish legal profession and some of the key political and economic Zionist institutions in Palestine.

The following case, known as the Shoshani affair, will set the scene for a discussion and analysis which follows the above guidelines.

SALLE D'ATTENTE

The colonial High Court of Justice of Palestine made known its preliminary judgment in the case of Sa'adia Shoshani and Morris Meoden vs. Council of Tel Aviv Township on 30 July, 1926.[1] Petitioners contended that the Council of Tel Aviv, in an attempt to expand the franchise in the municipal elections, misinterpreted the Township Order which stipulated that only "ratepayers" were eligible to vote. The Council of Tel Aviv, petitioners argued, applied the term to all taxpayers, whereas only taxpayers for immovable property were eligible to vote. The court ruled:

> The term ratepayer is taken from English Law and should be interpreted in its English sense. We do not find any general definition with the authorities we have had the opportunity of consulting but we do find that in English the term rate is always used in relation to some rate or tax levied on owners or occupiers of immovable property. If the intention was to give the franchise to all persons paying any sort of tax or imposition of a public nature the Township Order would have said so. As the Order used the word ratepayer we must assume that it used it in the only sense in which that word is actually employed.
> ... Mr Gorodisky (the petitioner) at this point states that he is instructed not to proceed any further in his application on the undertaking given by the Respondent which Mr Donkelblum offers that new elections shall take place in October next.
> No order.

Having offered its principled interpretation of the Township Order, the court compelled the Council of Tel Aviv to commit itself to new elections.² The petitioners, activists of the Tel Aviv Home Owners Association, further challenged the attempt of the Council to introduce progressive taxation for immovable property. They were successful in that petition as well, thereby effectively frustrating – through British legal aid – a planned tax reform scheme.³

Writing in the first half of the nineteenth century, the political philosopher Benjamin Constant celebrated the civic virtues of those persons fortunate enough to own landed property:

> [i]n order to be a member of the association, it is necessary to possess a certain degree of understanding and a common interest with the other members of the association. Men below the legal age are not deemed to possess that degree of understanding. Foreigners are not deemed to guide themselves by that interest ... Yet this principle requires a further extension. In our modern societies, to be born in the country and to have come of age is not sufficient reason to grant those qualities required for the exercise of the rights of citizenship. Those who are kept by poverty in eternal dependence, and who are condemned by it to daily labor, are neither more knowledgeable than children about public affairs, nor more interested than foreigners in national prosperity, of whose elements they are unaware, and in whose advantages they share only indirectly ... There must be a further condition in addition to those prescribed by the law of birth and age. This condition is the leisure indispensable for the acquisition of understanding and soundness of judgment. Property alone makes men capable of exercising political rights.⁴

The link between citizenship and ownership was at the heart of the political and legal struggles of mid-1920s Tel Aviv. Established in 1909 by middle-class Jewish residents of Jaffa, and designed as an affluent residential neighborhood, Tel Aviv rapidly multiplied its population under British rule and became, in fact, the bustling commercial, political and cultural engine of the colonization enterprise as a whole (although certainly not acknowledged as such, socialist Zionism advocating the supremacy of rural and agricultural settlements over bourgeois urbanism).⁵ This process, in itself, had often been to the chagrin of the old-timers and the pre-war founders of the town who subsequently lost their grip over what once was their own small residential community. Bitter conflicts had erupted in 1922, when the unification of Tel Aviv with seven surrounding neighborhoods had been negotiated. Some of these disputes concerned the future of the town's public property which was owned and maintained by the town's original settlers. Others erupted in regard to the united town's new constitution, which stipulated that persons who resided in Tel Aviv for more than six months and paid at least half a pound in municipal taxes yearly were eligible to vote in the municipal elections. The old-time property owners wanted to impose stricter terms, arguing that the new constitution allowed newcomers – unfamiliar with the town's problems and needs – a greater voice in the town's politics than they ought to have.[6]

A massive immigration wave between 1924 and 1926 further increased the population of Tel Aviv. (While 13,000 people resided in Tel Aviv in 1922, the town tripled its population within four years, reaching the 40,000 mark by 1926.[7]) These waves of Jewish immigration included middle-class urban settlers who infused Tel Aviv with the larger part of the private capital that flowed into the country. A significant part of this capital was invested in real estate property, thus creating unmet demand and unleashing skyrocketing prices. At the same time, Tel Aviv also became a magnet for propertyless workers.[8] By the mid-1920s, the most burning issue on the public agenda of these urban colonizers concerned the shortage of residential apartments, steep increases in rent, uninhibited speculation in land transactions, and the waning prospects of owning a home.

Economic conditions in the colonizing community were soon translated into a political struggle, pitting organized home owners against 'tenants' and 'neighbors' who formed their own political associations, seeking public control over prices and accusing speculators of betraying the national cause. The 1926 legal battle against the Town Council of Tel Aviv was a direct continuation of this ongoing political struggle.

Sa'adia Shoshani, the petitioner, embodied that particular kind of resident who was both an original founder of the town and well-to-do real-estate owner, who became increasingly concerned that the influx of newcomers would rob them of their privileged economic, political and symbolic status. Shoshani's success at court, therefore, was a truly embarrassing affair. Tel Aviv prided itself on being the first 'purely Jewish' urban settlement in Palestine, its mere existence symbolizing the essence of Zionist aspirations. Yet here was a founder, not one that could easily be dismissed as an outsider, who deliberately undermined the cherished Zionist effort to demonstrate the ability of Jews to maintain their affairs without colonial protection and intervention. Once the conflict came to light under British judicial scrutiny, the specific class-politics issue was transformed into a principled national concern.

Enormous pressure was exerted on the petitioners to waive their petitions. Throughout July 1926, in the shadow of the pending petitions, the National Council of the Jewish Palestinian community undertook to accommodate negotiations between the Town Council and the Home Owners Association. Representatives of the National Council, although careful to act as neutral arbiters, strongly emphasized the need to find a compromise that would enable the parties to settle the conflict at "a Jewish table."[9] Appeals were made to the petitioners' sense of national responsibility:

> The Home Owners Association ... try to undermine the autonomy of the Council and to subvert our whole existence in this country. It is common knowledge that our autonomy is not yet established in detail, and when the home owners oppose the franchise, which is the foundation of this autonomy, our enemies may more easily destroy our carefully and incrementally constructed enterprise ... we are used to tipsters and betrayers – but these always came from outside our camp, and the loathers of Israel never resided among us. I ask, therefore, will the Council express its opinion of these people? Will we express the contempt we all feel towards them, especially towards Shoshani who appeared here as a loather of Israel who undermines our whole edifice?[10]

Shoshani and his allies were condemned as traitors, as enemies of the community, and as an irresponsible gang of tipsters who were closer to the Arabs than to the Hebrew community. One had first to overcome a sense of scorn and disgust, some contended, before even dealing with such people; and Bugrashov, one of the town's most distinguished citizens, called upon his friends to "vomit those destructive people out of our camp."[11] When the decision of the court was made public, the daily press was flooded with manifestos by a multitude of public associations and groups, unanimously blaming the Home Owners Association for putting their narrow class interests before the national cause.[12]

Above and beyond the class-conflict issue, the public outcry opened up questions concerning the relationship between law and nationalism, the status of colonial law with regard to Zionist constitutional matters, the appropriate way to handle disputes and establish governing norms in the absence of full sovereignty, and questions concerning the public role of lawyers in the nation-building process. The general opinion was that the legalistic arguments raised by the petitioners' lawyer – according to which some voters were not eligible to vote because they did not own property or, worse, because they were not yet naturalized in Palestine (as the Township Order stipulated) – amounted to an outright betrayal of the national cause.[13] Harsh language had been used. Members of the Council excoriated Shoshani and his friends, who were members of the council, for turning to the British court. "There are now two contending parties before the Chief Justice," lamented one (Dr Bugrashov), "We shall soon face the destruction of our whole enterprise and you are the ones who provide ammunition to our destroyers." "The Hebrew community knows that the government puts hurdles on our way and it is therefore clear that we should not address the government unless absolutely necessary," argued another; "the war should be internal ... turning to outsiders when in conflict – well, this is treason."[14]

Moreover, the fact that Horace Samuel, lawyer for the petitioners, raised legalistic arguments that ran counter to the colonization enterprise, was perceived by many as a distinct professional trait, an inherent lawyerly tendency to ignore the general context of litigation and to unscrupulously exploit any legally valid argument which could benefit clients. Dickstein and Eisenstadt joined, or rather led, the attack on lawyers in the aftermath of the Shoshani affair. "The majority among this circle of educated and cultured people," wrote Dickstein,

> distanced themselves from public work and from dedicating time and energy to public issues. They are devoted to their own material wellbeing ... The lawyers consider the foreign court, in spite of its shortcomings, to be an arena of greater opportunities – they search therein for ancient rules and bygone formal demands which may be manipulated – than those offered by a Jewish national court of law where informal considerations of equity and justice are more important than the intricacies of legal manipulation.[15]

"It was the absence of a centralized political-legal organization that brought about the severe rupture among the Hebrew public in regard to the authorities' intervention in our national autonomy affairs a few months ago," wrote Eisenstadt. Lawyers were partly responsible: not only that, lawyers had been "keeping away from national-political activities and ignored their public duties," he wrote, "the majority among them are entirely under the spell of the flexible and convenient English law," believing "in all their hearts in the universal value of English law," and gradually bringing about our "political and cultural assimilation."[16]

Lawyers were blamed for being 'too' professional, turning their craft into a buffer that allowed them to keep politics at bay. But they were also blamed for furthering a general process of assimilation into the values and culture of "the West" and for compromising the distinction of the Zionist project. These two criticisms, in fact, were not so much at odds with each other as they first seem to be. Lawyers furthered a process of assimilation precisely because they bought into the universal, apolitical, and meta-cultural claims of the English Common Law. By adhering to it, they were at once able to think of their craft as dissociated from the politics of nationalism and to participate in the reproduction of English law as a universal gift.

The Shoshani affair, in short, promised to develop into a vendetta against the legal profession's dubious commitment to the national cause.

Its aftermath created the impression that the Jewish public in general and Zionist political elites in particular were now ready to acknowledge the value of developing autonomous legal mechanisms for resolving public-related disputes. The advocates of the Hebrew Law of Peace tried to capitalize on this mood. The following argument, developed by Paltiel Dickstein, situated the problem not merely in political, but also in cultural, terms:

> The [Shoshani] petition asked the court to define the term 'rate payer,' thus licensing the court to determine the voting rights of women and dependent members of the household. Ordinarily, this is a political-public question that each autonomous community resolves in itself ... Anyone who values self-determination as a foundation for political education and political life understands that we must first of all ensure that this will become an internal problem to be resolved by the internal forces of the community ... but we cannot treat the decision of the Palestine High Court in this way. No matter how much we tell ourselves that the government is ours and that the court is ours, we cannot ignore the fact that in this important public problem we had to submit to a foreign authority .... A *priori*, we cannot trust the decision of the Arab member of that court, if he indeed took part in the decision. After all, he is a member of a nation that hides its women behind veils, locks them in harems, and tolerates polygamy, so how could he resolve the question of women's rights for us? ... There are also British members in this court, and they occupy center-stage. And the British are the high-cultured nation of the day and they are supposedly in a position to resolve such questions. But I allow myself to doubt this assertion. Let us analyze for a moment the psychological elements that could have determined the decision of the British judges of this court ... England has a conservative character, and women in England, particularly women who had no possessions, were not eligible for the franchise until after the war. The judge who spent all his days knowing that only a tax payer, only the one who headed the economic unit, is a full rights-bearing citizen, must certainly have imposed these views on the Jews as well. If we further add that the emissaries of Britain in the colonies are used to seeing themselves as the sons of an elected race and to looking down on natives, it will not be unthinkable to imagine a certain thought passing through that judge's mind: Do these people deserve to be equal with us in their political democratic institutions? It is sufficient for them to be granted the same franchise laws that we had in England ten or

even fifty years ago, and even this will be a great cultural step for them.[17]

Dickstein's conclusion, therefore – based on a simultaneous cultural distancing from British colonizers and Arab colonized – was that the Jews should learn to entrust such future conflicts to the autonomous legal mechanisms of the community.

The urgent task, in practical terms, was to convince lawyers on the one hand and influential Zionist institutions on the other, that the Hebrew Courts of Peace were competent bodies whose jurisdiction should be both respected and expanded. In the next two chapters, I consider the responsiveness of these two social forces to the Hebrew Law of Peace. With these analyses set out, I shall be in a position to comment on the interplay of law, colonialism and nationalism in general, and on the Zionist colonizing project in particular, from a more informed perspective.

CHAPTER 6

LAWYERING THE NATION

The political colonization of Palestine by the British created new conditions and new expectations. The establishment of a functioning, 'Western-type' state apparatus in general and the reconstruction of the legal system in particular, enhanced a general rationalization process that was perceived by most Zionists as a blessed mark of progress and order. In this chapter, I take a look at an elite who may be termed 'local' (from a British perspective) or 'colonizing' (from an Arab perspective): namely the Jewish lawyers who played an active role in legitimizing colonial law and working to activate it as the hegemonic law of the land. Although these lawyers, like the Zionist community in general, occupied that unstable and ambiguous position as both colonized and colonizers, by and large they embraced the idea that law was a primary instrument at the service of the civilizing mission of colonialism. In this respect, most Zionist jurists perceived themselves as auxiliary agents for colonizing Palestine rather than as a colonized elite and, moreover, as agents who, through law, accomplished a national mission. Oppositional views, such as those expressed by the advocates of the Hebrew Law of Peace, as we shall see, were marginalized and rejected.

More generally, I hope this chapter will contribute to a literature of law and colonialism that increasingly treats colonial law as an arena of struggle among various social groups rather than as a mere instrument of colonial control. In this, I follow Nathan Brown, who argues that if we wish to understand colonial legal systems, we must pay more attention to local elites. Otherwise, he writes, we risk writing the colonized population out of their own history.[1]

Arthur Ruppin, a Zionist leader who headed the Zionist Palestine Office and who played a constructive role in the creation and operation of Hebrew Courts of Peace before the war, changed his attitude in its aftermath. In a 1921 meeting of the Palestine Zionist Executive which was devoted to the question of Hebrew law, Ruppin argued that

> things have now changed. The courts of the state have improved, they are not Turkish any more, and they are now open to hear everyone without prejudice. Moreover, the Hebrew Courts are changed, in the sense that every person has the right to become a judge, and naturally we cannot submit matters of public money to the jurisdiction of courts which base themselves solely on principles of pity and charity.[2]

Two elements in the above statement should be singled out. First, the idea that the legal system of the colonial state was accessible to all and was neutral in respect to the identity of litigants. Second, the idea that the Hebrew courts were inferior to state courts and untrustworthy precisely because Hebrew judges were drawn from the Jewish population at large and based their rulings not on rules but on "pity and charity," namely on substantive notions of equity and common sense. What we have here, in short, is a Zionist leader, authorized by a Zionist institution, who distrusts another Zionist institution because of the latter's embeddedness in the community.

Ruppin expressed a sentiment that was largely shared by many lawyers and was constantly transmitted by them to the general public and to relevant Zionist institutions. As far as lawyers were concerned, the very idea that an important function of the Hebrew courts was to generate compromises between parties, based on an embedded sense of equity rather than on the articulation of clear-cut legal solutions, proved the unsound character of the Hebrew Law of Peace. In the absence of the element of a rule-governed adversarial system, many lawyers treated Hebrew law with outright suspicion: "Facilitating peaceful compromises between contending parties is a good thing whose fruits are consumed in this world while their surplus remains for the after-world," wrote one lawyer, "and yet this is not Law, whose one and only foundation is in that justice which materializes in objective laws."[3]

In the shadow of the colonial state's law, lawyers repeatedly argued that the litigation and decision-making methods of the Hebrew courts worked to the detriment of the PZE. In 1926, for example, the PZE was sued by a former employee who asked for monetary compensation. Two lawyers advised against submitting the case to the jurisdiction of the Hebrew court. Zigfried Van Vriesland, a lawyer and the treasurer of the PZE, had been quite blunt: "We would have to pay more than we had planned to," he said, "at a Hebrew Court of Peace."[4] Harry Sacher, a prominent private lawyer who served as the legal adviser of the PZE, argued that the Hebrew court had no jurisdiction in such matters. On the basis of his advice, the PZE refused to litigate and explained that it had its own internal legal mechanisms for settling such disputes.[5] In another case, a plaintiff addressed a Hebrew Court of Peace against the Jewish National Fund (JNF). As a preliminary move, lawyers for the JNF announced that they would submit to the jurisdiction of the court only if it would decide the matter on the basis of Ottoman law and the relevant British amendments to that law.[6] In 1929, Van Vriesland submitted a secret report on the Hebrew law project which explicitly urged the PZE to distance itself from these courts because "in the case of the PZE, experience has shown that '*rachmones*' [literally: pity, but here used in a derogatory sense, using the Yiddish word for it] as one of the elements which constitutes the 'too common a sense' of the *Mishpat Ha'Shalom* (Law of Peace) judge, speaks generally in favor of the claimant against the PZE."[7]

The attitude towards the Hebrew courts seems at first to have been triggered by considerations of utility and efficacy and based on an instrumental approach to law. Lacking clear standards, let alone expertise, Hebrew courts failed to provide the certainty and rule-bound logic that lawyers and, arguably, public institutions needed in order to run their business. Yet it seems that more was at stake than mere calculations of utility. At the very least, instrumental considerations were merged with the more general idea that Hebrew law was in fact no law at all. Not only did it not 'pay' to litigate at a Hebrew court, it made no sense, as it had no stable foundation of 'objective laws' from which to argue a case:

> As far as the Hebrew Law of Peace is concerned, there are no such things as laws or rules which it applies. The laws do not provide any indication as to the principles upon which the judgment would ultimately be based. My inquiries with a number of Hebrew Peace judges revealed a variety of opinions on this subject. Some mention that 'justice and equity' is the law, others refer to 'public opinion', in itself divided as to 'workers' public opinion', 'teachers' public opinion', etc., others argue that the 'law of Israel' is the law, and at best, they apply the law of the state, corrected and revised in accordance with the mixture of the abovementioned sources. It is necessary to understand that this is a highly undesirable system. For the purposes of litigation, recognizing the Hebrew Law of Peace means handing over disputes to a compromising third party, whose common sense cannot be trusted more than the common sense of any other person ...

Recognizing the Hebrew Law of Peace, in general, does not benefit the idea of economic development, because this system encourages litigation. '*Dura Lex, Sed Lex*' [bad law is preferable to no law] is applicable to our people as well. A stable law tends to reduce litigation, and the waste of time and energy they entail, because people then try to live within the framework of that law. The real problem, therefore, is not the judicial tribunal, but the existence of law. When the law is bad, one should exert pressure in order to change it. The solution is not to run away from the problem by creating a lawless judge.[8]

In other words, the claim of the advocates of the Hebrew Law of Peace to speak in the name of the nation's culture was turned on its head by hostile lawyers. The idea of law-as-culture, I previously argued, was premised on the intellectual (and biographical) affinity between the Russian-born jurists of the Hebrew Law of Peace and the intellectual group of writers who emigrated to Palestine from Odessa and Warsaw in the 1920s. The latter were accepted and celebrated precisely because they had confined themselves to 'pure' cultural activities and because largely they conformed to the existing political parameters of the nation-building project.[9] The advocates of the Hebrew Law of Peace, on the other hand, operated in a sphere of activity that forever transgressed into the 'political.' Unlike literary practices, the establishment of an operative system of courts and the derivative claim to practice the actual shaping of social relations among individuals and between individuals and institutions could not be contained within a distinct cultural sphere. Professional lawyers, therefore, were ready to admit the abstract cultural value of law, but effectively robbed it of its practical value in the sphere of 'real life.' The cultural claim, I reiterate, was used against itself by state-oriented lawyers.

The emergent conception of Hebrew law as non-law severely impaired the ability of the Hebrew law advocates to transform nationalism into a negotiable resource that could be traded in exchange for jurisdiction and authority. Having robbed the Hebrew courts of their 'legal' character, lawyers had effectively dismantled the potential competition between the legal system of the state and the aspiring 'national' system of law. The door was now open for an unabashed state-centered concept of law, regardless of the identity of those who happened to occupy the offices of state at that particular time. Corroborated on the one hand by the conviction that the basic legal apparatuses installed by the British in Palestine represented an enlightened, neutral and universal system, and on the other hand by the conviction that the alternative was not really law, a positivist approach to law began to crystalize as a hallmark of the Zionist legal epistemology, shared by lawyers and political leaders alike.

Early signs had become apparent in 1920, when a group of lawyers convened to discuss the future of the Hebrew Courts of Peace. Speakers in that convention argued that the new legal order established by the British reduced the need to resort to Hebrew courts. In order to have a 'national' impact in law, some speakers argued, it was necessary to get rid of the "negative attitude to foreign tribunals and to integrate with the mandatory legal system by penetrating the courts of the state, mastering the English language, and lobbying the government to admit more Jewish judges to the bench."[10] This same position, minutely explained by a lawyer and a prominent Zionist leader, was published in the daily *Ha'Aretz* in the aftermath of the Shoshani affair. Bernard Joseph, who later became a minister in the Israeli government, apparently undeterred by the attacks on lawyers that followed Shoshani's 'transgression,' flatly rejected the Hebrew law-and-nationalism project and the idea that developing an autonomous national legal system was no less urgent than the need to develop an autonomous Hebrew educational system.

The Shoshani affair, he wrote, had been exploited by people who were "categorically opposed to submit Jewish affairs to the jurisdiction of the general civil courts operating in Palestine." This approach was not a national one, "but a mere mark of ghetto psychology" and "a remnant of exilic life." "Healthy nationalism," he wrote, "is one of the most important forces in the development of humanity, yet an abyss separates it from narrow chauvinism." Not only that, the avoidance of Mandatory courts was not a display of national responsibility, Joseph wrote, but it in fact amounted to being an anti-national act in itself: "There is nothing more dangerous to our future national life than the assumption that we are nothing but another Jewish congregation and that the government of this land is not our government and the general system of courts are not our courts." True nationalism, he wrote, depended on strengthening the ties to the institutions of the Mandatory state. We need "to work from the inside," he wrote: Jewish lawyers who would penetrate the governmental establishment, Jewish judges who would be appointed to the Mandatory courts, Jewish jurists who would shape the spirit of Mandatory law, rather than the establishment of "a government within a government." As to the Shoshani case, Joseph concluded, "if the law stipulated that only citizens of Palestine were eligible to vote, then the appropriate course of action for those who disagreed with that law would have been to urge the government to change it. Instead, they decided to excommunicate the Jews who raised the question."[11]

With Joseph's views in mind, we are now in a better position to make sense of the debate on the place of law and the role of lawyers in the Zionist national project. This debate was organized around two competing notions of nationalism in law. Countering the attempt to ground the legitimacy of Hebrew courts in their nationalist vocation, Joseph treated 'that' nationalism as no more than an exilic-bound sectarian insularity; countering the attempt to advance a claim on behalf of Hebrew autonomy in law, Joseph spoke in the name of another type of nationalism, one based on strong links to the institutions of the colonial state; and countering the claim that the vitality of law resided in a particular national culture (coexisting with state law and functioning as an active cultural force of civil society), Joseph spoke for a centralist and, arguably, a universal legal paradigm which abhorred the notion of "a government within a government."[12]

In sum, the Hebrew law was attacked on two fronts: it was no law, and it had no national value. The final link was made in 1929, in Van Vriesland's secret report. Having concluded that Hebrew law was no law, and having demonstrated its potentially negative social and economic impact, Van Vriesland added the following:

> Neither is there any political value in the *Mishpat Hashalom*. On the contrary, the government courts, though in many respects deficient, are the better of the two evils ... The Hebrew Peace Court, which dates from Turkish times, *is supported by a Russian point of view which considers a government the natural enemy of the people*. This does not seem politically the wisest attitude to adopt.[13]
> (emphasis added)

Michael Bakunin, in his *Statism and Anarchy*, defined anarchy as "the free and independent organization of all the units and parts of the community and their voluntary federation from below upward, not by the orders of any authority, even an elected one, and not by the dictates of any scientific theory, but as a result of the natural development of all the varied demands put forth by life itself ..."[14] To the extent that the advocates of the Hebrew Law of Peace tried to imagine a law that grew from below, in response to "varied demands put forth by life itself," Van Vriesland, keeping in mind the backgrounds of some of the Hebrew law advocates, had a valid point. But it also seems that Van Vriesland finally expressed an explicit and uncompromising appeal for an alliance with the colonial state as the 'wisest' form of nationalism.

Partha Chatterjee, tracing the trajectory of Indian nationalism, argues that bourgeois opposition to colonialism has always been ambiguous. There is a history of collaboration between the colonial state and the educated classes, he writes, "sealed by the marriage of law and literacy."[15] The dominant form of elite-nationalist politics in India was "social reform through the medium of the legislative institutions of the colonial state;" trying "to persuade British administrators to legislate on social questions by appealing to enlightened reason and ratinality."[16] In short, it was a nationalism disposed towards Western-colonialist notions of law and state. I believe a similar point can be made with respect to Jewish lawyers in colonial Palestine who, however small in number, seemed to have had a significant influence on key Zionist economic and political institutions in matters of 'law.' ("Our lawyer, Dr Donkelblum," wrote Van Vriesland in his report, "formally refused to represent us at the *Mishpat Hashalom* [Hebrew Law of Peace].")[17]

At this stage, however, it is important to make a key methodological point that guides the present study. This is that we are *not* dealing here with a confrontation between idealistic and altruistic jurists who recruited law to the national project, on the one hand, and instrumental and profit-seeking lawyers who neglected their national duties on the other hand. We are *not* dealing with people who 'shirked their national duties' – the expression itself being a conceptual weapon in an ongoing struggle as to what is law and what is nationalism – but rather with the *competing* conceptualizations of 'law' and 'nationalism' of various segments of the legal profession. On numerous occasions, the advocates and supporters of the Law of Peace argued that the difficulties of their cherished institution stemmed from the fact that many lawyers (and Zionist institutions, for that matter) neglected their national responsibilities and compromised 'national discipline.' Yet such arguments do not provide a sociological explanation; rather, such arguments should be treated as discursive moves which have been directed against other players in the legal field.

In either case, the uses to which terms such as 'law' and 'nationalism' were put by the lawyers of the day cannot be comprehended without linking them to the differential positions they occupied in the Palestinian legal field of the 1920s. In talking of a legal field, I have in mind Bourdieu's conception of a field as a set of dispositions that, however unstable they may be, structure the range of possibilities for the relevant actors within it and mark the boundaries of their legitimate action. The field, in this sense, both constrains and enables action. It is a space which is shaped through the practices of actors and at the same time it is that space which gives meaning and direction to the practices which are realized within it. The theoretical value of the field metaphor lies in that it anchors symbolic systems of meaning to the concrete practices and experiences of their carriers and, consequently, provides a blueprint for analyzing the way a given discourse is produced within a social universe that produces its own internal division of labor, structured hierarchies and differential positions. Ultimately, writes Bourdieu, the legal field is "the site of a competition for monopoly of the right to determine the law,"[18] and I employ this guideline in making sense of the role lawyers played in suffocating the Hebrew Law of Peace.

The growing reluctance of lawyers to steer clients to Hebrew courts and to facilitate the Hebrew law project has to be read in the light of the fact that the colonial state had launched a quite assertive program of professionalization in law, beginning in the early 1920s. In 1922, the government published an Advocates' Ordinance which regulated legal practice. The Ordinance provided a general definition of the "profession of advocates," established jurisdictional boundaries, forbade unlicensed persons from practicing law, and set the terms for obtaining a license to practice. The four primary requirements were to have attained the age of twenty-five, to have a "good character," to complete two years' service in the office of a lawyer licensed to practice in Palestine, and to be qualified by an examination "as to [one's] knowledge of law."[19]

Two years earlier, in 1920, a government law school had opened in Jerusalem, sponsored by Norman Bentwich, the colonial government's senior legal adviser. Studies at the law school had two levels: a basic level in which students received their education in Arabic or Hebrew (or both), covering areas of the law such as the Ottoman Majela, commercial and land law, criminal law, and civil and criminal procedure. Those who completed this level of study were ready to sit an examination and to be licensed as practitioners, but they were not entitled to a diploma, a formal degree in law. The formal degree was granted only to those who had completed the second level as well. Only English-speakers were admitted and they had to undertake a three-year study program which covered jurisprudence, English torts and contract law, and international law. In other words, the school's program was structured in a way that explicitly singled out the true full-fledged legal expert: only someone who was proficient in English, who had been familiarized with the notion of law as a theoretical body of knowledge, and who had actually mastered the essential principles of English law.[20]

Entry-level requirements to the government law school were gradually raised throughout the 1920s.[21] The stricter standards and the limit on the number of graduates were made in the name of quality considerations, and introduced in response to pressure exerted by practicing lawyers concerned with the prospect of the profession being flooded with too many lawyers.[22] There were many complaints about 'illegal' competition by unlicensed practitioners. In particular, they cited Article 3(ii) of the Advocates' Ordinance which left intact an Ottoman rule that allowed non-lawyers to "address the Court as a friend on behalf of a party not represented by an Advocate, but in no case shall such person have a claim enforceable at law, for remuneration for his service." Licensed lawyers considered that this provision threatened their representational monopoly. "Our experience in the last several years," complained one lawyer, "has been sufficient to show that persons who purport to act as 'friends' routinely represent parties at court. This state of affairs has deteriorated to the extent that such people dare to offer their services in public by publishing ads in the daily press." This situation was particularly grave, the writer argued, given that the law school contributed its share to a steep increase in the number of lawyers: "This situation requires that the government will improve the work conditions of lawyers and will establish – in accord with professional associations – regulations for their improvement. Both the government and the public have an interest in such improvements, because it is well known that the duties of lawyers require considerable responsibility, and the lawyer needs to be protected if he is to defend his clients' interests in a proper way."[23]

The Advocates' Ordinance and the establishment of a government-run law school, then, laid the foundation for a professionalization project under the auspices of the colonial state. This foundation in turn set the conditions for legitimate juridic participation in the Palestinian politico-legal sphere (for lawyers, officials, judges, legal representatives of political and commercial organizations, and for experts who were needed to manage the affairs of the colonizing community) on the basis of the commitment of lawyers to English law and on the basis of their ability to develop expert-based ties to the institutions of the colonial state. The growing suspicion of lawyers towards the Hebrew courts, then, should also be considered in light of the fact these courts displayed 'unprofessional' traits – let alone tolerating an unsteady mix of lawyers and lay persons in terms of personnel and institutional setting – precisely at a time when the market for legal services was perceived to be suffused with intensifying internal competition among certified lawyers as their numbers grew and external competition from other 'uncertified' competitors.

The advent of the professionalization process is key to understanding the attitude of most lawyers towards the Hebrew Law of Peace at the epistemic, and not merely at the systemic, level. Professionalization is a social process of closure and distinction on the basis of claims to expertise in a given field of knowledge and on the basis of a proven ability to solve problems which are in themselves constructed, organized and framed in a particular way. The primary purpose of professionalization in law is to secure a legally protected and legally recognized monopoly over the market of legal services; such monopoly is secured when lawyers are granted exclusive rights of representation and gain exclusive rights of access to the juridical and quasi-juridical arenas of the state.

The most crucial element in a professionalization project, at the epistemic level, is the availability of an abstract and theoretical body of knowledge which arguably ensures the reliability and the (at least) quasi-scientific foundation of professional practice. The ability to refer to such a body of knowledge, in fact, is what distinguishes a profession from a craft and allows the construction of professional identity. "The ability of a profession to sustain its jurisdictions," writes Abbott,

> lies partly in the power and prestige of its academic knowledge. This prestige reflects the public's mistaken belief that abstract professional knowledge is continuous with practical professional knowledge, and hence that prestigious abstract knowledge implies effective professional work. In fact, the true use of academic professional knowledge is less practical than symbolic. Academic knowledge legitimizes professional work by clarifying its foundations and tracing them to major cultural values.[24]

The study program in the Jerusalem Law School may thus be read as a declaration of the values relevant to the Palestinian legal expert: familiarity with Mandatory law from the perspective of the guiding principles of English law. In other words, the forms in which the body of knowledge considered to be the source of authoritative expertise was being produced and distributed, and the relations between the authorised producers of this knowledge and its consumers, operators and competitors, were the forms that constituted the legal field as a more or less distinct sphere of expertise.

In the colonial situation of 1920s Palestine, the establishment of a civil administration was accompanied by and sustained by the construction of a new legal order, yet one which was essentially based on importing 'ready-made' legal knowledge: the colonial law of the British empire with its references to the legacy of English law. The Mandatory government had a stake in the professionalization project of lawyers as part of its more comprehensive effort to secure a coherent legal system that would bring together and order under one conceptual and institutional roof the various elements of Palestine's previous legal forms. The colonial state, in other words, was not simply a major player in the construction of the legal field 'in abstract,' but also the center of gravity for a social process of professionalization. Lawyers, for their part, also had a stake in securing links with the law of the state: the unifying umbrella of English law defined and supplied that theoretical body of knowledge from which they could derive the legitimacy needed in order to secure a monopolistic position in the market of legal services. The idea that law may be created 'from below,' on the basis of commonsense, non-confrontational methods, and through interpretive creativity (of Jewish legal texts accessible only to a few) contradicted, therefore, the most basic elements of the professionalization project.

The advocates of the Hebrew law tried to remind their critics that the origins of the enlightened British legal order which they celebrated were rooted in a common-law tradition that could also be said to represent a growth from below, in itself grounded in culture and history. This argument, however, did not seem to be effective, and perhaps for good reasons. The British did not purport to import the common law 'in full' into the colonies, as the common law was indeed perceived by them to embody the traits of their own distinct culture. On the contrary, law of the colonies was supposed to be based on existing local laws (e.g., the Ottoman, in Palestine), revised and updated by formal colonial legislation (e.g., ordinances), and interpreted and developed, as a last resort, by appeal to English law. The legal systems of colonies, in other words, did not purport to embody the cultural and historical accumulated meaning of the English common law. These colonial legal systems, rather, were presumed to be empty vessels, the British 'only' providing a blueprint: an efficient and professional legal administration, local legislation, and the already 'complete' and 'final' symbols of English law. These empty vessels, in principle, were put at the service of the natives, to be filled with local flavor, or 'tradition,' or 'custom,' or 'needs,' or 'modernization' and so on. The irony, however, is that the so-called empty British colonial state vessel has sometimes been revered for an independent value of its own, 'fully loaded as is,' so to speak. It seems that this was the predominant attitude among Zionist legal and political elites in 1920s Palestine, who celebrated the means (state institutions) as ends (the state as a value), planting the seeds for a statist orientation to law, an approach that essentially treats law as an instrument of ordering and control and one which, at bottom, privileges the formal aspects of law over substantive content.

At any rate, a caveat is in order. We should also keep in mind that most lawyers are not driven by abstract principles. Lawyers are trained to frame anticipated and concrete conflicts in pre-given forms, to master rules, and to litigate in appropriate forums. Thus, a majority among Jewish Palestinian lawyers were wedded to English law by default; not because of any clearly articulated ideological disposition, but simply because they opted for what seemed to be the more rational and cost-effective way to conduct legal business on behalf of clients. Under the umbrella of the state law, Jewish practitioners developed a taste for the mastery of second-order rules, procedural devices, and evidentiary forms that ordinarily secure a bond among the players in the legal field. All these acquired habits were often frustrated in Hebrew courts, leading lawyers to complain about the 'unpredictable' notions of justice in those courts.

> The following episode may explain why Dr Donkelblum, a prominent lawyer who had a rich record of appearances in the Hebrew courts, eventually decided to steer his clients away from these tribunals.[25] Donkelblum argued for plaintiff in the case of Shrier vs. Epstein. Plaintiff argued that he paid money to defendant in return for an obligation to share ownership in a piece of land which defendant was about to buy from Geula, a real-estate company. The District Hebrew Court accepted the plaintiff's version, established a breach of trust between friends, and ruled that plaintiff was entitled to two-fifths of the said land. On appeal, defendant argued that according to the laws of the country, to Hebrew law, and even according to precedents of the Hebrew Courts of Peace, the sale of land required a definite form, namely, a formal written document. The High Hebrew Court of Peace ruled that Hebrew law (citing *Hoshen Mishpat*) established that in principle, land is acquired against the payment of money, but wherever and whenever custom is to write a formal deed, a sale would not be finalized prior to such formal action. "In the present case," the court ruled, "according to the circumstances of the time and the place, and mainly on the basis of the friendship which existed between the two parties, no formal document was needed in order to finalize the sale. Moreover, at stake was not the actual purchase of land, but a purchase of a promise to share a right to ownership because the land still belonged to Geula when the parties entered into the agreement." Consequently, the High Court of Peace established that plaintiff had a right of ownership in half the land.[26]
>
> Yet while plaintiff won the case, he was nonetheless about to lose the land. In a letter written by Donkelblum to the High Hebrew Court of Peace shortly after the decision was rendered, he complained that rumor had it that Geula was about to transfer the land to defendant, who happened to be its employee, without registering the plaintiff as a joint owner. Donkelblum, therefore, asked the High Court to warn Geula that it would be considered a shirker which disobeyed the judgments of the court and further urged the Hebrew court to advise the municipality of Tel Aviv, where the land in dispute was located, to decline granting owner the needed construction permit. Donkelblum attached to his letter a letter from Geula which stated that the company's regulations prevented it from registering said land as joint ownership and that it would therefore not submit to the court's ruling.

> Subsequently, Geula appealed the High Court of Peace to reconsider the case on procedural grounds, arguing that a few witnesses were prevented from testifying before the court in earlier motions. In reconsidering the case, the High Court of Peace reversed its earlier decision, establishing that plaintiff had no right of ownership because the negotiation between the parties was never completed prior to the purchase of the land by the defendant. This decision allowed the Hebrew Court of Peace to avoid much embarrassment and damage to its authority as it became clear that Geula was determined not to respect the earlier judgment. Yet it is also clear that Donkelblum had a good reason to be extremely frustrated with what could only be considered as a total blurring of law and politics.[27]

In short, litigation in the Hebrew Courts of Peace seemed to have robbed lawyers of some of the properties essential to their very identity as legal experts and as legitimate agents of representation. Here is an enlightening glimpse into another legal world, in another novel by Barry Unsworth, through the eyes of an inhabitant of that world and those of a foreigner:

> The lawyer listened quite impassively, looking sometimes at their faces, more often fixing his eyes on the far wall or down on his immaculate desk. When Harold had finished, he nodded slowly but without speaking. He was holding a pencil and he tapped softly with this upon the desk, causing quick reflections in its polished surface. "It is only a small thing, I know," Harold said, a little disconcerted by the silence. "But I thought it best to do whatever is to be done in legal form." "That is very wise," Mancini smiled suddenly. "Legal form resembles other virtues: when you have it, you don't always need to apply it. Without it there is no form at all, none whatever."
> ... "If they try to close the road, I will take them to court in double quick time," Harold said belligerently. "Double quick time? In Italy?" Mancini raised the hand holding the pencil and made a sweeping gesture round the room. "Look at those sofas and armchairs. Look at those rugs on the floor, they are Afghan. This office is in the part of town where the rents are highest. I have a house in Umbertide and a large villa in Apulia. All this has been paid for by people taking other people to court in double slow time."[28]

Max Radin, commenting on the hostility of American lawyers to newly established administrative agencies set up to eliminate complex legalistic practices in the 1930s, captured the essence of that hostility:

> What the lawyer undoubtedly misses is the air of the cock-pit, the chaude-melee of the tournament, the *strepitus judicili* which in all reformatory efforts, popes and emperors, philosophers and publicists, have always attempted to eliminate. It cannot be wholly eliminated because lawyers love it, as all craftsmen enjoy opportunities to exhibit their skill, as musicians love virtuosity, as aviators love stunts when they can do them.[29]

Radin spoke, I think, about precisely the same force that Pierre Bourdieu tried to capture through the sociological concept of "habitus": agents acquire the ability (or fail to acquire it) to make the 'right' movements in the space within which they operate. It is not simply a learned technical skill. It is an inscription into one's bodily movements and gestures, inseparable from one's words and utterances. It is a practice whose logic can no longer be articulated but only performed.

One such performance involved the ever-increasing attempts to challenge the rulings of Hebrew courts in state courts. As previously mentioned, the Hebrew Courts of Peace were regulated by the Arbitration Ordinance and their rulings were subjected to the reviewing powers of state court judges. This institutional arrangement allowed unsatisfied parties, guided by lawyers, to frustrate, or at least to delay and complicate, the execution of rulings of the Hebrew courts. Such practices had a snowball effect, as they led other prospective litigants to doubt whether litigation in the Hebrew courts was worth the effort to begin with. As far as lawyers were concerned, employing procedural and other delaying tactics in defiance of arbitrators' rulings was a perfectly legitimate application of their skills (and when they were accused of thus betraying the national cause, they routinely defended themselves by arguing that they were only obeying the dictates of clients). Yet these lawyerly tactics were devastating as far as the Hebrew Courts of Peace were concerned. A report presented at a general meeting of the Judges of the Hebrew Courts of Peace in 1927 thus stated that "in the past six months we have witnessed a decline in the number of cases brought before us, due to the war launched against us by a number of lawyers who lobbied for and succeeded in prolonging the procedure of validating our judgments by the district governmental court."[30]

Finally, a strict social dimension must not be ruled out. Training in the ways of the law of the colonizers also entailed at least some 'social' training in negotiating with British officials. In turn, effective representation breeds and often depends upon maintaining good professional and, preferably, social relations. The stake Jewish lawyers had in strengthening relations with colonial officials, in the absence of research, can only be generally inferred. A case in point is the general aura dispensed by the biggest and most influential Jewish law firm that existed in Palestine at the time, that of Sacher, Horowitz and Klebanoff. The firm had offices in Jerusalem and Haifa and maintained regular correspondents in London. Harry Sacher and Solomon Horowitz seemed to enjoy considerable clout both in Zionist circles and with British colonial officials. Sacher served as the official legal adviser of the Palestine Zionist Executive, as noted earlier, and his firm also provided extensive legal services to the Council of Tel Aviv, assisting it in litigation and in drafting and introducing proposed legislative measures to the colonial government.[31] In performing such services, the firm conducted all its correspondence with the Council of Tel Aviv in English, and did not fail to mention to the client that both Sacher and Horowitz could engage the Chief Justice in private chambers in matters of concern to the Council.[32] Sending such signals of professional status is also consistent with the spirit of Gad Frumkin's recollections. Frumkin was the first Jewish judge at the colonial High Court of Justice, and his published memoirs convey strongly the atmosphere of association with British officials at cocktail parties and other social events at which the ability of the Jew to integrate into the colonial administration was praised as a high mark of 'national' influence.[33] I believe it is not too daring to suggest, then, that Jewish lawyers were strongly socialized into developing strong links with the colonial state as at least one trait of their professionalism.

It is only from within the logic of their practice that we may ultimately understand the role of lawyers in suffocating the Hebrew courts. The formal, well-articulated ideas of some key lawyers notwithstanding, I think we have here an actualization of the positivist legal paradigm in its concrete and practical social dimensions. Max Weber noted almost a century ago that the culture of lawyering consists of a preference for the fixed and regular determinateness of all external rights and duties by a sovereign as a value worth pursuing in and of itself.[34] It seems that this craving for rules and order, orchestrated from above by a unifying power, is for lawyers a condition of their ability to secure a monopoly on representation. In this sense lawyers, and not theoreticians and jurisprudential experts, are the 'true' carriers of the positivist paradigm in law. Establishing a jurisdiction on the basis of a body of knowledge whose legitimacy and might is secured by the state, lawyers tend to develop and in turn to sustain the notion that there is no law but state law. Further, the contingencies of professionalization merge with notions of state sovereignty in a way that ensures that members of the legal profession will indeed act as agents of the state in the deepest sense of the term. Each motion, each act of representation on behalf of a client, is simultaneously an act of recognition of the validity, legitimacy and inevitability of state law.

Yet the colonial situation, where the state is by definition an 'alien force,' may complicate the ordinarily 'natural' disposition of lawyers towards the law of the state. Writing about the professionalization of American lawyers in the late nineteenth century, Larson observed that:

> It is therefore not coincidental that the American legal profession should have decisively moved toward professionalization in the Progressive era. The bureaucratization of the state apparatus, the movements for civil service reform, and the articulation of legitimacy principles which emphasized the role of expertise all contributed to establish the state's 'neutrality.' This, in turn, created a favorable ideological climate for the legal profession's assertion of neutrality and independence.[35]

The colonial situation, however, is potentially one of tension between colonizers and colonized, hardly propitious for conceiving the state as a neutral arbiter, let alone at times when the 'colonized' are deeply invested – symbolically if not practically – in a nation-building project. Indeed, I already noted that the advocates of the Hebrew Law of Peace regularly snapped at lawyers for their lack of national responsibility. But I also argued that we should treat this accusation as a discursive move in the field and not as an objective account of the role of lawyers in Palestine. Rather, as previously argued, the space Jewish lawyers occupied in the colonial legal field bred competing notions not only of what law was, but also of what nationalism was, thus effectively discounting the national value of the Hebrew Law of Peace by articulating a competing, state-centered, version of nationalism based, as we have seen, on the idea of law's impartial calculability if not on an unabashed notion of state neutrality.

To recapitulate, let me try to weave together the loose threads of this chapter. The general thrust has been that the emerging Jewish legal profession of colonial Palestine identified with and adopted the universalistic pretense of English law as a 'perfected' system of law. By extension, I argued that the professionalization of Jewish lawyers in Palestine was a process involving the development of institutional ties to the apparatuses of the colonial state. Subsequently, the Hebrew Courts of Peace became less and less appealing to lawyers as appropriate forums where they could exhibit and practice their skills. Given the strategic location of lawyers as gate-keepers who shaped the legal consciousness of individuals and given their ability to shape the legalistic dispositions of key political and economic institutions, lawyers played a key role in the decline of the Hebrew Law of Peace.

In the most direct and practical terms, Jewish lawyers distanced themselves from or suspected the Hebrew Law of Peace for strict professional reasons: the Hebrew law was not conducive to the rules of the legal game in which lawyers had been trained and, finally, amounted to being no law at all. I have also showed that these professional conceptions cannot be understood independently of the legal field in which those notions of professionalism crystalized and that, further, the colonial state was a major player affecting the construction of that legal field and its hegemonic notion of professionalism. However, at this point it is important to reintroduce the question of nationalism to this analysis. My point is, simply, that the emergent conception of what constituted nationalism-in-and-through-law was grounded in these acquired notions of professionalism and articulated from within them. Thus, the treatment of the Hebrew law as no-law, the apprehension at the lack of rules, the suspicion of common sense, and the downgrading of 'charitable' compromise, showed one face of a coin whose other face gave rise to a lawyerly version of nationalism which had practically been empty of content. Lawyers were talking about the necessity to withhold stable legal structures, frameworks and institutions, about the need for Jews to penetrate the justice apparatuses of the colonial state, and about affiliation with the colonial government 'as if it was ours,' as the epitome and true manifestation of Jewish nationalism in law. Yet these lawyers, in the last instance, said nothing about what Jews would have to say, presumably in a different way from others, *in* these institutions, *as* Jews, *about* the substance of law. Therefore in the final analysis, what was at stake was not only a confrontation between community and state law or between case and abstract law. The Hebrew Law of Peace, potentially at least, stood for much more than an insistence on the need to ground law in the community. Rather, it represented the idea that law was not an end in and of itself but a means to create a qualitatively different political culture.[36] In this respect, it truly challenged the conception of law which grounded it in an institutional framework devoid of concrete substance; a conception of law, finally, which consolidated one element of what is yet to be discussed in terms of statist-nationalism.

It was not the colonial state and its legal officers, but rather forces from within the Jewish colonizing community of Palestine that ultimately brought about the demise of the Hebrew Law of Peace. The conception of law suggested by the advocates of the Hebrew Law of Peace represented a *cultural,* as distinct from a *political* (or 'scientific') approach to law which corresponded to a broader nationalist orientation that emphasized the *cultural* rather than the *political* aspects of the national project precisely at a time when the latter form of nationalism – investing in the institution-building 'practicalities' of national revival – became the dominant orientation of the Zionist movement.

CHAPTER 7

NATION-BUILDING AND THE CONTAINMENT OF LEGALITY

In their analysis of the San Francisco Community Boards (SFCB), Fredric L. DuBow and Craig McEwen note that the SFCB were reluctant to rely on referrals from state courts and the police. Guided by the idea that ties between alternative justice mechanisms and state apparatuses may turn the former into an extension of the latter, the SFCB relied instead "on cases brought to it voluntarily by individuals or groups."[1] DuBow and McEwen further note that the SFCB also had little input from community organizations, such as schools, churches and neighborhood committees. "This fact," they argue, "may reflect the lack of commitment in these organizations to conflict resolution, but if that is the case, it is a lack of commitment that SFCB did little to change."[2] Coming to terms with the fact that the SFCB – basing themselves on community norms, local empowerment and self-organization – made little effort to tie into existing neighborhood networks, DuBow and McEwen argue that it had to do with the SFCB's view of urban life "in terms of estranged and individuated 'mass public' ... so the appeal was ... to individuals through organizations rather than to the organizations themselves."[3]

This is in sharp contrast to the Hebrew Law of Peace, which vigorously sought institutional input. The aim of the Hebrew law project was not to distance itself from state apparatuses per se, but to maintain a distance from those of the *colonial* state. Further, its mission was not to empower 'an estranged mass public' but, rather, to organize itself around a presumed community, thought of in terms of an awakening nation with a distinct collective identity. In other words, the Hebrew Law of Peace was premised on the notion that Zionism entailed a community which already existed as a 'real' social entity, albeit without an independent state of its own. In this sense, at least, the Hebrew Law of Peace was community-oriented only to the extent that community practices anticipated the eventual emergence of a sovereign state. With these premises in mind, the Hebrew Law of Peace endeavored to enlist the support of quasi-state Zionist institutions. Such support for its cause was crucial for financial reasons and for guaranteeing a steady flow of cases. Moreover, strong institutional links with other bodies of the colonizing community promised to signal to the public at large that the Hebrew Law of Peace was an essential ingredient of the national project, thereby strengthening the position of the Hebrew courts in their jurisdictional competition with both state courts and rabbinical courts. Zionist institutions, however, declined to provide the Hebrew Law of Peace with a much-sought-after stamp of officialdom.

Accordingly, the general purpose of this chapter is to explore the reluctance of Zionist institutions to facilitate the emergence of autonomous legal institutions. I begin with the Hebrew Law of Peace and then move on to consider some basic facets of another Zionist legal institution, namely the Comrades Law of the Hebrew Federation of Labor. In both cases, I show that efforts to enlist Zionist institutions in full and uncompromised commitment to the Hebrew law project, and similar attempts to secure the Comrades Law as a strong autonomous instrumentality within the Hebrew Federation of Labor, were largely abortive.

The argument I develop in this chapter is that, through a curious inversion, the adoption of the law of the colonialist state on the one hand and the gradual dismissal of attempts to create distinctly national systems of law on the other hand, concern two interrelated aspects of the nation-building project: an avoidance of legality which Zionist political elites nurtured since the beginning of the Zionist enterprise in Palestine, and general apprehension at the idea that an effective nation-building project could tolerate substantive popular inputs from below. It is the combination of these two analytically distinct dispositions, finally, that provides us with a blueprint for understanding the emergence of a state-centered version of nationalism as a crucial emergent process in the trajectory of Zionism.

I have already told the story of Sa'adia Shoshani and his friends who were publicly condemned as enemies of the national cause because they challenged the legality of the Tel Aviv municipal elections at the state's High Court of Justice (see Salle d'Attente). The Hebrew Law of Peace had its brief moment of glory, and, moreover, its moment of hope, in the aftermath of the Shoshani affair. In concrete terms, it had been emboldened by the role assigned to it in the forthcoming municipal elections which followed Shoshani's successful legal challenge. The

Executive Committee of the Town Council of Tel Aviv addressed the High Hebrew Court of Peace as follows:

> 5.11.1926
> To: The High Hebrew Court of Peace
> re: Elections.
> You may know that elections to the town council are scheduled to be held on 21.11.26. Needless to say, the executive committee exerts every possible means to ensure that the elections will be held on schedule and in full accordance with the town's constitution. Nevertheless, there are persons who spread rumors with the intention of destroying the public's trust in the integrity of the elections committee. Therefore, we ask you to consider the urgency and to summon today an emergency meeting of the executive committee of the High Court and to nominate from among the members of the High Court a committee that will supervise the list of voters and that will serve as a last instance for appeals in matters relating to voting privileges.
> Respectfully, D. Bloch[4]

The advocates of the Hebrew Law of Peace tried to capitalize on public sentiment against turning to the courts of the state by arguing that the jurisdiction of the Hebrew Law of Peace had to be expanded to include the public law aspects of the colonization project because 'public law'-related issues consisted of problems that "every autonomous public should resolve without recourse to external forces."[5] Thus in August 1926, at the same time that the Shoshani affair shook the colonizing community, representatives of the Hebrew Law of Peace and of the municipality of Tel Aviv negotiated the terms of their future relations. Yet the possibility of asserting a jurisdiction over public law-related issues was rejected outright by the municipality. Consequently, the representatives of the Hebrew Law of Peace drafted a document that would have at least ensured that the Hebrew courts would be the ones to decide whether or not a particular case fell within their jurisdiction. The suggested terms of agreement between the two bodies included the following:

1. Disputes concerning the actions of the municipality of Tel Aviv in its capacity as a public governmental body (including taxation matters, confiscation of land, licensing and permits) are not within the jurisdiction of the Hebrew Law of Peace which assumes to itself the adjudication only of those matters which derive from private relationships.
2. All the disputes that the municipality of Tel Aviv has or will have with individuals or with Jewish institutions in matters of a commercial nature, such as selling and buying, rent and leasing and relations with its own officials and all matters based on private law, the

municipality will refer to the Hebrew Law of Peace without conditions and reservations.
3. In disputes of the above type, the municipality as plaintiff hands over all disputes to the Hebrew Law of Peace and may turn to state litigation only if the defendant shirks.
4. In order to prevent shirking, the municipality will insert in all its contracts a clause requiring the parties to submit to the jurisdiction of the Hebrew Law of Peace.
5. Authority to decide whether a case is of a public or private nature is exclusively delegated to the Hebrew Law of Peace and the municipality of Tel Aviv, therefore, must submit to its jurisdiction in all cases and may object to said jurisdiction only in the course of litigation, but it cannot refuse to refer to the Hebrew Law of Peace prior to litigation.
6. The municipality will use its powers to influence other officials and institutions dependent upon it to refer to the Hebrew Law of Peace.[6]

The municipality of Tel Aviv, however, declined to accept even the terms of this already restricted document. In particular, it rejected the idea of inserting a compulsory litigation clause into its future contracts and declined to commit itself to influencing those dependent upon it to submit to the jurisdiction of the Hebrew courts. Ultimately, it only took upon itself to submit private law-related matters to Hebrew law, while omitting the words "without conditions and reservations," which were in the original draft. The municipality also narrowed the scope of article 3 (see above) by specifying that it would consider itself free to approach state courts in all matters of shirking that were not resolved within eight days. The municipality also reiterated the principle that in matters of a public nature the Hebrew Law of Peace had no jurisdiction and insisted on omitting the article that delegated to the Hebrew courts the power to decide whether a case had a 'public law' aspect to it.[7]

The links of referral that were established between the municipality and the Hebrew courts, in short, were of a far more restricted nature than the ones hoped for by the advocates of the Hebrew Law of Peace. In fact, the municipality applied a double standard in respect to the jurisdictional powers of the Hebrew Law of Peace. On the one hand, it refused to litigate as defendant in matters of taxation on the grounds that such matters were part of its prerogative as a governing public body.[8] On the other, it exploited the Hebrew Law of Peace as an instrument for recovering unpaid taxes: a report submitted to the municipality of Tel Aviv indicated that in the summer of 1928 alone, the municipality, as plaintiff, pursued two hundred tax collection cases in the Tel Aviv Hebrew Court of Peace, thus effectively using the court as an extended collection agency.[9]

The nature of the relations that existed between the Hebrew Law of Peace and the Tel Aviv municipality has been symptomatic of the relations it had with other Zionist governing bodies and institutions. From the early 1920s onwards, the advocates of Hebrew law lobbied the various institutions affiliated with the Zionist enterprise (e.g., the Jewish National Fund, *Hachsharat Ha'Yishuv*, the Anglo-Palestine Bank, the General Apotekai Bank, *Agudat Neta'im*, and *Hadassah*) to commit themselves to Hebrew law. Already in 1920, the Hebrew Law of Peace had sent to the Education Department of the Representatives Council (*Va'ad Ha'Zirim*, later replaced by the National Council) a letter of complaint which stated that "we demand the Hebrew public in Palestine to unequivocally obey our Hebrew law judgments and it is therefore inconceivable that our own central Zionist institution would not succumb to our decisions."[10] Yet by and large, Zionist bodies often used the Hebrew Law of Peace as an auxiliary mechanism for attaining institutional goals but without ever allowing it to develop into a full-blown autonomous arena. While several institutions provided funding to the Hebrew Law of Peace,[11] while some institutions litigated (often reluctantly) in its forums in matters having a 'private nature,' and while they publicly paid lip service to the importance of the Hebrew law system, any actual commitment to empowering the Hebrew Law of Peace was, at best, minimal.

Consequently, the advocates of Hebrew law routinely complained about a general "institutional shirking of national duties" and argued that "the attitude of the Palestine Zionist Executive and its affiliated institutions to the Hebrew Law of Peace is but a result of the fact that they do not adequately appreciate the national, cultural, political and practical importance of the [Hebrew law] institution."[12] This statement, however, should be read as an 'accusation' from within the field rather than as an explanation for the fact that the Hebrew Law of Peace had been unable to establish itself as the official legal system of the colonizing Zionist community of Palestine.

The immediate and most apparent reasons for the reluctance of Zionist governing institutions to fully submit to the jurisdiction of Hebrew law have already been discussed, albeit indirectly, in previous chapters. First, the rabbinical establishment exerted constant pressure not to validate the Hebrew Law of Peace as a national legal system.[13] Second, there were cases in which instrumental considerations of efficacy overruled all other considerations. In such cases, lawyers and officials tended to argue that public institutions were in fact under an obligation to opt for those judicial forums where they had better chances of prevailing.[14] Third, as discussed at length in chapter 6, the legal advisers of several key Zionist institutions routinely urged them to give preference to the courts of the state.[15]

Yet Zionist institutions had a deeper reason, although it was not articulated, for refusing to submit to the Hebrew law. It seems that officials and leaders of Zionist institutions realized that by submitting to the jurisdiction of Hebrew Law in administrative and constitutional matters they would permit the consolidation of an autonomous locus of power and that, consequently, their own political power would be somewhat restricted. A case in point concerned the public standing of the National Council (*Va'ad Le'umi*), a governing body recognized by the colonial government as a representative of the Jewish community. (The National Council was composed of representatives chosen from a larger assembly whose own members were elected in general elections by the Jewish community on the basis of proportional representation.) It seems that the National Council derived at least some of its political power from its very ability to serve as a quasi-juridical body and to function as a de facto arbitrator in disputes of national concern. The National Council, therefore, was reluctant to delegate powers to the Hebrew Law of Peace, well aware that the latter's judicial functions threatened to undermine its own powers.

> Another example in support of this view was provided by the Shoshani affair. Enormous efforts were made to settle the dispute 'internally,' in order to prevent the state's High Court of Justice from considering the matter and reaching a decision on the basis of state law. Yet the various parties involved in these efforts never tried to channel the case towards the Hebrew Law of Peace. Rather, all efforts were geared towards bringing the disputing parties to the negotiation table and to settling their differences under the auspices of the National Council, which took upon itself to serve as an impartial conciliator. The Hebrew Law of Peace had been approached in this affair only in its aftermath, after the National Council failed to sponsor a compromise and following the state court intervention that compelled the municipality to commit to new general elections. Only then, as mentioned earlier, was the Hebrew Law of Peace asked to serve as a supervising body over the lists of eligible voters, in fact performing a technical auxiliary role in the service of the municipality.
>
> A further example involved the Rishon-LeZion winery where strikes and bitter labor disputes had been frequent since 1921. The National Council declined to approach the Hebrew Law of Peace as a potential arbitrator and opted for the selection of an ad hoc board of arbitrators who were assigned the task of settling the case. The decision of this board, however, did not satisfy the workers and they asked the National Council to engage the Hebrew Law of Peace in the matter. The Hebrew Law of Peace was eventually asked to provide its 'expert opinion' on one particular point, again engaged only in an auxiliary role.

From this perspective, the preference for the law of the colonial state that many Zionist institutions displayed must be seen as a 'negative' rather than a 'positive' preference. That is, it was based on the tacit assumption that in crucial constitutional matters, the law of the state would *not* become a constitutive element because the force of public opinion and the sanctioning capacities of Zionist institutions would deter prospective claimants from bringing their grievances to the 'foreign' courts of the colonial state. In this respect, the Shoshani affair had been an exception that proved the rule; the public outcry that followed and the reprisals and attacks to which Shoshani and his accomplices were consequently subjected, clearly demonstrated this point. In short, *the thesis I propose here is that, given the particular conditions of state-building under the auspices of a hovering colonial state, the law of the latter was the option because the threats posed to governing political bodies by an emergent non-statist juridical body outweighed the risks posed to it by the ordering and disciplining capacities of the colonial law.*

I have in mind here an idea of the way political elites in control of key public institutions tend to create for themselves a space of unaccountability, a no-man's land where in the name of the national interest whole domains of decision-making, policies, exhibitions of authority and various types of relations are rendered immune from legal scrutiny. There are various ways of creating this space: defining issues as strictly 'political' (hence beyond the reach of formal legality), drawing a distinction between 'administrative' and 'judicial' matters, or challenging jurisdictions by creating 'internal' quasi-legal mechanisms.[16] These were blended in the case of Palestinian Zionism with the particular circumstances of building a nation under the protection of a foreign colonial power. That is to say, the formal existence of an autonomous colonial law and the simultaneous ethos of avoiding this law in matters of 'national' importance produced a very original way of creating spaces of unaccountability.

Consider, for example, the dilemma of Eliahu Zvi Cohen, a lawyer from Tel Aviv, who told his story to the press:

> I have a dispute with the municipality of Tel Aviv in a matter of taxation ... I had the option of doing nothing, exposing myself to a suit against me at a state court which would have ruled on the basis of the law of the state. I also had the option of taking the initiative by bringing forth a suit at a Hebrew Law of Peace. I opted for the latter option. But the Hebrew court notified me that at a meeting of its executive committee it resolved not to hear my case. It is odd that there is such a procedure which allows the executive committee to reach a principled decision that only the court itself

may reach in the course of actual litigation, and it is noteworthy that the Hebrew Law of Peace shuts itself to claims concerning matters that are thought to damage the national cause when they are brought before the courts of the state. Thus, I cannot submit my case to the state-court and yet the Hebrew Court would not listen to me as well. Are we to live in our national home without law? I wish not to be considered a traitor and a destructor and yet I am not allowed to litigate at a Hebrew court ... How should I act in such a matter in order to avoid, on the one hand, the spilling of my blood which the laws of Yisra'el [Jewish/Hebrew law] allow when one appeals to foreign law, and, on the other hand, being thrown into jail for failing to pay taxes according to the laws of Ottomania [state law in a derogatory sense]?[17]

Cohen's complaint was seconded by Paltiel Dickstein, who wrote that the situation Cohen described allowed "Jewish governing bodies to set themselves free from any form of judicial supervision, a situation that might lead to the uninhibited rule of these institutions."[18]

> In fact, it seems that the advocates of the Hebrew Law of Peace, realizing the reluctance of other institutions to submit to the jurisdiction of Hebrew courts in such matters, were careful not to assume such jurisdiction on their own initiative, fearing that failures would further diminish the standing of the courts. A case in point is one which I discussed at some length in chapter 2 and repeat here in a concise form.
>
> In 1926, Ben-Zion Ben-Aharon, a lawyer from Jerusalem, petitioned the High Hebrew Court of Peace in a matter concerning the judicial prerogatives of rabbinical courts. The petition was directed against the Town Committees of Jerusalem, Tel Aviv, and Haifa, the two Chief Rabbis and other Judges (*Dayanim*) of the High Rabbinical court. The petition involved a constitutional matter relating to the legal standing of judges in rabbinical courts. The matter never reached actual litigation because a majority among the members of the Executive Committee of the Hebrew Law of Peace decided that there were compelling strategic and political reasons not to hear the petition. For example, many thought that in agreeing to hear the petition the Hebrew Law of Peace risked humiliation because the parties involved were likely to refuse to litigate and thereby would undermine the prestige and honor of the Hebrew court. The solution was to defer the claim to a special tribunal of the National Council, which would have included representatives of the parties. Becoming defensive about the limited role of the Hebrew courts, Dickstein further explained that the resolution of disputes of a public character should be borne by the primary representative body of the colonizing community and that the Hebrew Law of Peace should not try to impinge upon that jurisdiction.

In sum, the politics of building the nation involved, among other things, a non-legalistic orientation to problem-solving, relying instead on informal methods of persuasion, 'friendly' discrete agreements, quasi-judicial forums, ad hoc arbitration, and 'internal' (and often unaccountable) mechanisms for the resolution of disputes. Ehud Shprinzak analyzed the *illegalism* of Israeli society in terms of a general instrumental approach to law and in terms of a tendency to downplay the importance of submitting to the rule of law. He grounded these behavioral traits, among other things, in the institutional practices of Israel's political elites.[19] Here, I do not focus on questions of obedience to the law, but on the creation of spaces of political action immune to legal scrutiny and on spheres of action that resisted reduction to legalistic forms of dispute resolution. The Hebrew Law of Peace, in this respect, represented an option which was incompatible with the dominant politics that guided the nation-building process. Specifically, the Hebrew Law of Peace had the potential to become a particularly potent locus of power because of its asserted claim to direct embeddedness in the community. As such, it promised (or threatened, depending on one's point of view) to become a legitimate regime of non-state law, not simply on the basis of its adherence to strict legalistic (i.e., neutral, 'objective,' apolitical) standards, but also because that it provided the public with a direct opportunity to check and review the actions of the political and economic institutions that had been managing the national project.[20]

Yonathan Shapiro argues that the thrust of political Zionism, in its concrete practices in Palestine, was to create strong bureaucratic institutions which recruited individuals to the national cause and expected them to display discipline and loyalty to the political leadership. In years to come, these typical forms of control and mobilization found expression in Israel's adherence to a formalistic type of democracy:

> The democratic idea has been naturalized (in Israel) in its collectivist version ... that is, by ensuring free elections that only guarantee the rule of the majority. This is the collectivist version of democracy. The individualistic-liberal aspect of the democratic idea, that which emphasizes individual and minority rights against the will of the majority, has been pushed to the margins of political thought. The constitutive element of the new society has been a procedural or formalistic democracy, not liberal democracy.[21]

I think that the way in which the Hebrew Law of Peace was contained by other Zionist institutions seems to corroborate this thesis. Further, I think that the matter goes beyond that of liberal-versus-procedural democracy and touches on the no less fundamental issue of the possibility of participatory democracy. In other words, the creation of a space of unaccountability in the case of the Zionist institutions goes beyond that of privileging the 'political' over the 'legal,' precisely because the 'legal' – in the context of a colonizing community – had been premised on notions of popular input and substantive notions of justice responsive to a reconstructed and imagined national culture. In the last instance, therefore, the case of the Hebrew Law of Peace (like that of the Jewish Federation of Labor's Comrades Law, to be discussed below) attests to the way in which Zionism has been premised on a consistent impoverishment of 'civil society' or, in concrete terms, upon a political-statist notion of regimentation devoid of substantive possibilities for direct popular input from below.

A prime example of this politics of nation-building-from-above may be seen in the trajectory of the Comrades Law that was operating in the 1920s alongside the Hebrew Courts of Peace. The following section describes the Comrades Law in its essentials and accounts for the way it was overwhelmed and contained by the political organs of the Hebrew Federation of Labor.

THE COMRADES LAW

The Ideal

The General Federation of Hebrew Workers in Palestine (*Ha' Histadrut Ha'klalit Shel Ha'ovdim Ha'Ivriim Be'eretz Yisrael*, hereinafter: Histadrut) was formed in 1920 by a number of political groups (prime among which were the Zionist–Socialist Association of the Workers of Eretz Yisrael (*Achdut Ha'Avoda*) and Ha'poel *Ha'tza'ir* (the 'Young Worker'). While it had 4,433 registered members in 1921, it had doubled its membership by 1923, and again by 1926, when it had 16,000 members. By 1927 it had 22,538 members (family members not included) out of an overall Jewish population of roughly 140,000 by that year, and it reached the 30,000 mark in 1930.[22] By the second half of the 1920s, the Histadrut incorporated 73 per cent of the total number of Jewish wage-earners in Palestine, becoming the strongest organizational, economic, and political organ of the colonizing community.

In 1923, the Histadrut formally established its own internal legal system and resolved to instruct its members to hand *all* their disputes and grievances over to the jurisdiction of a Comrades Law (*Mishpat Haverim*).[23] The Comrades Law consisted of three judicial instances: a 'Limited Comrades Law' (*Mishpat Haverim Metzumtzam*), in which three judges considered disputes between individual members of the Histadrut, a 'Broad Comrades Law' (*Mishpat Haverim Rachav*), in which five judges considered appeals from the lower instance and had jurisdiction over disputes among institutional organs of the Histadrut or between individual members and such organs (these two instances were

135

to function as a two-tiered juridical system attached to geographically organized Workers' Councils), and a High Comrades Court, which functioned as a court of appeal with additional exclusive jurisdiction for providing reasoned opinions to the Histadrut's Acting Committee (*Va'ad Ha'poel*, the Histadrut's top executive organ) in matters of fundamental constitutional importance. Judges of all instances were elected in confidential votes taken in the local Workers' Councils.

The jurisdiction of the Comrades Law applied to all types of disputes among members, not only those directly relating to their activities as members of the Histadrut, thus assuming in effect the force of a compulsory and all-inclusive dispute-resolution mechanism for members, organs, and affiliated institutions. In this respect, the projected jurisdiction of the Comrades Law partially overlapped with that of the Hebrew Law of Peace. In practice, however, the two systems cooperated quite closely and did not engage in overt jurisdictional conflicts. The Comrades Law also asserted itself as part of the general nationalistic activity undertaken in Palestine: it assumed the duty to express general social norms and customs and to provide a popular outlet from the tendency of the state to "be involved in everything" and to "leave nothing beyond its reach."[24]

Moreover, in a remarkably similar way to the Hebrew Law of Peace, activists of the Comrades Law also appealed to the "powerful desire that always characterized the history of the Hebrew People to enjoy autonomy in the resolution of disputes and to be free from foreign tribunals ... [hence] the Hebrew court was always a pillar of national existence in exile, substituting popular trust for coercion." In this spirit, the Histadrut has been imagined as a micro-society which, "according to the example set by the Hebrew public of medieval times," assumed the regulation of the lives of its members.[25]

Speaking about the joint purposes of the Comrades Law and the Hebrew Law of Peace,[26] Yisrael Bar Shira – a lawyer who acted as the primary public voice of the Comrades Law – added a class-centered dimension to the general 'national' mission of legal revival: both systems, he argued, aimed to recreate Hebrew Law on non-religious grounds and to articulate a "progressive secular law." Jewish traditions in exile were invoked in order to sustain this image as well: "Hundreds of years ago," wrote Bar Shira, "our people already had special courts for workers and artisans. The Jewish working class was autonomous to regulate its own affairs ... and judges were elected by the members of the various workers' societies from among the general judges of the public as a whole."[27]

As for the type of judicial discretion that judges were expected to employ, Bar Shira suggested adopting, *mutatis mutandis*, section 4 of the new Soviet Civil Procedure Code which stipulated that in the absence of a clear law, judges were to rule in accordance with "the general politics of the workers' and farmers' government." Accordingly, Bar Shira articulated the principle that judges of the Comrades Law should render judgments, essentially based on a sense of justice and common sense, in accordance with "the general principles of the Histadrut's legislative acts and the general politics of the Histadrut's leadership."[28]

The projected ideal of the Comrades Law, in short, consisted of popular tribunals whose judges were responsive to the needs of workers, employed informal methods of adjudication, and, in particular, were ready to assume an active role in protecting the interests of workers. "One should come to terms with the identity of those who appeal to Comrades Law," wrote Bar Shira:

> ... [w]orkers far removed from legal education and legal understanding, let alone legal sophistication. Exhausted after a hard day's work they go at night to the Comrades Law in order to claim their rights from their comrades. And if the lawyer of the other party, or the other party himself, when he is so equipped, would try to confuse him and fail him with legal tricks, he would always be able to do so ... therefore, we must turn the judge into one who is more than a passive onlooker at a competition he cares little for, into one who instructs the parties, consciously teaching them the rules. The judge must act as an adviser to the weaker party who is not familiar with formalities and must not himself become a slave of this formality.[29]

Bar Shira therefore proposed in concrete terms departing from the dominant models of adjudication that barred judges from rewarding parties with more than they had originally asked for. The Comrades Law, in short, was to apply socialist notions of legality and substantive notions of working-class justice. Succinctly summarizing the projected image, one the Comrades Law proponents described it as *"the civil legal apparatus within the Histadrut,"* namely, the voice of 'civil society,' the "conscience of the Histadrut" vis-a-vis the political organs of the Histadrut which were structured along bureaucratic statist lines.[30]

The Reality

The history of the Comrades Law was not a history of assertive independence in relation to the political organs of the Histadrut, nor has it been sympathetic to the voices and concerns of individual members vis-a-vis institutional authority. On the contrary, within a short period of time, the Comrades Law has largely become an instrument of discipline and control in the service of the organization, while attempts to constitute it as autonomous were effectively blocked both at the local level (by the politically oriented Workers' Councils) and at the national level (by the Acting Committee of the Histadrut).

In actuality, the officials and judges of the Comrades Law showed very little interest, if any, in the development of an alternative socialist law. "The socialist tradition of popular justice," writes Merry, "springs from Marxist–Leninist theories about the potential of popular tribunals to empower the masses to deal with rule breaking and to educate them in the forms of a new socialist society."[31] As 'educators', judges occasionally inserted ideological lecturing-style statements into their decisions. Consider, for example, a case of violence between two neighbors in the settlement of Petah-Tiqwa. The disputants hit each other, but there had also been physical damage to property and violence against the wife and children of one of the disputants. The records of the trial reveal that the judges, after hearing a considerable number of witnesses, could not reach a conclusive decision. Eventually, the judges decided that they were not competent to rule in the 'legal' issue concerning the damage to property (referring the parties to a rabbi) but only in the 'factual' matter of personal violence. They resolved to fine one of the disputants and yet concluded with a general statement:

> The Comrades Law together with the Workers' Committee hereby expresses its dismay with comrades Firstenberg and Steinberg for their anti-social, impolite, and irresponsible behavior which hurts the dignity of the Histadrut, as they allowed this dispute to develop without bringing it at the outset before the Comrades Law. Failure to behave patiently and nicely towards each other in the future may lead the Histadrut to resort to harsher measures that may lead to their exclusion from the Histadrut.[32]

More commonly, however, 'educational' decisions had to do with attempts to discipline workers who deviated from the formal norms and regulations of the Histadrut. Consider, for example, the case of the Haifa Labor Bureau against the Carmel Group. The Carmel Group consisted of a number of construction workers who directly contracted with employers, without first referring their employment opportunities to the Labor Bureau which operated within the Haifa Workers' Council. Labor Bureaus were assigned the sensitive task of coordinating and distributing available jobs to unemployed workers. Workers, accordingly, had to register at the local bureaus and were subsequently placed on waiting-lists. The process was ridden with conflict and many disputes erupted around attempts by workers to bypass the waiting-lists, counter-disciplinary measures by the Histadrut, and complaints concerning the fairness of the allocation process and the justice of the Labor Bureau's officials. In the case of the Carmel Group, the Comrades Court ruled:

> Obtaining work by bypassing the organized organs of the Histadrut may lead to competition among workers and to decreasing wages which destroy the worker and demoralize the organized working class, undermine the authority of the Histadrut, and provide exploiters with ammunition in their war against the Histadrut. Obtaining work without the mediation of the Histadrut deeply subverts the institutions of the worker in his struggle to consolidate work-contracts and obstructs a just division of labor.[33]

While it is possible to read such cases in terms of the educational functions of law, namely teaching workers about the importance of workers' solidarity, it is also evident that in such cases the overriding rationale was to consolidate and defend the centralizing authority of the Histadrut. Nevertheless, the jurisdiction of the Comrades Law over such disciplinary issues was challenged by local Workers' Councils, worried about their own disciplinary powers. Bureaucrats holding positions of authority in local Workers' Councils were reluctant to delegate authority to the Comrades Law. Thus, a letter sent to the Comrades Law from the Jerusalem Workers' Council flatly determined "it is inconceivable that the Comrades Law would hear appeals concerning waiting-lists, and that it would review the actions of committees and secretaries of local councils or would pass judgment over the administration of our various bureaus. Bureaus and officials are only responsible to the Jerusalem Workers' Council whose executive committee has the exclusive authority to consider such matters."[34]

Similarly, the Construction Workers' Association affiliated with the Jaffa Workers' Committee revolted against the involvement of the Comrades Law in the matter of comrade Kushnir. The Construction Workers' Association expelled Kushnir from the Histadrut after he was found guilty of conspiring with an independent contractor to "exploit workers" on a private basis. Similar charges had been brought against Kushnir by a member of the Construction Workers' Association, who turned to a Comrades Law tribunal. The Comrades Law reached the same conclusion as the one reached by the Association. Nonetheless, the Jaffa Workers' Council challenged the authority of the Comrades Law to consider the matter and opined that the Comrades Law stepped beyond its jurisdiction. "Complaints against undisciplined workers," the Workers' Council wrote, "were strictly the concern of local committees whose decisions could only be appealed to the higher executive bodies of the Histadrut."[35]

> *Sexual Harassment and Comrades Justice*
>
> In 1927, following a series of accusations against an official of the Jaffa Workers' Council who was in charge of allocating financial aid to workers, the Council nominated a five-member board of inquiry. The board eventually submitted a secret report in early 1928, summarizing the allegations of various witnesses. Most of the allegations concerned the attempts of the official to kiss female comrades, to visit them at night in their private homes, and to make indecent propositions while promising financial aid to those who complied and threatening not to provide aid to those who refused. The board heard thirty-two witnesses who described the said deeds, and concluded that most charges were unfounded and that the official was only guilty of general indecency. The board thereby suggested temporarily removing the official from his position and offering him one which would not involve direct contact with the public.
>
> The board did not include any 'educational' statements in rendering its decision. One board member refused to endorse the findings and conclusions. Rather, he published the whole story in an opposition publication, arguing that the decision was based on political considerations and that the whole process was marred by the fact that "a number of female comrades refused to testify in full because they were ashamed to do so." Subsequently, the minority member of the board was brought to trial by the Jaffa Workers' Council, this time before a Comrades Law Tribunal which found him guilty of unlawfully publicizing secrets from a judicial chamber. Upon conviction, he was removed from the list of persons eligible to serve as a Comrades Law judge. It is noteworthy that the original harassment case was not handled by a Comrades Law Tribunal. Rather, the Jaffa Workers' Council opted for an ad hoc quasi-judicial board of inquiry. The council thus retained its power to decide on the identity of the judges and, at least according to the opinion of the minority member, indirectly to shape the result. It is also noteworthy that members of the Comrades Law did not protest this tactic and, further, facilitated it in later decisions against the recalcitrant member of the board.[36]

In substantive issues pertaining to rights of employees in disputes with the Histadrut (as employer), the Comrades Courts were typically as rigid and as formalistic as any other 'bourgeois' court. Consider the case of Sara Agi. Agi was a cleaner at the offices of the Jerusalem Workers' Council (JWC). She was laid off without compensation on the grounds that she was not a monthly wage-earner but only a part-time worker who could show no formal documents relating to her work. It was alleged that she was laid off because she was not fit for the job. Agi argued that she had been working in the same offices for seven years, beginning her employment with the local Labor Bureau which was then dismantled and integrated into the Jerusalem Workers' Council which retained her as an employee. The Workers' Council argued that, in any case, Agi had worked for only four-and-a-half years in its service and that "the JWC never assumed upon itself the obligations of former bureaus and cannot be held responsible for the plaintiff's former years of employment." The judges of the first instance (one of whom was Golda Meirson (Meir)) established Agi's principled entitlement to compensation for four-and-a-half-years' employment.

The Jerusalem Workers' Council appealed the decision on grounds that it had not been under any binding obligation to pay compensation at all. The court of appeal upheld the decision of the lower instance and went as far as to establish Agi's entitlement to compensation on the basis of seven years' employment. Still, the court abstained from awarding Agi additional compensation on grounds that she had not appealed the decision of the lower instance.[37] In other cases as well, the idea that judges should assist the 'weaker' parties to a dispute and should actively intervene in cases where lack of legal sophistication worked against the substantive interests of workers was rarely applied in the tribunals of the Comrades Law.[38]

Some cases relating to the rights of employees were litigated at Hebrew Courts of Peace which routinely awarded laid-off employees compensation in the equivalent of one month's salary for each year of work. In fact, it seems that at least in some cases the Hebrew Law of Peace was more sympathetic to the rights of employees than the representatives of the Histadrut.

Consider the case of Erlich vs. Bureau for Public Works, which was litigated in a Hebrew Court of Peace in 1923. The bureau, an organ of the Histadrut, was represented by Dr Zmora, who was also the chief executive of the Comrades Law. Plaintiff asked for compensation for three years of work, calculated on the basis of one month's salary per year. Zmora objected, arguing that "this principle of granting one month's salary for each year of work is not recognized by the Bureau," suggesting instead compensating plaintiff with only one month's salary. The judges, faithful to the Hebrew Law of Peace's tendency to seek compromises, awarded plaintiff more he had been offered by the Histadrut but less than he had originally asked for. Both parties appealed, and on appeal Zmora protested the conciliatory practices of the judges, arguing that judges who sat as arbitrators could not enforce such compromises but were under an obligation to make an either/or judgment. In short, the idea of the trial as a winner-takes-all battle seems to have guided the legalistic outlook of the Comrades Law's most senior executive.[39]

Dr Moshe Zmora

Moshe Zmora, a lawyer, served as the Histadrut's General Counsel as well as the Secretary of the High Comrades Court. In this latter capacity, Zmora was the active force behind the policies and administration of the Comrades Law. At the same

> time he retained the right to private practice. At a certain point, he tried to enlist the law firm of Harry Sacher to the service of the Histadrut. The Histadrut, according to this plan, was to become a full-time retainer of Zmora and Sacher. The legal fees were fixed by Zmora at 60EL per month, a huge amount by the standards of the day. These fees were to be paid jointly by the Acting Committee of the Histadrut and the Jaffa and Haifa Workers Councils. Ben Gurion, upon seeing the terms of the agreement, apparently cancelled it.[40]

Particularly telling was the decision of the High Comrades Court in the matter of Solel-Boneh. Solel-Boneh, initially called the Bureau for Public Works, was incorporated under the ownership of the Histadrut and functioned as its largest contracting company. In June 1927 it went into bankruptcy, throwing the Histadrut into a severe fiscal and moral crisis. Following the collapse of Solel-Boneh, a few former employees sued the company claiming that they were entitled to compensation also for their years of employment at the Bureau. As far as the rights of employees were concerned, they argued, "Solel-Boneh and the bureau were one and the same." The first instance accepted the claim and established plaintiffs' right to full compensation. Solel-Boneh appealed the decision to the High Comrades Court, sending David Remez, a senior executive, and Dr Krongold, a lawyer who was also one of the executives of the Comrades Law, to argue on its behalf. Dr Zmora, the highest executive of the Comrades Law, but also Solel-Boneh's legal adviser, remained behind the scenes. On appeal, the High Comrades Law reversed the decision of the lower instance. In its laconic decision, the court ruled that Solel-Boneh, "in its present situation, could not pay workers compensation due to them for their years of employment in the Bureau for Public Works."[41]

The decision was so shockingly unexpected that the Tel Aviv Comrades Court asked the High Comrades Court for further clarification, "without which the decision would remain incomprehensible to our comrades." Dr Krongold, who represented Solel-Boneh at the trial, replied to that letter in his capacity as the deputy-secretary of the Comrades Law:

> Dr Zmora and the undersigned did not take part in the case either as judges or as secretaries. The under-signed appeared as an advocate for Solel Boneh. Dr Zmora, who is the lawyer of Solel Boneh could not take part in the case. Therefore, I do not know the reasons for the decision of the judges. The meetings of the judges are confidential, there are no protocols and it is therefore impossible to know their reasons ... I am also not satisfied by the decision because the court did not provide a clear answer as to the

responsibility of Solel Boneh towards the Bureau for Public Works. I argued that such responsibility did not exist, neither legally, nor morally, and I explained my position.

Of course, the court should decide whether a claim is justified and not to inquire into a defendant's ability to pay. But I can understand that in certain cases the court may not validate a legal right and on the other hand validate a moral right – known in English law as Equity. And in such cases the court may also morally evaluate the condition of a defendant and rule that, although the plaintiff had a moral right, this right could not be granted under the circumstances. This is how I understand the decision in this case. I understand that the court did not recognize the plaintiffs' legal right, but recognized their moral right on the basis of equity, and yet resolved not to validate it because of the situation of Solel Boneh.

These, of course, are my personal speculations ...[42]

This remarkable answer, so it seems, was quite remote from Bar Shira's original ideal of what the Comrades Law should have looked like. In the case of Solel-Boneh, the ideal of judges who would actively employ judicial reasoning in accordance with "the general politics of the Histadrut's leadership" – namely, in accord with some envisioned socialist principles – has come full circle, turning the court into an instrument for denying workers' rights.

By 1928, however, a significant part of the case-load of the Comrades Law consisted of hundreds of routine cases, briefly summarized and processed on standard forms, in which members of the Histadrut were sued for failure to pay taxes to the organization or to pay back loans granted them by the Histadrut's Savings and Loan Fund. These cases resembled neither an elaborate judicial proceeding nor a popular-justice process.[43] Further, the more such cases were processed by the Comrades Courts, the less satisfactory they seemed to be. A letter from the Histadrut' Savings and Loan Fund to the Jerusalem Workers' Council thus complained that "while we are obliged by law to submit collection cases to the Comrades Law, this system does not function ... many of our comrades smile when they see a judgment against them ... of all the judgments in our favor this year there were no more than two comrades who complied and paid their debts. We had to resubmit all other cases to the courts of the state for judgment and execution ..."[44]

In contrast to the ideal articulated by a few enthusiasts, the main issues on the agenda of the Comrades Law in the 1920s concerned the lack of respect displayed towards the system by individuals and institutions alike, the tendency of judges not to show up for designated trials, the system's chaotic administration and chronic lack of resources, and the urgent need to establish more rigorous procedures and operational rules. Most of the discussions held by the activists and judges of the Comrades Law during the 1920s, in short, dealt with procedural and organizational matters, while only a handful were concerned with ideological and conceptual issues of the type outlined in the 'ideal' above.[45] These administrative concerns, as well as the frequent complaints about the Comrades Law being far from revered, were only outward manifestations of the fact that the Comrades Law had been marginalized from within the Histadrut and that its jurisdiction had been constantly eroded by direct and indirect measures.

In fact, the jurisdiction of the Comrades Law had been formally defined in a way that ensured the immunity of Histadrut's executive bodies from effective judicial review. First, the Acting Committee of the Histadrut, its highest political body, was formally exempt from the review powers of the Comrades Law. Second, article 7 of the Histadrut's Constitution stipulated that the Acting Committee of the Histadrut had a final say in all matters relating to its activities and operations. Third, an article in the Comrades Law's own Constitution stipulated that the Acting Committee had the authority to decide which organizational matters were beyond the jurisdiction of the Comrades Law. Fourth, the ultimate sanction which the Comrades Law could inflict, namely revoking membership in the Histadrut, could be appealed to the Histadrut's General Council. Finally, in contrast to article 14 of the Histadrut's Constitution, which established a principled duty to litigate at the tribunals of the Comrades Law, the regulations of other institutional bodies of the Histadrut (e.g., Hevrat Ha'ovdim) stipulated that disputes relating to their specific activities be resolved by their own internal mechanisms.[46]

Attempts to change this dismal state of affairs, which ensured the superiority and privileged standing of clerks and bureaucrats vis-a-vis the judicial organs of the Comrades Law, were effectively blocked. In the course of the 1930s, the jurisdiction of the Comrades Law was further eroded as the Acting Committee moved to transfer whole areas of disciplinary control to newly established disciplinary tribunals (e.g., tribunals responsible for prosecuting members suspected of 'communist sympathies' or even workers' groups charged with employing wage-labourers at their cooperatives and settlements). These administrative moves, Bar Shira argued, turned the Comrades Law of the Histadrut into just another bureaucratic apparatus for pursuing members who did not pay their taxes, thus effectively giving the kiss of death to the idea of a national-socialistic legal system. Hard-pressed, Bar Shira eventually resorted to 'bourgeois law,' completely reversing his earlier line of argument:

> Scientific socialism rejected Montesquieu's separation-of-powers doc-trine which distinguished the legislative, the executive and the

judicial branches of government. Indeed, the law by and large expresses the interests of the ruling class and serves that class. Lenin even added that the imperative to govern requires the creation of a law that obeys political authority. Still, it should be otherwise in our movement.[47]

In sum, the trajectory of the Comrades Law of the Histadrut demonstrates the degree to which, in both jurisdictional and substantive terms, law has been marginalized and made subservient to the political leadership of the Histadrut. Let me reconnect the conclusion of this section, then, to the remainder of the chapter.

Before moving to consider the Comrades Law of the Hebrew Federation of Labor in some detail, I suggested that the trajectory of the Hebrew Law of Peace testified to mainstream Zionism's consistent impoverishment of 'civil society,' premised as it was upon a political-statist notion of regimentation devoid of substantive possibilities for direct popular input from below. I think that the history of the Comrades Law also confirms the argument. Rather than living up to the projected ideal of socialist law and popular justice, functioning, as one advocate-idealist put it, as "the civil apparatus of the Histadrut," the Comrades Law had mainly served the cause of organizational centralization, providing little space, if any, for alternative voices from below and very little room for challenging the entrenched practices and policies of the Histadrut's bureaucratic organs. The fate of the Comrades Law, in this respect, reflected the tendency of the Histadrut to operate as a quasi-statist institution; it was concerned with strong bureaucratic tactics and with rigid practices of centralization rather than with social reforms and novel popular experiments; with 'nation-building,' and not with providing a framework for 'a new society.'[48]

With the analysis of this chapter in mind, we may now appreciate from yet another perspective an argument that has repeatedly informed this book: it was not the colonial state but rather forces from within the Jewish colonizing community of Palestine which brought about the containment, and ultimately the demise of an autonomous Hebrew law.

In various chapters of the book I have looked at three forces which formed an unintended coalition against vesting Hebrew law with considerable jurisdictional powers (the force of strong coalitions always lies precisely in the coincidence of each party's own *distinct* concerns): the rabbinical establishment of the orthodox nationalists, the embryonic Jewish legal profession of Palestine, and the quasi-statist politics of the Palestinian Zionist movement (both socialist and bourgeois).

For the orthodox, the Hebrew law represented a threat of an order that could not be matched with the law of the colonial state. The law of the latter had no claims to national representation, in fact grounding its legitimacy in its universal neutrality related to questions of history and identity. The law of the colonial state, in short, did not compete with orthodox interpretations of Jewish texts and orthodox versions of tradition and legality. Hebrew law, on the other hand, by its very label, opened up the possibility of a non-orthodox negotiation over the memory (hence the meaning) of Judaism to be carried out from outside the rabbinical authority structure. Orthodox nationalists in general, and rabbinical courts in particular, had strong vested interests in marginalizing the non-religious version of Hebrew law.

The orthodox interest coincided with that of many Palestinian Jewish lawyers. Lacking training in Jewish law, licensed to be experts in the positive laws of the colonial state, bred to think of their ethical obligations to the immediate interests of their individual clients, and uneasy with the open-ended and – at times – anti-professional orientation of popularly oriented tribunals, many lawyers shied away from the Hebrew Law of Peace. The effort, as we have seen, was to overcome all of these so-called 'shortcomings' by stressing the national duties of the profession. The success of this effort, however, depended on the active support of other national institutions, support the latter withheld.

I have considered in this chapter the degree to which Zionist elites and bureaucracies, socialist and non-socialist alike, developed an instrumental approach to law which overrode concerns with the substantive capacity of law to act as a constitutive element in the shaping of the community, in the reconstruction of its past, or in the articulation of its future social arrangements. Law, as far as 'order' was concerned, could well be activated by the colonial state. Law, as far as the management of nation-building was concerned, could not, and should not, have replaced the regulation of the community by the political and bureaucratic managers of the project.

In this respect, the Hebrew Law of Peace, and the Comrades Law for that matter, went against the grain of mainstream Zionism. Whether we look at the relationship of Jewish lawyers to the institutions of the colonial state or at the internal dynamic of Zionist quasi-state institutions, we come up with a configuration in which, with law at least, structure and form won over substance. Zionist politicians, executives, and administrators were more interested in the perfection of quasi-state institutions and in building bridges to the institutions of the colonial state than in forms of legality that provided both a check on the institutional structure of the nation-building project *and* an alternative way of imagining the nation. In other words, the creation of a space of unaccountability, in the case of Zionist institutions, goes beyond that of privileging the 'political' over the 'legal,' because the 'legal' – in the context of a colonizing community – had been conceived as a constitutive site for the invigoration of a reconstructed and imagined nation, rooted specifically in the distinctive historical experiences of Judaism-without-sovereignty. Both in form and content, in short, the story of law in Palestine is in fact a story about the triumph of statist-nationalism, a configuration in which state structures stand as the ultimate representation of the nation. It is also a story, finally, about the impossibility of a Jewish nation distinct from the state apparatus that it established in Palestine, on the one hand, and from a transcendental Jewish religion, on the other.

CHAPTER 8

DEAD LAW AND STATISM: A SUGGESTED LESSON

The reader will no doubt have noticed in this book a romantic, if not naive, longing for an alternative cultural and political course that Zionism could have taken. Indeed, I cannot deny a normative desire to celebrate the Hebrew Law of Peace as an affair which offered an opening for an anti-colonialist, non-statist, popular form of justice which would have grounded itself in an alternative imagined 'authentic' and non-chauvinistic national past. Perhaps one should not be apologetic about normative yearnings, yet the sociologist in me insists on rebelling against this reading. So, rather than uncritically celebrating a lost possibility, my intention has been to develop a second-order sociological imagination of the visions and projections and practices that accompanied the Hebrew Law of Peace. In this sense, a certain loss of distance between researcher and subjects was perhaps inevitable. Yet the discourse about community does not necessarily carry a genuine promise of solidarity and is not necessarily more humanizing than a statist discourse. The same principle holds also when applied to the discourse on modernized Judaism. In either case, such projects of the imagination are not less embedded in trajectories of power, jurisdiction, control, interests and authority. My intention, in short, was to chart the ideas contained in the Hebrew law project and to push further the imagination of its adherents as a means of exploring Zionism's route to statist-nationalism.

In this final chapter I shall opt for some distance, perhaps less evident in previous chapters; a distance from which I shall try to offer a more general reading of the Zionist colonization movement in Palestine; a reading which, I hope, will tie up some of the loose ends.

Let me begin with a methodological statement. The November 1996 issue of *Art in America* ran an article entitled "Ars Moriendi." It alerted art historians to the simple fact that despite efforts of conservation and in spite of the general myth about the immortality of art, most art is by now dead. Accordingly, the writer advised art historians to take note of dead art because 'understanding dead art may be illuminating for understanding what we are living with.'[1] Put in the most simple and straightforward terms, I have converted this notion to an invitation to think of the Hebrew Law of Peace as *Lex Moriendi*, as dead law, as a silenced option which did not simply illuminate unrealized possibilities and roads not taken, but, positively, provided us with a perspective from which to explore and problematize that which has been taken for granted or has been conceived of as inevitable for the nation-building process.

In this sense, I have not been overtly concerned in this book with the possibility, or impossibility[2] of popular justice per se, nor have I been preoccupied with identifying the exact species of popular justice for(u)ms into which the Hebrew Law of Peace could have been classified.[3] In fact, I believe that the case of the Hebrew Law of Peace defies classification. The Hebrew Law of Peace adopted a non- and even anti-statist posture and yet prepared itself to become a foundation for the future legal system of the Hebrew state. It was grounded in community norms and lay justice and at the same time considerable efforts to professionalize along conventional parameters were made. It spoke in the name of substantive justice, but the decisions it rendered were often marked by narrow formalism. And it searched for an authentic historical specificity by relying on notions and concepts which had been borrowed from German legal historicism and romanticism.

My method of inquiry, therefore, was to examine the reactions which the Hebrew Law of Peace provoked in various social circles. The responses to the different ideational and practical directions which the Hebrew Law of Peace placed on the agenda interested me more than the 'what if' question with respect to the substantive possibilities opened up by the system. In other words, the methodological principle which I have activated here was premised on the idea that it was through the consideration of the *responses* – more than through the consideration of the actual gestures which instigated those responses – that we may learn something about the trajectory of the colonizing and nation-building movement.

Specifically, I emphasized the methodological merit of studying the Hebrew Law of Peace as a system which problematized, in principle at least, the inevitability of state law. The Hebrew Law of Peace, at times intentionally and at times by default, testified to a rupture, however fragile and tentative, in the image of law as a sword, as a manifestation of the state's power to 'take life.'[4] It has done so both in a concrete sense

– defying allegiance to the law of the colonial state – and in a symbolic and imaginary, but no less profound, sense in its articulation of law as a communal practice which may flourish independently of state sovereignty. It was primarily in response to this problematization of state law and legal instrumentality that some of the constitutive elements of hegemonic Zionism came to light.

Thus, above and beyond the substance which popular justice for(u)ms and so-called indigenous legal systems and customary-law tribunals voice, the articulation of social relations, myths, symbols, and identities by non-state law alerts us to the fragility and historicity of the cultural and political forms which emerge out of the bondage between state power and legal instrumentality and, further, it sensitizes us to explore both the dynamics and the implications of those cultural and political forms.

As previous chapters sought to clarify, the study of dead law (or marginalized law for that matter) seems to be a particularly potent device when applied to the question of nationalism and nation-building projects. In a sense, the Hebrew Law of Peace was 'just' another platform upon which agents executed the nation-building drama. Yet the fact that this platform has been marginalized, both in real time and in the national historiography that followed, provides an opening for thinking about the specificity of the societal forms which emerge and consolidate when the nationalist drive is primarily organized around the practice and idea of the state. In this respect, the case of the Hebrew Law of Peace – existing as a non-state, if not (as I have said) at times anti-state, form of law – served me as a methodological device with which to explore strong statist orientations within Palestinian Zionism.

Statism, in general, is a cultural and political orientation which posits symbols and practices of statehood and sovereignty as the organizing matrix for national self-determination and for the constitution of a national identity at the collective and individual levels. As I tried to show in chapters 6 and 7, statism often breeds a reversal of means and ends; the state is not perceived merely as an instrument for the pursuit of social goals, but appears as if its mere functional existence and its ability to sustain mechanisms of violence and order embodies the vigor of the nation. Statism, in this respect, is a 'content-empty' version of nationalism.[5] Hence, statism as a primary nation-building practice does not only entail specific organizational forms: it is also an epistemological condition, a way of experiencing the nation and its environment which bears on the constitution of collective identity and on the positing of and the disposition towards the nation's 'others.'

Of course we may ask: Can it be otherwise? Is it not inevitable that nationalism, especially in colonial situations, will breed statism? Edward

Said writes: "The establishment of nationalism includes the refurbishing of one's past, the invention of traditions and the recapturing of cultural, geographical or political territory that was taken by others. Nationalism also involves, in this phase, setting up institutions that approximate or will become the institutions of state."[6] We are not talking, then, about an either/or question but about a question of priorities and emphases and the way they are established and played out in the trajectory of national movements.

For example, a religious outlook often tends to downplay statism as a core nationalist practice and to reject the identification of nationalism with the institutions of state which express it. Rather, it asserts that "the national consciousness realizes itself in the symbols and practices of religion."[7] Zionist writings, and writings about Zionism, have also extensively dealt with the historic tension between 'political,' 'practical,' and 'cultural' Zionism. The two former trends tended to instrumentalize the nation-building project; investing in the creation of state-like institutions, in the material colonization of the territory, and in obtaining empyreal support for the Jewish cause (while occasionally dissenting as to whether the 'political' effort should precede or follow actual settlement). 'Cultural' Zionism, on the other hand, sought to prioritize the spiritual aspect of the nation-building project, defining the cause as a search for the meaning of Judaism, rather than as an effort to provide relief to particular Jewish communities in the Diaspora.[8]

However, the Hebrew Law of Peace seems to have transcended this conceptual opposition. Concerned with the resolution of disputes, with regulation and discipline, and ultimately with setting the stage for a full-blown legal system, the Hebrew Law of Peace was certainly engaged with the pragmatic aspects of the nation-building project. At the same time, the advocates of the Hebrew Law of Peace considered law as much more than an instrument of regulation and control. Institutions of law, according to their vision, were ones through which it was possible to dramatically enact the nation through performing its distinct culture, tradition, and distinctive spirit. Yet it is in response to this latter aspect of the Hebrew Law of Peace, belonging more or less to what in ideational terms is referred to as 'cultural' or 'spiritual' Zionism, that I was able to explore a set of statist dispositions.

Statism-in-law had three distinct aspects. First a statist orientation that was carried and sustained by lawyers and jurists who privileged state law over non-state law; an orientation that effectively meant that the law of the colonial state, regardless of content, was preferred over the possibility of developing national law from below. Second, a statist orientation sustained by political elites who invested in the creation of authoritative quasi-state institutions and were apprehensive about the possibility of subjecting the affairs of the nation-building project to independent legal scrutiny. Both statist manifestations, in other words, converged to suffocate effective manifestations of community-based justice.

However, there was also a third statist aspect which was extracted from analyzing the trajectory of the Hebrew Law of Peace, one that had less to do with the organizational aspect of statism and more to do with its epistemological side. This aspect opened up for discussion the relationship between Zionism and its internal 'other,' namely Jewish life in the Diaspora. It had been exhibited by the rejection of secular Hebrew law which would have been modeled on an alternative memory of Jewish tradition in the Diaspora. Associating Jewish life in the Diaspora with the absence of sovereignty – hence with an inferior and degenerate state of being – served in the negation of that form of existence as a vital counter-image against which the nation-building project organized itself around notions of sovereignty.

Let us recall the words of Paltiel Dickstein when he tried to reason in favor of a non-state legal system:

> How can a national Hebrew law exist among the waves of the Anglo-Arab legal sea? ... The puzzlement with this phenomenon is only a product of those legalistic views which are grounded in the premises and principles determined by eighteenth- and nineteenth-century science. Yet in medieval times, the coexistence of legal systems and the functioning of one legal system within another one had been common ... It is also well-known that the Jews enjoyed self-determination in law in their various countries of residence, especially in Babylon, Spain and Poland.[9]

Dickstein invoked three arguments in favor of non-state law: First, non-state law as an essential cultural component for a nation-building project and as a guarantee against cultural assimilation under colonial rule; second, non-state law as a communal reality that was denied by the legal positivism which flourished under the organizing regulatory power of sovereign states; and, finally, non-state law as a national tradition and as a constitutive element of the nation's memory of itself. These arguments, in turn, were potentially addressed to three social groups: lawyers and jurists who developed an explicit preference for the law of the colonial state and for institutional links with the legal and administrative machinery of that state; Zionist politicians and bureaucrats – both socialist and bourgeois – who relied on the law of the colonial state for general ordering functions while creating spaces of illegality within their own quasi-state institutions; and, last, orthodox rabbis, who opted for state protection of rabbinical courts and for relegating all other juridical issues to the justice system of the colonial state.

These social forces, each with its own distinct motives, nonetheless converged into a critical coalition which transmitted statism as the dominant mode of the nation-building project. Throughout this book I have relied on the notion that meaning is created in the course of praxis, often in an haphazard way and certainly with unintended consequences. It is in this sense that the attitude of each of these groups towards the Hebrew Law of Peace created an on-the-ground picture of the formative *practices* which shaped statism as a dominant national orientation. In this way, statism becomes a prism for exploring three elements of Jewish nationalism which are rarely discussed in relation to each other: the nature of Jewish secularism, the impoverished character of Israel's civil society, and the question of Zionism *and* colonialism and Zionism *as* colonialism. To be sure, I am not thinking here in terms of causality. Rather, the focus on statism which the story of the Hebrew Law of Peace allows for invites us to consider the co-presence and the possibly mutually constitutive force of the various *distinct* drives to invest in the state; as an idea, as a symbol, as an institutional matrix, as a blueprint, and as a political and cultural ordering device. Thus, another methodological statement which seems to be in order is that I consider power politics, professional interests, and religious/secular ideological competition as interactive and overlapping dimensions that combine to create a certain reality. In analyzing the response to the Hebrew Law of Peace, I thus offer an interpretive sociology that builds on conjecture rather than on a strictly cause–effect dynamic. These conjecture, finally, is made possible by of my conviction, set out in these pages, that in a deep way the Hebrew Law project ran against the grain.

But where is the nation? The rise and fall of the Hebrew Law of Peace invites us to rethink one of the most crucial constitutive elements of Zionism, namely the way Judaism – as identity and memory – was conceived and activated by the nationalist-colonizing forces of Palestine. In chapter 2, I used illustrations from Abraham B. Yehoshua's novel *Voyage to the End of the Millennium*.[10] I read the scene of the trial – centered as it was around the identity of those who passed judgment in matters relating to Jewish life – as an opening for an alternative imagination of Jewish life in the Diaspora. The trial, I argued, provided a model of communal self-regulation that undermined the image of Jewish law as a rigid, formal, authoritative and unidimensional form of religiosity. In this respect, the trial in the novel unleashes Jewish tradition from its reductive association with the strict dictates of a rabbinical regime. "In the typical historical reality," writes Goldman, "there is no comprehensive authoritative framework recognized by the nation as a whole. The validity and the degree of institutionalization of rabbinical authority depended on the authority of the communities and on the contingent status of the rabbinate in the various communities."[11]

Likewise, perhaps the most crucial gesture of the Hebrew Law of Peace, with far-reaching and unanticipated consequences, had been to model itself on an imagery of Jewish legal autonomy that refused allegiance to the rabbinical version of what Jewish tradition was all about. By emphasizing the communal input into the history of Jewish law, by searching for lay tribunals, by pointing to actual practices of conflict-resolution to which latter-day rabbinical authorship had to adapt, by suggesting that a whole tradition and memory had in reality been monopolized by a rabbinical structure of authority that consistently denied the plural and disorganized development of Jewish law, the Hebrew Law of Peace in fact negotiated the meaning of Judaism and the way to memorize Jewish traditions in the Diaspora.

The Zionist wing of Jewish orthodoxy understood only too well what was at stake. The advocates of the Hebrew Law of Peace not only challenged rabbinical monopoly over the interpretation of Jewish texts, but also tried to re-negotiate the defining terms of the nation's collective memory of its past practices, organizing principles, and cultural heritage. The response, therefore, was bitter and aggressive precisely because of the proximity of the Hebrew Law of Peace to the orthodox version of the Jewish-turned-into-Hebrew law. In both versions, the ability of the Jews to retain non-statist forms of legal autonomy served as proof of the very existence and vitality of the nation. Yet in the orthodox version, the antiquity and resilience of Jewish law were always related to the commanding ability of rabbinical scholarship and judgeship. The Hebrew Law of Peace, and to some degree the Comrades Law as well, questioned this narrative, practically asking who the judges will be. This anticipated Rabbi Elbaz' question in Yehoshoua's fictional drama, a question which was nothing so much as a way of asking who was to shape the memory of the nation and how Judaism would be developed and maintained as a form of collective identity. It is not surprising, therefore, that orthodox rabbis sought to discredit the Hebrew Law of Peace as a distortion and that latter-day orthodox scholarship treated it as no more than a naive and inconsequential episode.

Yet the challenge of the Hebrew Law of Peace also worked against the grain of basic trends in secular Zionism. Let us recall Bernard Joseph's conception of nationalism-in-law. Bernard Joseph, a lawyer and a politician, attacked the public call of the Hebrew law's advocates to abstain from litigating in the courts of the colonial states. The avoidance of state courts, he wrote, was nothing but "remnants of ghetto psychology" and a "vestige of exilic life:" "Nothing is more dangerous to our future national life than the assumption that we are *nothing but another Jewish congregation* and that the government of this land is not ours and the courts of the state are not our courts" (emphasis added). Joseph, in short, sought to ground "true nationalism-in-law" in stronger links to the apparatuses of the colonial state's legal machinery. To that end he invoked – and this is the crucial point here – the notion of a congregation, not of a community, which immediately brought to mind and associated Judaism with *both* religion and non-sovereignty as the high marks of collective existence in the Diaspora.[12]

I would like to dwell for a while on the alarm inherent in the possibility of becoming "nothing but another Jewish congregation." I would like to do it in the shadow of a counter-alarm: one voiced more than twenty years later, upon Israel's declaration of independence, by the philosopher-sociologist-theologian Martin Buber, who asked: "We have a State. But where is the Nation in this State?"[13]

What is there in the space between these two 'alarms'? While Joseph considered an alliance with the colonial state to be a matter of national interest, and while he identified the national project with an ultimate takeover of the state, Buber abhorred that identification as an empty shell, as a daunting, content-free reduction that would have invited national chauvinism, the impoverishment of the Jewish destiny, and a chronic inability to come to terms with Palestine's 'Others,' namely Palestinians–Arabs.

It may be plausible to argue, and some guidelines will be offered in what follows, that Buber's scenario was realized and Joseph's triumphed.

Between Buber's search for the nation (emphasizing his notion of the 'inter-human') and Joseph's rejection of 'the congregation' lies a space of critique and inquiry concerning the relational structure of nation-state and religion which emerged in the course of colonizing Palestine. Baruch Kimmerling, a sociologist, argues that Zionism's most fatal failure lies in its inability to dissociate the Jewish nation from Jewish religion; that the central component of the national identity is Jewish and that Jewishness, in turn, is a synonym for Jewish religion. Therefore, when he writes about secular identity in Israel, he doubts whether there is any substantive existential meaning to being a secular Jew and whether this term is not a contradiction in terms.[14]

Amnon Raz-Karkutzkin, a historian, argues along somewhat different lines that Zionism did in fact dissociate nation and religion, but that it did so by identifying the notion of the nation, and in turn reducing it to the idea and actuality of the state. He argues that the move away from religious identity was carried out by invoking symbols of state sovereignty: sacrifice, soil, blood, conquest, and the redemption of the land.

The result is that the secular, alternative answer to the question of who is a Jew comes through fulfilling military duties in the service of the state. Raz-Karkutzkin, in other words, does acknowledge Zionism's distanciation from and negation of religion, but also emphasizes the idea of state sovereignty as the essence of the Jewish nation and as a substitute for religion.[15]

While Kimmerling thus articulates the historic impossibility of realizing secular Judaism, Raz-Karkutzkin articulates the historic impossibility of realizing a non-statist secularism. From the two arguments we can distill an aspiration to the possibility of a national identity which would have been distinct from the state (as an idea and a structure) on the one hand, and from religion (identified with an orthodox rabbinical structure of authority) on the other hand. Put differently, we may distilll from these two arguments a counter-factual image: a certain existential space, a certain sphere of experience 'in-between' state and religion which was not allowed to develop; a space, moreover, that would have transcended that fusion of state and religion which brought about particularly belligerent results in the colonization of Palestine and in the future management of the state of Israel.

These arguments, in short, may be read as a search for Buber's 'nation:' a possible sociohistoric configuration in which to search for the possibility of re-asserting a Jewish identity and Jewish solidarity that would not be reduced to either statist or religious nationalism. It is in fact a quest for what it means to be Jewish, a standpoint from which Jewishness cannot be avoided, denied or repressed – being, as it is, a central element in memorizing the past and experiencing the present – but from which it must be negotiated and revitalized along non-statist and non-religious lines.

Along these lines, I submit that the Hebrew Law of Peace represented a quest along such lines. It thus not only alienated Jewish orthodoxy, but also deviated from the principles around which secular Zionism has sought to constitute itself. Secular Zionism identified exilic life both with the absence of sovereignty and with a religious form of life. Thus, with the repudiation of exilic life, the Zionist at once resisted religion as a constitutive element of the new national identity and affirmed sovereignty as the organizing principle of that identity. In this sense, Jewish secularism in Palestine derives from this dual gesture in respect to the Diaspora.

The Hebrew Law of Peace, however, offered a disturbing narration which destabilized the 'religious' and 'non-sovereign' elements which were attributed to the Diaspora. First, its very celebration of non-statist Jewish law problematized the tendency to degrade the absence of sovereignty as a necessarily inferior form of national existence. Moreover, its celebration of the communal nature of Jewish-turned-Hebrew law '*secularized*', *or at least pluralized*, the character of Jewish life in the Diaspora. In both gestures, implicit and partially articulated as they were, the Hebrew Law of Peace subverted the imagery of exilic life against which secular Zionism sought to constitute itself; it fractured the unity of exilic life which was needed in order to define the coherence of Zionism.

First, in its non-state model of law, the Hebrew Law of Peace stood for a 'disturbing' representation of national life. Zygmunt Bauman, in his *Modernity and the Holocaust*, discusses the emergence of a 'conceptual Jew' in Europe. He argues that the conceptual Jew represented the defiance of order and the specter of chaos and devastation. As a concept, the wandering Jew embodied "the horrifying consequences of boundary-transgression, of not remaining fully in the fold."[16] It seems that the Jew, although forever a 'guest,' was at the same time Europe's fantastic projection of the 'native' who refused to be spatially tamed. And it seems that it was precisely this fantastic projection that was embraced by Zionists who sought a solution to the Jewish problem by means of sovereignty. It is in the context of the conceptual Jew that the devotion of the Zionists to notions of sovereignty has to be grounded. Insofar as sovereignty orders national identity into contained spaces and marked boundaries, it offered an antidote to the image of the conceptual Jew that Jews internalized. Thus an established Zionist position was that "eighteen hundred years of exilic life, without sovereignty, cannot be erased. They deeply affected us. Yet our national character had not been determined there, but here, when we were once settled in this land."[17] Hence, one way of reading Joseph's apprehension at the possibility of becoming 'just another congregation' is to read that daunting image in terms of being spurned by a non-sovereign community neither located in space nor grounded in reference to a state.

Second, in its community-based notions of Jewish law, the Hebrew Law of Peace destabilized the imagination of exilic life as essentially religious and decisively governed and regulated by an orthodox rabbinate. Here, one should read Joseph's apprehension as a reference to the congregation in its religious-disciplinary sense. Yet again, the exilic Jew 'had' to be religious in order to create a space for a secular Jewish person who, to a considerable degree, acquired that secular identity through distanciation from religious practices and customs. In emphasizing 'secular' aspects of Jewish life in the Diaspora, the Hebrew Law of Peace thus disturbed the opposition of associations and identifications around which the new identity could be forged.

Still, the crucial point here is that the repudiation of exilic life as religiously governed was not only a means of constituting secular nationalism. Negation forever presumes an affirmation of that which is being negated. Ahad ha'Am, a Zionist thinker who from an early stage warned against the vices of statist-nationalism, identified this curious relation of rejection and affirmation in one of his early essays. Secular Zionists, he wrote, tended to think that nothing of importance took place during exilic life and that no substantial cultural progress could be assigned to Judaism since the sovereign times of antiquity. Consequently, he stated, the secularists, in spite of their anti-religious sentiments, shared with religious Jews the same reductive approach which posited religion as the sole heritage and property of the nation's spirit in its exilic phase.[18]

Zionist repudiation of exilic life, perceived as lacking in cultural development (apart from the strictly religious), furthered a historic consciousness which not only associated the Jewish past with religion but also affirmed the role of the orthodox rabbinate as the historic leader of the nation in the period between antiquity and modernity. The orthodox rabbinate was legitimated as the authentic representative of the Jewish people in its non-sovereign form, as the legitimate keeper of tradition, and as the valid custodian of Jewish memory through thousands of years of non-sovereign existence. Secular Zionists hardly ever challenged or competed over *that* particular historic memory because their own identity *qua* secular was derived from it. Thus, secular Zionism had typically turned only to the symbols and myths of the biblical sovereign past when it needed 'religious' symbols; to the biblical stories of conquest, heroism, war and national liberation from oppression.[19] This particular adoption and use of the biblical past did not threaten the orthodoxy because it did not imply an attempt to re-negotiate the meaning of Judaism as a form of communal existence, nor had it challenged the orthodox monopoly over the definition of the nation in its non-statist, non-sovereign sense. Consequently, the Zionist orthodox rabbinate benefited from the secular repudiation of exilic life, thus securing for itself a strictly religious definition of Judaism.

It is this cultural arrangement, finally, that has made possible the secular–religious Zionist alliance, the state–religion structure which undergirds and still holds Israeli society today. As we have seen in previous chapters, already in the 1920s, under the auspices of the colonial state, Zionism organized itself around a secular–religious construct that had been, to a large extent, a caricature of the two concepts alike: secularism reduced to statism and religion reduced to a monolithic system of meaning. In the process, both the secular and the religious acquired narrow, monolithic and static meanings which together silenced and ruled out a rich social complexity. (For example, in the case of Jews from North Africa and Asia who immigrated to Israel en masse in the early 1950s and who had no place within this binary secular–religious structure. Defined as 'traditionalists,' this opposition played a role in relegating them to the domain of the unenlightened who had yet to be educated – either by European-born secularists or a European-born religious establishment.) It is in this sense that the version offered by the Hebrew Law of Peace, however fragmentary and unstable, represented an attempt to invoke law as a means of imagining a nation which would have been distinct from state and religion but, working as it had done against the grain of both secular and religious Zionists, it was declared non-law and, worse, anathema to the national project.

We may now ask where society is. In his *Nation-building or a New Society?* Zeev Sternhell posits a tension between socialism, as a world-redeeming universal world view, and nation-building, as an orientation that forever flirts with particularism and chauvinism.[20] If there ever was such a tension in the history of Israel's labor movement, Sternhell argues, it had been decisively resolved in favor of national socialism: a praxis which harnessed the socialist principles of equality and social change as content-less symbols at the service of the nation-building project. Given that the leading Zionist socialist party – Achdut Ha'Avoda – had assumed the leadership of the Jewish Federation of Labor back in the 1920s, and given that the Jewish Federation of Labor, in turn, had been the unrivaled organized force behind the colonization project, Sternhell's analysis offers much more than an account of Zionist socialism. Rather, it constructs a platform for making sense of the colonizing community's statist form of social organization.

Sternhell is unambiguous. The socialist-national 'revolution,' he argues, was about the acquisition, consolidation, centralization, and bureaucratization of power, preventing both individuals and voluntary organizations in civil society from having a significant independent ability to shape national politics. Socialist ideology, he writes, was an effective instrument for regimenting workers, not in order to bring about a comprehensive change in inter-human relations or in order to promote workers' rights, but in order to advance the conquest of Palestine by ensuring, first and foremost, uncompromised loyalty to the leadership of the party and the Jewish Federation of Labor.[21]

Sternhell writes that this pattern was already established in the 1920s; the purpose was to establish a Jewish state in Palestine and the means to achieve it were realized through a strong political and economic organization in which a political party and a quasi-state apparatus were, for all practical purposes, one and the same. Sternhell's terminology, however, seems to imply that a nation-building project *is* a statist form of organization. It has been one of my purposes in this book to problematize, through the study of law, this taken-for-granted (con)fusion. In this sense, therefore, Sternhell's analysis is not only a critique of national socialism but also an analysis of statism as the hegemonic orientation through which the nation has been imagined and mobilized. And studied.

The labor movement derived its strength from its ability to organize and to discipline propertyless laborers and settlers, mostly young immigrants to Palestine, who depended on the party and on the JFL for employment, for a whole range of social services, and, arguably, for a sense of identity and solidarity. Ideologically, workers (especially agricultural workers and frontier settlers) were praised as the pioneering heroes of the national revolution. Pragmatically, the labor movement's ever-growing bureaucracy enlisted the support of clerks, administrators and functionaries who were directly employed by the quasi-state machinery. In tandem with the concentration of power in and around this quasi-statist structure, Zionist historiography has mainly attended to the Jewish Federation of Labor, and the dominant socialist parties and their 'pioneer' and working-class constituencies, acknowledging and affirming the centrality of these forces to the understanding of the nation-building project. Critics have also worked from within this research paradigm. Thus, for example, Shapiro (1996) talked about these centralized and highly bureaucratized political parties and quasi-statist institutions in terms of an analytically distinct 'political system;' this system had to be analyzed independently of both the state – the colonial (and even the sovereign Jewish) state – and civil society (that of the colonizing community), because it alone dominated the colonization of Palestine and the nation-building project in the name of which it had been undertaken.[22]

Accordingly, the colonial state has not been considered crucial for understanding the distribution of political power within the colonizing community, let alone for understanding the dynamics of the nation-building project.[23] Likewise, social groups and classes which were external to the sphere of influence of the labor parties have also remained understudied. The middle classes, the so-called 'civil circles' of the colonizing community, all those who were part of 'disorganized society,' so to speak – merchants, medium-size land- and home-owners, commercial and industrial people, and professionals – were by and large left out of the research paradigm through which the colonization of Palestine and the political economy of Israeli society had been studied. 'Society,' so to speak, is almost absent from the 'polis-centered' analysis (and arguably for the self-perception) of statist Zionism and its follow-up historiography.[24]

Nonetheless, it is agreed that the middle classes wielded considerable economic power. Waves of Jewish immigration to Palestine in the 1920s brought about a massive flow of private capital which considerably outweighed the public capital which had been received and dispensed by leading Zionist institutions in general and the labor movement in particular.[25] In general, the social composition and the demographics of the colonizing community changed considerably in the course of the 1920s, as middle-class immigrants settled in the cities and contributed to an urbanization, commercialization and small-scale industrialization process. Available data, therefore, show that a substantial proportion of the private capital flowing to Palestine was invested in private land acquisition and in urban construction, especially in and around Tel Aviv.

Still, while urbanization became indispensable for the actual colonization of Palestine, and while the new commercial and industrial enterprises created new employment opportunities for a rather pressed working class, and while even 70 per cent of JFL members resided in and around Tel Aviv in the 1920s, the dominant ideology degraded or simply ignored the role and importance of the middle-class city-dweller as far as nation-building was concerned.[26] Rather, it was the organized laborer, and in particular the pioneering rural colonizer of the frontier, who enjoyed the status of standing at the vanguard of the nation-building project and was the one in whose name the labor movement claimed a leading role in managing the affairs of the colonizing community. It is therefore also commonly agreed that the middle classes failed to transform their relative economic power into meaningful political power and that they remained politically weak throughout the colonization period (and beyond, also after independence).[27]

At times, it is argued that the middle classes simply consented to the ideological and organizational role which had been assumed by the labor movement. This consent has been said to rest on the fact that, on the one hand, the labor movement was indeed the only seriously organized force that was capable of looking after the collective interests of the national movement and that, on the other, the organized labor movement never seriously challenged the ability of private capital owners to develop a de facto capitalist economy. Thus, not threatened in their economic domain, the middle classes gave over the political affairs of the nation into the hands of the labor movement. It is sometimes argued that the middle classes failed to develop a counter-ideology and that they succumbed rather than consented to the hegemonic role of the labor movement. In either case, the scholarly wisdom is that the middle classes were politically weak and, in this respect at least, they are relatively inconsequential for understanding the dynamics of the actual nation-building project.

Beyond the ideological explanations for their reputed political weakness, it has also been suggested that the middle classes failed to create a strong and effective political party that would have vied for a more substantial voice within the political system of the colonizing community. Thus, it has been shown that the middle classes created a multitude of small parties, associations, and small-scale organizations and institutions that were poorly coordinated. In particular, some attention has been given to the political parties of the middle classes, showing that they failed to draw massive support and to create an effective political machine.[28] Little attention, if any, has been given to their professional associations and various Chambers of Commerce and Industry, a point to which I shall shortly return.[29] Little attention has been given to urban and local politics, where the middle classes had a much greater voice (often a dominant one) than in national politics. And, finally, little attention was given to the fact that middle-class politics were slanted towards the colonial state.

I think that the lines of inquiry taken and not taken insofar as the middle class was concerned result directly from a research paradigm that by and large accepted the labor movement's terms for measuring power, importance, status, and influence. The conceptualization of the middle class as politically weak has been *a priori* determined by considering party politics within the political system of the colonizing community to be the overriding criterion for evaluating the trajectory of Palestinian Zionism. However this 'weakness' acquires a somewhat different meaning in light of the possibility that the urban middle classes were in fact independent of that political system and that, consequently, this independence rendered "their participation in the power struggles, some of which focused on the allocation of material resources, unnecessary and irrelevant."[30]

This book, obviously, cannot overcome a long-standing research void, neither when it comes to the role of the colonial state nor when it comes to the 'civil circles.' But I would like to at least develop a possible research hypothesis.

Let us look again, then, at Bernard Joseph's insistence that the duty of lawyers, and of those they represented, was to establish stronger links with the legal and administrative machinery of the colonial state: to seek more jobs at its employment, to have Jewish judges sitting in state courts, to have a voice in legislative reforms, and to resort to state courts for the resolution of disputes. In short, to treat the government of this land as belonging to the Jews. In previous chapters, we have seen that Joseph's call reflected the general attitude of the organized Jewish legal profession towards the colonial state. To the extent that this disposition has been at least minimally indicative of the disposition of other professional groups, and to the extent that we may at least minimally generalize from this as to the orientations of the so-called civil circles, we have to rethink the relationship between the colonizing community's owners of private capital (and 'professional capital') and the apparatuses of the colonial state. We have to rethink, in other words, the paradigm through which to consider spheres of power and influence that shaped the nation-building project.[31]

This paradigmatic shift is partially encouraged by post-colonialist accounts of the typically well-nurtured links, often mediated through law, between colonizers and the bourgeois elements of colonized people. India, writes Chatterjee, has had a history of collaboration between the colonial state and the 'educated classes;' a fact which considerably compromised the Indian bourgeoisie's opposition to colonialism.[32] And Peter Fitzpatrick describes the introduction of the common law to British colonies, in the name of order and enlightenment, as serving the interests of the metropolitan bourgeoisie, later to be exploited by "indigenous class elements who were good in using the law to their own advantage."[33] The Palestinian case, however, has been unique in that the nation's acknowledged political elites emerged out of the parties and institutions of organized labor which by and large functioned independently of the colonial state (albeit with its tacit approval). Nonetheless, and precisely because of the openly socialist orientation of these political nation-building elites, it is plausible to expect that the material interests of the Jewish middle class would have been wedded to the economic policies of the colonial state. It was the colonial state, operating along the parameters of a capitalist economy, which could have provided the structural matrix for the development of the Jewish middle class. Still, it is noteworthy that very little research exploring relations between the colonial government and the 'disorganized,' namely middle-class, forces of the Jewish colonizing community, has been undertaken.

As a general hypothesis, therefore, I posit that the Jewish middle class, or influential elements thereof, invested political effort in, and targeted, the colonial government rather than investing in the nation-building politics of a system in which they had little stake. This hypothesis is at least tentatively corroborated when we consider the fact that Zionist governing bodies constantly targeted the colonial government for budgets, contracts, and employment opportunities within the various bureaus and offices of that government. It is further corroborated when we consider the nature of Jewish urban politics and the management of direct economic interests by the Jewish middle class.

While 'national' politics were largely managed by the National Council and, gradually, by the dominant political parties, the middle class had not only a stake, but a considerable voice when it came to local politics, namely, the management and control of townships and municipalities. This has been particularly evident in Tel Aviv, in which the middle class – self-employed, merchants, home-owners and professionals – dominated local politics through most of the 1920s.[34] In the most direct sense, it is evident that as far as local politics were concerned, it was the colonial government which had been the local politicians' and officials' primary focus for local empowerment prerogatives and budgetary allocations alike. An example is the way the Council of Tel Aviv handled the constitutional crisis that followed the decision of the High Court in the Shoshani affair (see Salle d'Attente).

The Council of Tel Aviv instructed the law firm of Sacher, Horowitz, Klebanoff to prepare a draft of a new Tel Aviv Township Order and to negotiate its acceptance by the colonial government. Accordingly, Solomon Horowitz wrote to the Chief Secretary that "during the course of litigation ... many obscurities and inadequacies in the Tel Aviv Township Order became apparent, and the necessity of completely recasting the Order is evident if the work of the Township is to be carried on efficiently and free from constant litigation as to the rights and powers and obligations and duties of the Local Council."[35]

Most urgent was the need to ensure the voting rights of women, because the court's ruling meant that wives of 'ratepayers', if not ratepayers themselves, could be excluded. Horowitz wrote, therefore, that "so far as the protection of the rights of the wives of ratepayers is concerned, I have followed and adopted the provisions of section 4(3) of the Representation of the People Act 1918 and Section 7 of the same Act ... my clients are most anxious that this may be dealt with by the government as one of extreme urgency ..."[36] A draft of an amended Order was attached, and in another letter, addressed to the Township of Tel Aviv, the firm notified its clients that Horowitz was about to meet the Chief Justice privately in order to expedite the handling of that matter. The proposed amendment was accepted and duly enacted by the government within three weeks.[37]

Throughout the 1920s Sacher's firm was engaged in drafting, introducing, and negotiating the legislative framework for the administration of Tel Aviv. And above and beyond the interest to be found in detailing the ability of that specific firm to establish strong relations with colonial officials,[38] I think it should be clear that both lawyers and clients became acutely aware that, at least as far as local politics were concerned, all relevant issues of budgetary allocations, taxing, policing, and setting the rules for the political game had to be channeled through and negotiated with the colonial government. I believe the same principle holds when it came to other sought-after legislative measures and reforms as well.

Perhaps most significant were organized middle-class activities in respect of British economic policies in Palestine. The colonial government of Palestine was primarily interested in facilitating the empire's strategic interests, in promoting British exports, and in ensuring that the state's budget would be maximally if not exclusively based on local revenues. Thus, for example, the tariff policy was strictly designed to increase the internal revenue, while specific taxes were structured to give concealed preference to British products. These policies hindered the development of local industries and threatened to dump in Palestine British goods against which local industry could not compete. Consequently, the Manufacturers Association, organized in 1921 by a group of Zionist advocates, invested considerable efforts in pressuring the government to protect particular industries and firms, to abolish customs for industrial equipment and machinery, to raise protective tariffs, and to introduce various laws that would have compromised the unabashed laissez-faire policy of the colonial government. (Gross writes: "In democratic Europe the climate of opinion was already moving away from economic liberalism, a trend that was evidenced by the growing demand for government action in additional areas and the consequent increase in budgets. But this new climate had little effect on the overseas possessions of the same democracies.")[39]

It seems that the activities of the Manufacturers Association and other similar interest-specific bodies were instrumental in the introduction of legislative reforms designed to encourage local industry and to enhance production activities. Direct encouragement of local industry began in 1924 with the exemption of many types of industrial machinery from customs duty and this, in turn, opened up a local campaign for the protection of industries from foreign competition. Gross reports that these pressures, which were at times aided by local civil servants (specifically the Director of Customs and Trade), were aimed not only at local government but also at the Treasury and the Colonial Office in London, which were steadfast in adhering to a laissez-faire (that is, empyreal-biased) policy in the colonies. He further reports that throughout the 1920s, "the industrial interest obtained a series of concessions:" raw materials for industry were gradually freed from duties, and, in 1927, "the policy of protecting local industry was initiated and the familiar phrase 'infant industries' became part of the fiscal language of Palestine."[40] Generally speaking, therefore, the multiplicity of middle-class organizations and professional associations, typically serving researchers as proof of political weakness, may be looked upon as a rather effective means of appealing to the colonial government in the particular interests of various middle-class groups.

Finally, given that a major policy directive of the colonial government, in line with empyreal strategic interests, was to develop the country's infrastructure, and given that other colonial interests required the establishment of a full-blown system of state apparatuses, we have to keep in mind that the colonial government became a major employer not only of unskilled labour (by maintaining public works[41]) but also of professionals, administrators, clerks and technical experts. Shapiro, accounting for the 'weakness' of the middle classes, argued that their complacency was due to their transformation into a subservient bureaucratic class in the service of various institutions that had been under the control of the Jewish 'socialist' political elite.[42] Shapiro had in mind employment by the institutions and bodies of the colonizing community alone. Yet there is no reason to assume that the colonial state did not create even wider and more lucrative employment opportunities. We have seen such interests explicitly expressed, and to some extent attained, by the Jewish legal profession. There is no reason to assume otherwise in respect of other employment opportunities opened up to the middle classes by the colonial government. In fact, available data and research indicate that Jews were quite extensively employed by the colonial state, that the Jewish Agency and the National Council constantly lobbied the government for more openings, and that an ongoing political struggle was carried out by various Jewish bodies and organizations to ensure adequate representation of Jews in the various instrumentalities of the colonial state.[43]

Lobbying for more governmental openings for Jews was not based on material interests alone. Rather, this path was sought in the name of nationalist interests: Greater employment opportunities entailed a capacity for greater absorption of Jewish immigrants into the country and also insured a fair representation of Jewish interests vis-a-vis Arab ones.[44] Thus, it was not only lawyers who developed a nationalist stance which called for stronger links to the colonial state. Rather, the disposition of the legal profession, in this respect, mirrored the general disposition of professionals and the Jewish middle class as a whole.

Jacob Reuveny, who has compiled the most extensive up-to-date employment data, found that Jews were significantly overrepresented in senior and intermediary governmental positions in the beginning of the 1920s, in fact double their proportion of the overall population. Changing policies and massive Jewish immigration diminished this overrepresentation throughout the 1930s and 1940s; employment data for 1945 showed that out of a total number of 30,000 government employees, 5,355 were Jews (excluding 3497 Jews employed by the state's police and 'civil guard' service). While this number, not insignificant in itself, does not seem to be overwhelming, Reuveny further makes the point that the "Jewish achievement was more qualitative than quantitative:" Jewish presence in the apparatuses of the colonial state was distributed over a wide variety of positions and skilled occupations and allowed Jews to acquire professional knowledge, considerable income, and managerial powers.[45] The presumed weakness of the middle class is therefore somewhat mitigated when we consider its ability to penetrate and occupy key positions which provided access to sources of information and allowed it to master administrative capabilities that were not exhausted with the establishment of the state of Israel. When we compound those direct employment openings with other routes through which the colonial state was in a position to enhance middle-class powers (e.g., financial assistance to Jewish institutions, local government and Jewish education and health services, and general industrial and commercial contracts) we get a different perspective from which to evaluate the 'weak' politics of the Jewish middle class.

Further, the strong middle-class disposition towards the colonial state must also be considered in light of the demographic changes that took place in the colonizing community during the immigration waves of the mid-1920s. These waves consisted of a considerable number of urban-oriented settlers whose arrival signalled the transformation of the colonizing community into a society of strangers. In a previous chapter, I analyzed nationalism as a disciplinary device and explained how the Hebrew Law of Peace relied on internal, rather intimate, forms of discipline in order to secure public adherence to its authority. This authoritative ability diminished with the changing demographic composition of the colonizing community, especially given the orientation of the newcomers towards the colonial state (and its legal machinery) as a source of distributive benefits. Thus, the collapse of the Hebrew Law of Peace, in a final analysis, must also be considered in light of the demographic and political changes brought about by these waves of immigration of the mid-1920s.

In sum, I instance the relationship of the Jewish legal profession in Palestine with the state-managed system of justice to introduce and highlight the more general issue of the relations between the Zionist middle classes and the colonial state. However, in the last case there is a point in arguing that the statist character of the nation-building project indeed led to the relative disappearance of 'society.' As mentioned earlier, the dominant political elites of the colonizing community derived their powers from disciplined organized workers and cadres of subservient bureaucrats who did not challenge their legitimate authority to handle and manage the nation-building project. The forces of 'disorganized society,' however (namely the middle classes), invested in interest-specific politics directed at the colonial state. In this respect, the subservient 'apolitical' service class that Shapiro referred to in analyzing the political system of the colonizing community was at least partially born also through the direct links between the Jewish middle class and the colonial state. Professional and commercial associations thus learnt to lobby state bureaus, to access and manipulate relevant business information, and to effectively adhere to strict economic and professional concerns. At the same time, they were content to remain in the shadows of what was considered to be the politics of nation-building, deferring to the so-called socialist elite in all that pertained to national affairs. Given that the same political elite was able to capture the apparatuses of the state after independence and to define its role in terms of a nation-building mission (coupled with a national emergency rhetoric), it effectively undermined the ability and willingness of the middle class to have a voice in national politics. Therefore, while the Jewish middle class was successful in laying the groundwork for a capitalist economy and for a consumerist 'bourgeois' lifestyle, an un-societal political culture had developed by educating both the 'civil circles' and organized labor to defer, in 'national' policy-making, to the nation's political elite. It is in this sense that we may indeed ask 'And where is society within this state?'

The *Jews were not colonized.* Bernard Joseph and the advocates of the Hebrew Law of Peace all had something to say about the dark side of exilic life but each activated that dark imagery in light of a different agenda. For the advocates of the Hebrew Law of Peace, the Jews of Palestine were at a risk of displaying the lowly exilic habits of bowing their heads to the idols of the presumably enlightened gentiles and of passively depending on the latter's ordering and policing devices. For Joseph, the problem of exilic life was closure and xenophobia, displayed by the outdated attempt to remain within the bounds of a closed 'community.' These different conceptualizations of the dark side of the Jewish past bred different politics and, moreover, a different epistemological posture: while the advocates of the Hebrew Law of Peace feared cultural colonization by the British, Joseph saw the high road to national self-determination as passing through an alliance with the colonial state. Thus, while the advocates of the Hebrew Law of Peace lamented the danger of being colonized under the conditions prevailing in Palestine, Joseph asserted that the Jews, under the same prevailing conditions, were not colonized.

We were not colonized. This denial was constitutive of the Zionist nation-building politics of the 1920s. We were not colonized, first and foremost, because Zionism was not about becoming 'just another congregation' in Palestine but rather about infiltrating, with the consent and support of the infiltrated, the apparatuses of the colonial state as if it were ours. Hence Zionism was in tandem with the general aims of the colonial state: colonialism presupposed, first, the dispersed and disorganized existence of natives who were yet to be pacified and civilized and, second, the existence of a wilderness which should be ordered, that is to say, fixed and named and mapped – by an officializing white gaze. For Zionists, the native to be tamed had always been the Palestinian Arab, and the land to be ordered and mapped had always been a Palestinian Arab one.

In many Zionist narratives, the new Hebrew immigrant from Europe was but another representative of Europe who faced a primitive Asian East. Zionist colonization, in turn, was based on construction and cultivation of a desolate land against which a Hebrew civilization constructed itself. Moreover, the Zionist was not colonized because it was exilic Jews – a rootless pariah people – who occupied that space, at least metaphorically; and the identity of the Zionist, as noted before, was constructed as its antithesis. Nurit Gertz observes that "the reaction to the image of the exilic Jew is also revealed when that Jewish identity – rejected and negated by the Israeli – is projected into the Arab ... he is passive, not a fighter, not rooted in his land, and not a people like other peoples."[46] Thus, Joseph's apprehension at being 'just another congregation' was at once directed at the Jewish ghetto in the Diaspora and at the possibility of sharing common existential ground with colonized Arabs. The two must not be separated, as the attitude towards the past shaped the understanding of the present.

In more than one sense, therefore, 'the Jews have never been colonized.' First, through an alliance with the colonial state, not only politically but also through an identification with what the British imperium stood for, namely a civilizing, benevolent force of the West whose destiny was to order by means of an "officializing white gaze." Since the 1920s, the Zionist attitude towards the Arab had been shaped through the prism of statism and sovereignty; for all practical purposes, this prism presupposed a constitution of an 'Other' and the treatment of that 'Other' in governmental terms: policing, containment, and control over territory. And a dialogue is forever hindered when one collectivity speaks to the Other through the prism of sovereignty.

Second, in an existential sense. The refusal to be 'just another congregation' also referred to the 'other' congregations of Palestine; Zionism's 'Others' were colonized. Positing the 'Other' as colonized, while denying one's own situation as being colonized, could not but profoundly affect the relationship between the Palestinian Jew and the Palestinian Arab. At the very least, this socially constructed existential gap between Jews and Arabs ensured that they would not share the same experience under colonial rule and would not develop a subsequent joint reservoir of memories.

But a caveat is called for. I am not suggesting that the Hebrew Law of Peace represented a potential – in law – for Arab–Jewish solidarity. The basic anti-colonial stance of at least one of the Hebrew law's principal advocates, Shmuel Eisenstadt, had been linked with an early 1920s' vision of Jewish law as part of an overall cultural crusade that would have united the "people of the East" in a joint effort to incarnate "an authentic and bold Eastern Law, which feeds upon the roots of Eastern religion and which inserts order into Eastern life." Indeed, this romantic and essentialized Western-centered conception of the East had been a quite explicit theme of cultural Zionists in Palestine. It was mainly voiced through Brit Shalom, an intellectual movement active between 1925 and 1933. Brit Shalom, following Martin Buber, spoke in the name of invigorating Judaism rather than in the name of a Jewish state ideology, argued for a distance from Western civilization and advocated an integration with the East as a key to Jewish–Arab coexistence.[47]

Yet voices such as Eisenstadt's had already disappeared from the self-presentation of the Hebrew Law of Peace by the mid-1920s.[48] By and large, the advocates of the Hebrew Law of Peace abstained from reflecting upon the implications of their project with respect to Palestinian Arabs. Although Arabs were not excluded from Hebrew Courts of Peace and although there were a handful of recorded cases in which Arabs litigated in these courts, there was nothing in the deeds and ideas of the Hebrew law's advocates which suggested that they had developed an alternative way of conceiving Arab–Jewish coexistence in Palestine. On the contrary, it seems that on this front, at least, the jurists of the Hebrew Law of Peace joined forces with the rest of the legal profession, degrading the image of the Arab lawyer and the Arab scholar. A review essay in *Ha'Mishpat Ha'Ivri*, a law journal controlled by the advocates of the Hebrew Law of Peace, illustrates this point. Commenting on the publication of a ne Palestinians–Arab law journal in Jaffa, Yitzchak Nofech wrote that most of the articles were primitive and childish, suitable only for the undeveloped reader, who tasted only a few grains of modern civilization, and judging by the articles' logic and the depth of thought, they may be suitable for mediocre schoolchildren in Europe, and may be boring even for them – yet if we measure this journal by the standards of the dormant and lazy East, we may consider it as a sign of progress and of desire for high culture, of a wish to learn and absorb European views – And for us the Jews, the journal may serve as an instrument for getting to know our neighbors' level of progress and the problems which occupy them in law. And since it is in the land of Israel that we constitute our national home, it is inescapable that we shall be influenced by the Arabs, for better or worse, and we must learn their views and culture. (emphases added)[49]

It is not that the Hebrew Law of Peace stood for a viable option. Rather, my point is simply that the search for 'authenticity' that the Hebrew Law of Peace represented, and especially the distance from colonialist culture for which it stood, unsettled – and hence brought to the surface – some of the basic tenets of hegemonic Zionism. The most salient was that the experience of the colonizing community in Palestine had never been one of being colonized by the British Empire. "Anticolonial nationalism," writes Prakash, responded to European rule by "asserting its claim to history" and by projecting "a distance from Europe."[50] Dominant Zionism, however, asserted a claim to sovereignty molded on the European model of the nation-state and imagined itself, by and large, as part of the West. Consequently, the fundamental Zionist experience was one of sharing in the colonial rule over Palestine. While later years, the 1930s and especially the 1940s, saw intense conflicts between the British government and the Zionist leadership, and while it ceased to be legitimate to associate with British officials and officers in those later years, this fundamental experience had not changed. By then, Zionist statism had already fully determined that the Arab Palestinian community would be conceived through a governmental prism of containment and control.

It is also in this light that the possibilities and impossibilities of a post-Zionist post-colonial discourse should be considered. Post-colonialism, among other things, puts the question of 'who speaks' at the center of the narrating process.[51] To the extent that post-colonial discourse supposes the ability of the formerly colonized to articulate an alternative experience, to write new histories and to disclaim and override former narratives, a post-Zionist post-colonial discourse faces a serious challenge in that the Palestinian Jew and the Palestinian Arab cannot relate to a shared experience under British rule, an existential stance which precludes in yet another way the possibility of sharing a destiny.

It is not surprising, therefore, that those who speak in the name of post-Zionism – as an intellectual agenda, a political perspective, and an organizing discursive reference point – mainly engage the post-colonial voice as a self-reflection on the colonialist. In other words, they speak from the perspective of the former colonialist who tries to come to terms with the colonial legacy: unmasking past repression, evaluating one's identity by looking at the construction of a colonized 'Other,' and trying to write a history, a jurisprudence, a literature, an art, and a revisionist politics of regret.

Still, we have never been colonized. And this profoundly shapes the way the post-Zionist discourse is organized and carried out. For what makes this discourse so challenging is neither the way it shatters old Zionist narratives, nor its new revisionist vocabulary, but rather its bold, and still embryonic search for the possibility of a Jewish nation in Israel, one whose terms of invention are not essentially implicated with the power structure of the state. One which ultimately may be conceived and narrated as if it were at once colonizing and still internally colonized in respect to its failure to experience itself in the in-between of state and religion.

Let me finally state the idea somewhat differently. The trajectory of Zionism has been one that failed to produce a Jewish Israeli. First, there never has been a (colonized) Jewish Palestinian. Then, there never has been a (colonialist) Jewish Israeli. To be sure, there are various social groups whose members experience themselves as Israeli Jews. These social groups are distinct from each other in that they entertain varying forms of relations between being an Israeli and being Jewish. At one extreme, there are those who try to radically break away from the legacy of Judaism. At the other, there are those whose Israeliness is no more than a formal burden (or, at best, an instrument). Most are somewhere in between. And within that in-between, this book has been about a silenced search for a hyphen, hyphen for Jewish-Israelis who experience their nationhood apart from the institutions, practices and symbols of the state on the one hand and apart from a transcendental religion on the other hand. A hyphen, finally, designed precisely for those who may develop, or at least sense, the experience of being colonized as an experience that may inspire a new paradigm within which to interact with Palestinian Arabs.

NOTES

INTRODUCTION

1 Jean-Jacques Rousseau (1712–1778)(1985) *The Government of Poland.* Indianapolis: Hackett Publishing, pp. 5–6.
2 I 'discovered' the above text only upon near-completion of this book. It was suggested to me by Bonnie Honig, to whom I owe many thanks for a thorough reading of key parts of the manuscript.

1 MANDATE PALESTINE: THE ENIGMA OF THE MISSING COLONIAL STATE

1 I outline only a general mood here. There are exceptions, especially among young writers of the 1990s, e.g., Assaf Likhovski (1998) "Between a 'Mandate' and a 'State': On the Periodization of the History of Israeli Law," *Mishpatim* 29(2), pp. 1–34.
2 Nathan J. Brown (1995) "Law and Imperialism: Egypt in Comparative Perspective," *Law and Society Review,* 29(1), pp. 103–126, 104.
3 See chapter 6 on the role of lawyers and chapter 7, fn 20.
4 Moshe Lissak, Anita Shapira and Gabriel Cohen (1995) *The History of the Jewish Community in Eretz-Israel Since 1882, The Period of the British Mandate, Part Two.* Israel Academy for Sciences and Humanities and the Bialik Institute: Jerusalem.
5 See the review of Tom Segev in *Ha'Aretz Literary Supplement* 30.8.95.
6 Meron Benvenishti "Ore'ach Hod Malchuta" (Her Majesty's Guest), *Ha'Aretz* 6.3.97, p. B 1.
7 On the cruelty of British soldiers towards the Arab population in crushing the Palestinian uprising see A. J. Sherman (1997) *Mandate Days: British Lives in Palestine 1918–1948.* Thames and Hudson: London. Sherman's account is based on private letters of British soldiers and policemen who were stationed in Palestine.
8 Gideon Biger (1983) *A Crown Colony or a National Home: The Impact of British Rule on Palestine 1917–1930, A Historical-Geographical Account* (Moshavat Keter o Ba'iit Leumi: Hash'pa'at Ha'shilton Ha'briti Al Eretz Yisrael 1917–1930 Bchina Geographit-Historit). Yad Ben Zvi: Jerusalem; Jacob Reuveny (1993) *The Administration of Palestine Under the British Mandate 1920–1948: An Institutional Analysis.* Bar Ilan University: Ramat Gan (Heb); Edwin Samuel (1957) *British Traditions in the Administration of Israel.* Anglo-Israel Association. Vallentine, Mitchell: London, p. 33.

9   See Lockman, situating Zionist nationalism within colonialist discourse, who in passing writes: "The British–Zionist alliance was never free of conflict and would break down just before the Second World War as the two parties' interests diverged. It is nonetheless clear that it was British colonial rule over Palestine which, in the face of growing Palestinian Arab nationalist opposition to Zionism and demands for self-determination, opened the way to Jewish immigration, land acquisition, and the development of the Yishuv's infrastructure and economy on a scale that would have been unimaginable had Palestine either remained under Ottoman rule or achieved independence under the Arab government." Zachary Lockman (1995) "Exclusion and Solidarity: Labor Zionism and Arab Workers in Palestine 1897–1929," in: Gyan Prakash (ed.) *After Colonialism*. Princeton University Press: Princeton NJ, pp. 211–240, 222.

10 "The Mandate of Palestine" in: Raphael Patai (ed.) (1971) *Encyclopedia of Zionism and Israel*. McGraw Hill: New York, pp. 757–760.

11 See Yigal Elam (1979) *HaDerech Ha'Zionit el ha'Ko'ach (The Zionist Way to Force)*. Zmora Bitan: Tel Aviv; Boas Evron (1988) *A National Reckoning*. Dvir: Tel Aviv. One of the most telling episodes on this account concerns the Zionist reaction to the Peel Report of 1937 (*Palestine Royal Commission Report*, presented by the Secretary of State for the Colonies to Parliament by command of His Majesty July 1937). The Peel report, which was essentially sympathetic to Zionist aspirations and, moreover, to Zionist achievements in Palestine since the beginning of the British Mandate, concluded that a partition of Palestine had become inevitable in light of the Jewish–Palestinian national conflict. It proposed, therefore, to divide the land between two sovereign and independent states, and to thereby discharge Britain of the obligations it took upon itself in the Mandate. This proposal was met with fear and anger on the Zionist side, not only because it compromised the dream of Greater Israel, but also because it exposed the Jewish community to dangers it was not yet ready to face on its own, thus leaving most Zionist leaders unprepared to part ways with a Mandatory regime that could easily be conceived as the hallmark of Zionism's political achievements up to that point. See, e.g., chapter 6 in: Yigal Elam (1975) *An Introduction to Zionist History*. Lewin-Epstein: Tel Aviv (Heb).

12 Curiously enough, some research along these lines focused on the constitutive role of the British colonizers vis-a-vis the Palestinian Arab population. See, Baruch Kimmerling and Joel S. Migdal (1993) *Palestinians: The Making of a People*. Free Press: New York; Ylana N. Miller (1980) "Administrative Policy in Rural Palestine: The Impact of British Norms on Arab Community Life, 1920–1948," in: Joel S. Migdal (ed.) *Palestinian Society and Politics*. Princeton University Press: Princeton, NJ.

13 Anita Shapira (1992) *Land and Power: The Zionist Resort to Force 1881–1948*. Oxford University Press: New York, p. 131. A number of sociologists and historians, both 'conservative' and 'revisionists,' have noted this absence in recent years but have not developed a research agenda in this direction. See e.g., Ilan Pappe (1996) "Ha'Zionut be'Mivchan ha'Teoriot shel ha'Leumiut" (Zionism in the Context of Theories of Nationalism,) in: Pinchas Ginosar

and Avi Bareli (eds) *Tsionut: Pulmus Ben Zmanenu (Zionism: A Contemporary Debate)*. Ben Gurion University: Beer Sheva, pp. 223–263; Moshe Lissak (1996) "'Soziologim 'Bikort'iim' ve'Soziologim 'Mimsadiim' ba'Kehila ha'Academit ha'Yisraelit: Ma'avakim Idiologiim o Si'ach Academi Inyani?" (Critical Sociologists and 'Establishment' Sociologists in the Israeli Academy: Ideological Struggles or a Substantive Academic Discourse?) in: Pinchas Ginosar and Avi Bareli (eds) *Tsionut: Pulmus Ben Zmanenu (Zionism: A Contemporary Debate)*, Ben Gurion University: Beer Sheva, pp. 60–98; Baruch Kimmerling (1993) "Yachasei Hevra u'Medina be'Yisrael" (State and Society in Israel), in: Uri Ram (ed.) *Israeli Society: Critical Perspectives*. Brerot: Tel Aviv, pp. 328–350 (Heb).

14 Some research on the economic role of the colonial state in Palestine – with a revisionist potential that has not been picked up by historians and social scientists – was done by Nachum Gross (1982) "The Economic Policy of the Mandatory Government in Palestine," *Discussion Paper 816*, Maurice Falk Institute for Economic Research in Israel: Jerusalem. Also see: Amotz Morag (1967) *The Financing of the Israeli Government: Development and Problems*. Magnes: Jerusalem, pp. 1–28; Jacob Reuveny (1993) *The Administration of Palestine Under the British Mandate 1920–1948: An Institutional Analysis*. Bar Ilan University: Ramat Gan.

15 Nicholas B. Dirks (1992) "From Little King to Landlord: Colonial Discourse and Colonial Rule," in: Nicholas B. Dirks (ed.) *Colonialism and Culture*. University of Michigan Press: Ann Arbor, pp. 175–207, 202–3.

16 Yoram Shachar (1995) "History and Sources of Israeli Law," in: Amos Shapira and Keren C. DeWitt-Arar (eds) *Introduction to the Law of Israel*. Kluwer Law Int'l: The Hague, pp. 1–10, 4.

17 Uri Yadin (1962) "Reception and Rejection of English Law in Israel," *International and Comparative Law Quarterly*, 11, January 1962, pp. 59–72; Assaf Likhovski (1995) "In Our Image: Colonial Discourse and the Anglicization of the Law of Mandatory Palestine," *Israel Law Review*, 29(3), pp. 291–359.

18 Nicholas B. Dirks (1992) "From Little King to Landlord: Colonial Discourse and Colonial Rule," in: Nicholas B. Dirks (ed.) *Colonialism and Culture*. University of Michigan Press: Ann Arbor, pp. 175–207, 177.

19 Ibid., p. 182.

20 Daniel Friedmann (1975) "Independent Development of Israeli Law," *Israel Law Review*, 10(4), pp. 515–568.

21 Sandy Kedar (1998) "Majority Time, Minority Time: Land, Nationality and the Law of Adverse Possession in Israel," *Iunei Mishpat* 21(3), pp. 665–746 (Heb). Kedar further adds that the method was named after Sir Robert Torrens who applied it to southern Australia in the second half of the nineteenth century. For more details and references see Kedar 1997, fn. 19–21. This legal framework, for example, severely limited the Bedouin indigenous population's ability to prevent the state of Israel, years later, from registering their lands as state property: see Ronen Shamir (1996) "Suspended in Space: Bedouins under the Law of Israel," *Law and Society Review*, 30(2), pp. 231–257.

22 Gershon Shafir (1989) *Land, Labour and Origins of the Israeli-Palestinian Conflict 1882–1914*. Cambridge University Press: Cambridge; Zachary Lockman (1995) "Exclusion and Solidarity: Labor Zionism and Arab Workers in Palestine 1897–1929," in: Gyan Prakash (ed.) *After Colonialism*. Princeton University Press: Princeton, NJ, pp. 211–240. Lockman argues that in order to make sense of the Zionist colonization of Palestine we need to look both at the labor market strategies and "the ways in which the 'Arab worker' and the Arab working class in Palestine were represented, and the roles they were made to play, in labor-Zionist discourse. At a crucial stage, it was to a significant extent in relation to those (always contested) representations of Arab workers that labor Zionism articulated its own identity, its sense of mission, and its strategy" (p. 213).
23 Dan Horowitz and Moshe Lissak (1978) *Origins of the Israeli Polity*. University of Chicago Press: Chicago, p. 16.
24 Ibid., p. 17.
25 Ibid., p. 6.
26 Zachary Lockman (1995) "Exclusion and Solidarity: Labor Zionism and Arab Workers in Palestine 1897–1929," in: Gyan Prakash (ed.) *After Colonialism*. Princeton University Press: Princeton NJ, pp. 211–240, 212.
27 Gershon Shafir (1993) "Land, Labor and Population in Zionist Colonization: General and Specific Aspects" in: Uri Ram (ed.) *Israeli Society: Critical Perspectives*. Breirot Publishers: Tel Aviv, pp. 104–119 (Heb).
28 Ibid., p. 108.
29 Ibid., p. 109.
30 Ran Ahronson (1996) "Settlement in Eretz-Yisrael – A Colonialist Enterprise?" in: Pinchas Ginosar and Avi Bareli (eds) *Zionism: A Contemporary Debate (Tsionut: Pulmus Ben Zmanenu)*. Ben Gurion University: Beer Sheva, pp. 340–375 (Heb).
31 Ibid., pp. 342–343.
32 Ibid., p. 345.
33 *Palestine Royal Commission Report* (Peel Report) (the Secretary of State for the Colonies to Parliament by Command of His Majesty) July 1937, p. 47.
34 Dan Horowitz and Moshe Lissak (1978) *Origins of the Israeli Polity*. University of Chicago Press: Chicago, p. 38.
35 John Hayes Holmes (1929) (1977) *Palestine To-Day and To-Morrow: A Gentile's Survey of Zionism*. Arno Press: New York, pp. 153–154, 152. Also cited in Assaf Likhovski (1995) "In Our Image: Colonial Discourse and the Anglicization of the Law of Mandatory Palestine," *Israel Law Review*, 29(3), pp. 291–359, 299.
36 Nicholas B. Dirks (1992) "Introduction," in: Dirks (ed.) *Colonialism and Culture*. University of Michigan Press: Ann Arbor, pp. 1–25, 9. Also see Edward Said (1978) *Orientalism*. Penguin Books: London.
37 Nurit Gertz (1995) *Captive of a Dream: National Myths in Israeli Culture*. Am Oved: Tel Aviv, pp. 38–43 (reporting on dominant narratives during the 1948 war); Gertz argues that literary texts of the 1920s and 1930s tended to romanticize the East and its Arab incarnation (see, e.g., her references to Itamar Even-Zohar (1988) "The Growth and Crystallisation of a Local and Native Hebrew Culture in Eretz Yisrael 1882–1948," *Cathedra* 16). However, it seems

to me that by the 1920s the representation of the East as a backward-looking culture occupied notable space. Moreover, the more the East had been concretized in the actual living Arab native, and the actual dirty and chaotic Arab town, the more the disrespectful attitude assumed the upper hand (see, e.g., the idea behind the establishment of Tel Aviv in 1909, when bourgeois Jews planned a neighborhood that would be distinctly different in style and order from neighboring Jaffa). Examples are cited in Nurit Gertz (1988) *Literature and Ideology in Eretz Yisrael During the 1930s*. Open University of Israel: Tel Aviv, p. 59 (Heb).

38 Cited in: Yigal Elam (1975) *An Introduction to Zionist History*. Lewin-Epstein: Tel Aviv, p. 35 (Heb).
39 Lockman (op. cit., pp. 214, 226, 236) traces the influence of European colonial discourse on Zionism, arguing that the land was represented as essentially empty, the indigenous population as lacking in rational agency, and the Arab workers as essentially degraded. He cites Zionist leaders who referred to the 'lowly state' of the Arab workers and to their 'primitive culture' and describes how this discourse shaped the identity and consciousness of the emerging Jewish working class; speaking on the one hand about the duty to educate Arab workers and to pull them out of their degraded state, and on the other about the need to exclude Arabs from the Jewish employment sector in order to prevent the Jewish worker from falling into that same state.
40 David Malouf (1994) *Remembering Babylon*. Vintage Books: New York, pp. 8–9.
41 Ibid., pp. 129–130.
42 Amitav Ghosh (1997) "The Indian National Army," *New Yorker*, June 23 & 30, pp. 63–66.
43 Gyan Prakash (1992) "Writing Post-Orientalist Histories of the Third World: Indian Historiography is Good to Think," in: Nicholas B. Dirks (ed.) *Colonialism and Culture*. University of Michigan Press: Ann Arbor.
44 Ibid., p. 359.
45 Partha Chatterjee (1986) *Nationalist Thought and the Colonial World*. University of Minnesota Press: Minneapolis.
46 See Nurit Gertz (1995) *Captive of a Dream: National Myths in Israeli Culture*. Am Oved: Tel Aviv, p. 43 (Heb).
47 Yael Zerubavel (1995) *Recovered Roots: Collective Memory and the Making of Israeli National Tradition*. University of Chicago Press: Chicago.
48 Paltiel Dickstein (1927) "Tchiyat Mishpatenu Beyadenu" (Our Legal Revival is at Our Own Hands), *Ha'Aretz* 1.6.27, p. 2.
49 Shmuel Eisenstadt (1910) "Le'Korot Ha'Mishpat Ha'Ivri" (The History of Hebrew Law) in: *He'Atid: Me'Asef Safruti Mada'i Le'berur Inyanei Ha'Yahadut ve'Ha'yehudim (The Future: A Literary Collection of Essays on Jews and Judaism)*. Sinai: Berlin, pp. 194–208, 208.
50 Paltiel Dickstein (1927) "Tchiyat Mishpatenu Beyadenu" (Our Legal Revival is at Our Own Hands), Part 1, *Ha'Aretz* 1.6.27, p. 2, Part 2, *Ha'Aretz* 2.6.27, p. 2.
51 Assaf Goldberg (1954) "Mishpat, Am, ve'Lashon" (Law, Nation and Language), *Hapraklit*, 1, February 1954, pp. 139–152, 142.

52 Assaf Likhovski (1998) "The Invention of 'Hebrew Law' in Mandatory Palestine," *American Journal of Comparative Law*, x/vi, Spring 1998, 2, pp. 339–79.

2 WHOSE TRADITION? IMAGERIES OF THE PAST IN HEBREW LAW

1 Memorandum by Jacob Thon, manager of the Zionist Palestine Office, 1.10.19, CZA J1/48. The memorandum also stated "the great importance [of the courts] for our internal autonomy and new cultural life" and committed the judges of the court to the fusion of "modern law" with "Jewish traditional law" that would be based "on our old legal conceptions and inspired by the Jewish spirit." The memorandum referred to J. Thon, Mordechai Eliash, Daniel Auster, Dr Donkelblum and Dr Yisrael Mani as the active jurists of the courts. On the history of the Hebrew Law of Peace, as recorded by one of its central advocates, see: Paltiel Dickstein (1964) *Toldot Mishpat ha'Shalom ha'Ivri* (Publishers: Tel Aviv. Hebrew Law of Peace).
2 Open letter by Moshe Gissin, published in *Ha'Or* 24 Menachem Av, TR'A (1910) pp. 1–2. For another instance in which Kook's judicial role alienated the secular "new generation," see: Yossi Avneri (1985) "Ha'Rav Avraham Yitzchak Hacohen Cook, Raba shel Yaffo, Tarsad-Tarad" (Rabby Kook, The Rabby of Jaffa 1904–1914) *Cathedra* 37, pp. 49–82. Avneri also discusses the growing tension between the 'old' and 'new' Yishuv in the context of the Hebrew Law of Peace.
3 Avneri, ibid. Also see: Sha'i Agnon (1976) *Me'Azmi el Azmi*. Shoken: Jerusalem; Mordechai Ben Hilel Hacohen (1925) *Mishpat Ha'shalom Ha'ivri*. Tel Aviv; for a sociological analysis see: Menachem Friedman (1978) *Society and Religion (Hevra ve Dat: Ha'ortodoxia Ha'lo Tzionit Be'Eretz Yisrael 1918–1936)*. Yad Ben Zvi: Jerusalem. Friedman writes, "The establishment of (the Hebrew Court of Peace in 1909) already expressed the distrust of the Zionist leadership of the new Yishuv in rabbis and rabbinical law" (ibid., p. 75). On the attempts of the rabbinical establishment to prevent the opening of a Hebrew Court of Peace in Jerusalem in 1919, see Friedman, ibid., pp. 116–117.
4 Friedman, ibid., p. 75, citing A. Loidolpol.
5 Memorandum of the Hebrew Law of Peace to the XV World Zionist Congress in London, 1927. CZA K11/361.
6 Abraham Cordova (1980) "The Institutionalization of a Cultural Center in Palestine: The Writers' Association," *Jewish Social Studies*, 1980, pp. 37–62. Cordova argues that the crystalization of this cultural center (e.g., the establishment of the Writers' Association) was characterized by a general adherence to the basic definition of the situation as set by the labor movement: 'Culture' was an important aspect of the nation-building process as long as it was clearly demarcated as a 'non-political' activity or, alternatively, as an activity that bore no elements of political dissent. The members of the Odessa and Warsaw centers who emigrated to Palestine, accordingly, by and large conformed to the existing political order. They were neither critics of the social order nor had they ventured to offer 'cultural' alternatives to the

paths of nation-building that gradually assumed shape under the hegemony of the labor movement.
7 Prime importance has been given to two compilations: *Even Ha-Ezer* and *Hoshen Mishpat*, which are part of the *Shulhan Arukh* (Set Table). For a sociological narration of the history of Jewish law, see: Max Weber (1978) *Economy and Society* (Max Rheinstein ed.). University of California Press: Berkeley, pp. 823–828.
8 Menachem Elon (1988) *Jewish Law: History, Sources, Principles*. The Jewish Publication Society: Philadelphia, p. 2. Community discipline sometimes involved the sanction of excommunication when dealing with recalcitrant members of the community and the often strict prohibition against litigating in non-Jewish courts (see: Louis Finkelstein (1964) *Jewish Self-government in the Middle Ages*. Philipp Feldheim: New York). Marianne Constable refers to a Synod of Rabbis "of Troyes, of Dijon, of Auxerre, of Sens, of Orleans, of Chalons, of Rheims, of Paris, of Melun, of Etampes and their neighborhoods; of Normandy, of the Coast of the Sea, of Anjou, of Poitou; and of the great men of Lothair" (who) ordered the excommunication of "every man or woman, far or near, who summon his neighbor before a Gentile tribunal, or compel him through Gentiles, whether lord or common man, ruler or official, unless the consent of both has been given beforehand in the presence of pure Jewish witnesses." Marianne Constable (1995) *The Law of the Other*. University of Chicago Press: Chicago, p. 19.
9 See the position of jurists and lawyers in chapters 6 and 7 of this book.
10 Paltiel Dickstein (1926) "Mishpat ha'Shalom ha'Ivri" (The Hebrew Law of Peace), *Hamishpat ha'Ivri*, 1, pp. 147–150, 148.
11 Paltiel Dickstein (1949) "Lesium Pe'ulot Batei Mishpat Hashalom ha'Ivri" (The End of the Hebrew Courts of Peace), *Hapraklit*, 6(1–12), pp. 156–159, 158.
12 Memorandum of the Hebrew Law of Peace to the XV World Zionist Congress in London, 1927. CZA K11/361, p. 5.
13 Shmuel Eisenstadt (1910) "Le'Korot Ha'Mishpat Ha'Ivri" (The History of Hebrew Law), in: *He'Atid: Me'Asef Safruti Mada'i Le'berur Inyanei Ha'Yahadut ve'Ha'yehudim* (The Future: A Literary Collection of Essays on Jews and Judaism). Sinai: Berlin, pp. 194–208, 201.
14 Marianne Constable (1994) *The Law of the Other*. University of Chicago Press: Chicago, p. 9.
15 Abraham B. Yehoshua (1997) *Voyage to the End of the Millennium*. Sifria Chadasha: Kibutz Meuchad (Heb).
16 Ibid., pp. 78–79.
17 Ibid., p. 80.
18 Ibid., p. 82.
19 Ibid., p. 99.
20 Ibid., pp. 103–104.
21 Ibid., p. 111.
22 Ibid., p. 130.
23 The original text promulgating this ordinance has been lost, yet Jewish tradition ordinarily ascribes it to Rabbenu Gershom (R. Gershom b. Yehouda of Mayence), a rabbinical scholar and law-giver who fostered the organization

of synods for German and French communities in the tenth century. Contemporary historians, however, dispute the immediate circumstances that produced this ordinance as well as the details of its temporal and territorial applicability. The ordinance's first known appearance in writing was only at the time of Rashi, an eleventh-century scholar, and some speculate that it actually originated at that time in response to the First Crusade and the growing pressure on Jews from their Christian 'superiors.' I believe that is indeed the case; the ordinance was referred to R. Gershom only in order to increase its enforceability among the dispersed Jewish communities of medieval Europe, hence the setting of cross-cultural conflict of this story. Also see: Louis Finkelstein (1964) *Jewish Self-government in the Middle Ages.* Philipp Feldheim: New York; Zeev Falk (1961) *Marriage and Divorce.* Mif'al ha'Shichpul: Jerusalem; Elimelech Vestreich (1998) "Polygamy and Forcing a Woman to Divorce in the Rulings of Ashkenazi Scholars of the Eleventh and Twelfth Centuries," *Mechkarey Mishpat,* 6.

24 Yael Zerubavel (1995) *Recovered Roots: Collective Memory and the Making of Israeli National Tradition.* University of Chicago Press: Chicago, p. xviii.

25 Gadi Elgazi makes this point about law in asking: "How to settle the ongoing invention of tradition with the ongoing forgetfulness of the fact that it is being invented, a forgetfulness which is a condition for validating 'tradition' as such?" in: Gadi Elgazi (1997) "Tavnit Nof Moladeto: Nicolaus Cusanus, the Farmers of the Mossel and Rural Law," in B. Z. Kedar (ed.) *Hatarbut.* Shazar Center: Israel, pp. 123–139, 127–128.

26 *Ha'tor,* 7(40), p. 2 (1.7.27); 2(13), p. 3 (1922). On the attitude of Zionist institutions towards the Hebrew Law of Peace see chapter 7.

27 *Ha'tor,* 22(33), p. 14 (10.8.28).

28 *Ha'tor,* 7(40), p. 1 (1.7.27).

29 Menachem Elon (1994) *Jewish Law.* The Jewish Publication Society: Philadelphia. Elon further adds that the term Hebrew law was used as early as the end of the nineteenth century. Elon also defines the term as "denoting that part of the *Halakhah* that corresponds to the areas of law that make up the *corpus juris* of other legal systems today," using the term to distinguish between the civil and religious aspects of Jewish law (ibid., p. 110).

30 *Hator,* 8(21), p. 8 (11.5.28). Also see: A. Y. Shirman (1922) "Mishpat Hashalom," *Hator,* 2(13), p. 2.

31 Assaf Likhovski (1998) "The Invention of 'Hebrew Law' in Mandatory Palestine," *American Journal of Comparative Law,* 46(2), pp. 301–335, 302.

32 Paltiel Dickstein (1927) "Split Opinions among Judges" (Hilukey Deot Be'Hitya'azut Shoftim), *Ha'Mishpat,* 1, pp. 315–317.

33 Elon, ibid., p. 444.

34 Paltiel Dickstein (1949) "Lesium Pe'ulot Batei Mishpat Hashalom ha'Ivri" (The End of the Hebrew Courts of Peace), *Hapraklit,* 6(1–12), pp. 156–159.

35 See e.g., *Encyclopedia Talmudit* pp. 72–99; Hilel Ben-Sasson (ed.) (1976) *The Jewish Community in the Middle-Ages.* Zalman Shazar: Israeli Historical Society: Jerusalem.

36 Elon, op. cit., p. 31, fn 100. See: Eliezer Goldman (1997) *Mechkarim ve'Iunim: Hagut Yehudit Be'avar U'ba'hove* in Dani Statman and Avi Sagi (eds) Y. L.

Magnes: Jerusalem. Goldman argues that the existence of a rigid Jewish legal codex is a myth and that rabbinical authority throughout the ages had been quite loose and dependent on local ordering and community practices, (ibid., p. 78).
37 Ehud Luz (1985) *Parallels Meet, Religion and Nationalism in the Early Zionist Movement (1882–1904)*. Om Oved: Tel Aviv, p. 237 (Heb).
38 Paltiel Dickstein (1925) "On the Hebrew Law of Peace," in: P. Dickstein (ed.) *The Hebrew Law of Peace*. Hebrew Law of Peace Publishers: Tel Aviv, p. 14 (Heb).
39 Those present at the first meeting (October 26, 1926) were Messrs Rosenboim, Horgin, Rosenthal, Rapoport, Friedenberg, Yaacobson, Meir, Bebkov, Epstein-Halevi, H'at and Dickstein. Two expert witnesses were also invited: Messrs Belkovski and Gorodiski. At a second meeting (December 7, 1926), the above were joined by Messrs Ben-Hillel Ha'Cohen, Zeiger, Gluskin, Azaria, Shershevski, and Soferski. Messrs Salomon, Duchan, Shmeterling and Ben Zvi, all jurists and lawyers, expressed written opinions. See protocols of the High Hebrew Court of Peace, State Archive, 76/P, box 629.
40 Rosenbaum, 2nd meeting
41 Freidenberg, 1st meeting.
42 Horgin, 1st meeting.
43 Gluskin, 2nd meeting.
44 Dickstein, 1st meeting.
45 On the inability of the Hebrew Law of Peace to secure itself a standing in matters of public law, see chapter 7.
46 *Ha'tor*, 7(9), p. 2 (19.11.26).
47 Shapira writes that with the formal establishment of rabbinical courts under the auspices of the colonial state, the Hebrew Courts of Peace came to an end. Yet the fact is that the Hebrew Courts of Peace were still active and highly visible in later years. However, Shapira's view does reflect a true sentiment: already in the 1920s there were many who thought that the formal state-protected establishment of rabbinical courts signaled the ultimate demise of the Hebrew Courts of Peace. Anita Shapira (1995) "Political History of the Yishuv, 1918–1935," in: Moshe Lissak, Anita Shapira and Gabriel Cohen (eds) *The History of the Jewish Community in Eretz-Israel Since 1882, The Period of the British Mandate, Part Two*. Israel Academy for Sciences and Humanities and the Bialik Institute: Jerusalem, pp. 1–61.

INTERREGNUM

1 Barry Unsworth (1995) *Morality Play*. Norton: New York.
2 Ibid., pp. 61–63.
3 Ibid., pp. 71–75.
4 Ibid., p. 79.
5 Michel Foucault (1972) "The Discourse on Language," in: *The Archeology of Knowledge*. Pantheon Books: New York.
6 Ibid., pp. 221–223.
7 Unsworth, ibid., p. 78.

3 STATE LAW AND COMMUNAL JUSTICE

1. Marianne Constable (1995) *The Law of the Other*. University of Chicago Press: Chicago.
2. Ibid., p. 7.
3. Ibid., p. 16.
4. Ibid., p. 25.
5. Ibid., p. 26.
6. Ibid., p. 67.
7. Ibid., p. 27.
8. Paltiel Dickstein (1925) "On the Hebrew Law of Peace," in: P. Dickstein (ed.). *The Hebrew Law of Peace*. Hebrew Law of Peace Publishers: Tel Aviv, p. 17 (Heb).
9. Sally Engle Merry (1988) "Legal Pluralism," *Law and Society Review*, 22(5), pp. 869–896.
10. Paltiel Dickstein (1926) "National and Governmental Courts," *Ha'Aretz*, 5.9.26, p. 2: "Even if the British would have imposed a Hebrew system of laws and appointed Jewish judges (however unfair to the Arab population), this system would not have fulfilled the true national interest because it would only lead to assimilation with the colonized majority." I read the above as an indication of the idea that a national-Hebrew distinction, from both British colonizers and Arab colonized, was prioritized over a state-imposed legal system.
11. Ibid., p. 2.
12. Constable, op. cit., p. 18.
13. Elon, op. cit., p. 15, fn 39.
14. Constable, op. cit., p. 19.
15. Alan Hunt (1992) "Foucault's Expulsion of Law: Towards a Retrieval," *Law and Social Inquiry* 17(1), p. 5. Hunt's formulation was offered in the context of his polemic against Foucault's "expulsion of law."
16. See, e.g., Carol J. Greenhouse, Babara Yngvesson and David M. Engel (1994) *Law and Community in Three American Towns*. Cornell University Press: Ithaca, NY.
17. A resolution to that effect was taken by the first convention of the Hebrew Law of Peace in 1922: "The convention declares the duty of the Hebrew public in general and the public institutions in particular to bring their disputes before the Hebrew Law of Peace and not to shirk it whether as plaintiffs or defendant." Resolutions of the First Convention of the Repre-sentatives of the Hebrew Courts of Peace, 9–10 Shvat, TRP'B, 1922, in: P. Dickstein (ed.) (1925) *The Hebrew Law of Peace*. Hebrew Law of Peace Publishers: Tel Aviv (Heb).
18. The sanction was formalized in the official regulations of the Hebrew Courts of Peace. Articles 20–23 read as follows: "Article 20: Whenever a defendant refuses to litigate or to comply with a decision of the court, the court tries to force him to do so by invoking the power of public institutions. When this does not suffice, the court notifies the High Hebrew Court of Peace and delivers to it all relevant documents. 21: The High Hebrew Court of Peace, on

the basis of said materials, decides to notify committees and public institutions and/or to publish the shirking. When the relevant material does not suffice to produce a decision, the matter is referred back to the lower court, so that all possible means are used to coerce the shirker into obeying the court. 22: In case of shirking – the plaintiff is entitled to demand that the court issue a note to that effect. 23: The Hebrew Court of Peace will not accept any complaints from a shirker until obedience is forthcoming. Where a shirker seeks to redeem himself, and the local Court of Peace finds grounds for removing the stigma, the matter is resolved by the High Hebrew Court of Peace." See: Regulations of the Hebrew Courts of Peace, in: P. Dickstein (ed.) (1925) *The Hebrew Law of Peace*. Hebrew Law of Peace Publishers: Tel Aviv (Heb).

19 See State Archive 76(P) (unclassified box), document of The Jewish Committee of Jaffa, 17 Sivan TR'P (1920). The letter, addressed to the Hebrew Law of Peace, sought to coordinate sanctions: Hebrew Courts of Peace would not consider applications made by persons who did not pay their taxes to the town committee, and the latter, in turn, would not assist those who refused to litigate in the Hebrew Courts of Peace. A handwritten comment in the margins of the document, added by Shmuel Pen, the chairperson of the Jaffa Court of Peace, dismissed the proposal: "One should not mix judicial matters with tax collection issues. The Hebrew people are not allowed to use the courts of the state and under no circumstances should we decline their turning to us because it would turn them to the courts of the government ... the Hebrew Law is one of the trademarks of national revival, and we must educate the people to use it and to respect its judges. The honor of our institution is degraded when we engage in matters relating to collection of taxes."

20 Data published by the Hebrew Courts of Peace established the rate of shirkers for the 1920s at 5–8 percent of total litigation rates. See *Hamishpat ha'Ivri*, 2 (1927), pp. 251–252.

21 In one case, defendants who were summoned to trial wrote the Tel Aviv Hebrew Court of Peace that they would submit to its jurisdiction only if they would be notified in advance as to the identity of the judges who had been assigned to sit in judgment. The reason for setting such terms, they wrote, was due to the fact that the Court's Chief Secretary (Paltiel Dickstein) was biased against them: "We are better prepared to be included in the list of *shirkers*," they wrote, "than to allow the secretary to torture us." The embarrassment was all the greater because the writers of the letter, Sa'adia Shoshani and Avraham Eitan, happened to be two prominent members of the community, and as such were also included in the Hebrew Court of Peace's list of judges. They were consequently removed from the list, and a letter announcing them to be *shirkers* was sent to the plaintiffs. State Archive, 76 (P), Box 635, File 200.

22 Paltiel Dickstein (1925) "On the Hebrew Law of Peace," in: P. Dickstein (ed.) (1925) *The Hebrew Law of Peace*. Hebrew Law of Peace Publishers: Tel Aviv, p. 9; also see a protocol of a meeting of Hebrew law judges who raised similar complaints (in particular see Bebkov and Yaacobson) in State Archives, 76/P Box 643.

23 A letter from Daniel Auster, Chairperson of the Hebrew Law of Peace, to the Hebrew Law of Peace in Zichron-Ya'acov, 8.1.20. CZA J1/50. The same general recommendation, to prefer "education" and "persuasion" over state enforcement, was also formalized in the official regulations of the Hebrew Law of Peace.
24 See note 18, above.
25 State Archive, 76 (P), Box 644, File 744 (1925) Dr Haya Fogel vs. The Town Council of Kfar-Sava.
26 CZA J1/50 A letter from Daniel Auster to Eliahu Berlin 28.6.20.
27 CZA J1/50 21.7.20.
28 J1/50 A letter from Daniel Auster to Eliahu Berlin 28.6.20.
29 Notice No. 32, 17.2.20.
30 See document dated 29.11.26 (CZA J1/50).
31 The Arbitration Ordinance (*Palestine Gazette* 172, 1.10.26) validated proceedings in which the parties did not name particular arbitrators but only a designated arbitration court, thereby indirectly legitimizing the institutional standing of the Hebrew Courts of Peace which could now operate even in the absence of pre-arranged judges to which the parties consented beforehand. Various archival documents indicate that activists of the Hebrew Law of Peace, together with officials of the Zionist Executive, were deeply involved in negotiations prior to the enactment of the ordinance and seem to have had a considerable impact upon its eventual content. See, e.g., a letter from the Hebrew Law of Peace to the Zionist Executive of 22.4.26, acknowledging the constructive input of the latter (CZA J1/50). The advocates of the Hebrew Law of Peace hoped that the new ordinance would increase the volume of litigation in their courts: see protocol of 1926 judges' meeting (State Archive 76(P), Box 643).
32 A detailed account of the memorandum submitted to the Chief Justice was published in the daily *Davar*, 19.8.27, p. 1.
33 In the case of Bella Vermouth vs. David Brumberg. See Paltiel Dickstein (1964) *Toldot Mishpat ha'Shalom ha'Ivri* (*The History of the Hebrew Law of Peace*). Yavne: Tel Aviv. Another decision of a Jerusalem court, in which the Hebrew Courts of Peace were referred to as legitimate forums in which liquidators could sue and be sued, was also noted with favor in the Hebrew press; see *Davar*, 4.7.27, p. 9.
34 Norman Bentwich (1926) "Recognition of Hebrew Law in the Constitution of Eretz-Yisrael," *Hamishpat ha'Ivri*, 1, pp. 129–136.
35 Merry: 1988.
36 For a detailed analysis of the political negotiations leading to the establishment of the Chief Rabbinate see Menachem Friedman (1978) *Hevra ve'Dat* (*Society and Religion*). Ben-Zvi: Jerusalem, pp. 112–126.
37 Ibid., p. 118.
38 Yisrael Kolatt (1994) "Religion, Society and State at the Time of the National Home" in Almog, Reinhartz, Shapira (eds) *Zionism and Religion* pp. 329–372, 343.
39 Kolatt, ibid., p. 350 on the standpoint of Ben Gurion.
40 For detailed accounts of the events leading to the British initiative and the response of various Jewish groups thereof, see: Anita Shapira (1995)

"Political History of the Yishuv, 1918–1935" in Moshe Lissak, Anita Shapira and Gabriel Cohen (eds) *The History of the Jewish Community in Eretz-Israel Since 1882, The Period of the British Mandate, Part Two (History of Jewish Settlement in Eretz-Israel Since the First Aliyah)*, pp. 1–61 in particular 25–34; Shulamit Eliash (1985) "The Chief Rabbinate and Ha'Mizrachi During the Mandate," *Cathedra* 37, pp. 123–148; Kolatt, op. cit., pp. 329–372.

41 *Ha'Tor* 2(13), p. 4. On the decision of the Hebrew Law of Peace not to assert jurisdiction over the Chief Rabbinate see chapter 2.
42 HCJ 3269/95, PD 50(4), 590. Katz vs. The Jerusalem Regional Rabbinical Court.
43 Ibid., p. 596.
44 See: Menachem Mautner (1999) "A Rabbinical Court in Netivot", in Adi Ophir (ed.) *Fifty to Forty-Eight*, Van Leer: Jerusalem, pp. 467–475 (Heb); (forthcoming) "Between Netivot and Jerusalem" *Teoria u'Bikoret (Theory and Critique)*; Issaschar Rosen-Zvi (1998) "The Subject, the Community and Legal Pluralism" *Iunei Mishpat*.
45 In this respect, the current heated debate between the orthodoxy and the Jewish reform (mainly North American) communities follows the rules of an already established game. The debate, conducted in the state's legislative and judicial arenas, is mainly on the question of "who is an authorized rabbi?"
46 Yael Zerubavel (1995) *Recovered Roots: Collective Memory and the Making of Israeli National Tradition*. University of Chicago Press: Chicago, p. 21.
47 Friedman, op. cit., pp. 126–127.
48 Zerubavel, op. cit., p. 18.
49 Shapira, op. cit., p. 34.
50 Kolatt, op. cit., p. 44.

4 CELEBRATING AUTHENTICITY AND PRACTICING HYBRIDITY

1 In his diary, Eisenstadt described the first meeting of the society in 1918 and the decision to invite Dickstein to settle in Moscow and join the project. Eisenstadt then recorded his first impression of Dickstein: "Our friend Paltiel Dickstein also came from the south to reside in hungry and pain-ridden Moscow, to contain himself within the narrow confines of the Halakah. It was the first time I met him: silent, slender-faced, well-mannered, a concise and realistic style, a true understanding of our legalistic problem. I think he will adapt to our collegial work ... he does not boast twice a day over his personality and over the depth of his work, and the spiritual serenity that surrounds him leads me to trust him more than I trust others. The neglected science of Hebrew Law cries for collective work and perhaps within a few days we shall so be engaged." Lavon Archive, File (4)-104–13–5 Hebrew Law Society in Moscow, under S. Eisenstadt.
2 The Hebrew Law Society was founded in 1918 by Rabbi Yaacov Mazeh, Dr Yehouda Yonowitz, Asher Gulak, Shoshana and Yosef Persitz, and Shmuel Eisenstadt. This cooperation between secular and orthodox Zionists was in itself rare. While the Russian intelligentsia considered the cultural question to be the most important one confronting Zionism, orthodox Zionists

tended to identify with the Zionist movement precisely because its mainstream center prioritized instrumental politics over cultural endeavors (See: Ehud Luz (1985) *Parallels Meet: Religion and Nationalism in the Early Zionist Movement (1882–1904).* Am Oved: Tel Aviv). Indeed, cooperation in the Hebrew Law Society began to falter as soon as the orthodox members realized that Dickstein and his friends envisioned a national secular Hebrew law. On the intellectual history of the society in Palestine, albeit one that does not detail the tensions between secular and orthodox members, see: Assaf Likhovski (1998) "Mishpat Ivri ve'Idiologia Zionit be'Eretz Yisrael ha'Mandatorit" (Hebrew Law and Zionist Ideology in Mandatory Palestine), in: Menachem Mautner, Avi Sagi and Ronen Shamir (eds) *Multiculturalism in a Democratic and Jewish State.* Ramot: Tel Aviv, pp. 633–659.

3   Shmuel Eisenstadt's private diary, Lavon Archive file (4)–104–13–5.
4   The findings are based on a review of all cases handled by the High Hebrew Court of Peace between 1922 and 1927, at the peak of this court's activities. Findings concerning lower-tiered courts are based on a seriatim reading of all Tel Aviv area files between 1922 and 1927 and samples of cases handled by other local and district courts. Source: State Archive, File No. 177 (Box 235) January 22, 1923.
5   Max Weber (Max Rheinstein ed.) (1978) *Economy and Society.* University of California Press: Berkeley, p. 826.
6   Elon, op. cit., p. G6.
7   State Archive. Also see the case of Bodizki vs. Hak (district Haifa), State Archive 76(P), Box 636, files 203, 258, 263: Plaintiff sued for breach of contract. Seller contracted with plaintiff and sold the disputed land to a third party. The contract stipulated a penalty for such a breach. Defendant claimed that he promised to sell to the third party before making the contract with plaintiff. The court ruled that plaintiff was aware of the promise made to the third party and only a formal written contract was needed to complete the sale to said third party. Thus, although the court held to a principled position that contracts had to be respected, it also held the case as "an exception" and decided that "the third party had a moral right to the land" and acquitted defendant from charge of breach. On appeal, the decision was reversed. The court ruled that the fact that plaintiff had prior knowledge of the promise to the third party had only "moral implications," citing *Hoshen Mishpat* as a source of the rule that one who bought an object which another had sought to buy was "mean" (*"rasha"*) and yet this condemnation was insufficient to nullify the contract. The court also referred to its own precedents and to German and English law. On a further appeal, under a special procedure, parties submitted detailed legal briefs based on Jewish law. Also see files 259, 250, 251, in 76 (P), Box 636 and files 252, 235 in P/635 (e.g., file 235, Ha'Haklai vs. Kupat Poalim: A principled ruling according to which a fine for breach of contract, although specified in the contract, was void when it was unreasonably high, on the basis of *Hoshen Mishpat.*
8   Neta Ziv, upon reading this chapter, noted that the phenomenom described above is also relevant for understanding the present-day predicament of non-orthodox Jews in Israel. In the absence of non-orthodox Jewish studies,

the educational system of Israel tends to reproduce ignorance which feeds back into the inability of non-orthodox Jews to negotiate the meaning of Judaism and to claim a position from which to reconstruct Jewish memory and tradition.

9   Most of these efforts were abortive. Thirty judges served on the Hebrew High Court of Peace interchangeably until 1927, yet only ten had legal education and only eight were licensed to practice as lawyers. The courts operating outside the larger settlements had no lawyer-judges at all, and in Tel Aviv, where sixty-one judges served interchangeably on the local Municipal Court (the lowest instance) and the District Court (mid-level instance) until 1926, only five lawyers and three persons with legal education assumed judgeship duties. See: Paltiel Dickstein (1964) *Toldot Mishpat ha'Shalom ha'Ivri* (*The History of the Hebrew Law of Peace*). Yavne: Tel Aviv, chapters 7–8; *HaMishpat*, 1, 1927, pp. 191–192.
10 Paltiel Dickstein (1949) "Lesium Pe'ulot Batei Mishpat Hashalom ha'Ivri" (The End of the Hebrew Courts of Peace), *Hapraklit*, 6(1–12), pp. 156–159.
11 *Ha'Aretz*, 1.6.27, p. 2, "The Revival of our Law is at Our Hands."
12 See, e.g., file 179, 5.2.23, in which the court reversed a substantive decision on grounds that the appeal had not been submitted within the time specified in the procedural regulations of the Hebrew Law of Peace. In fact, there were times when lawyers pressed the court to be less formalistic, urging it to adhere to the principles of "finding out the truth on the basis of the consciousness of the heart," often to no avail, see, e.g., State Archive 76(P), Box 556, File 198, 10.6.23 Weitzman vs. Goldberg. Also see early correspondence between Daniel Auster and the Hebrew Court of Haifa, instructing them on new procedures, urging them to strictly follow formal requirements (letters of 6.5.20 and 20.5.20 (CZA J1/45.)
13 The first edition of the Hebrew Law Regulations (1922) had 117 clauses. The 1924 edition added another 38 clauses, and the revised 1927 edition a further 274 clauses. A committee of five (Bebkov, Berlin, Dickstein, Yaacobson and Rosenboim) invested seven months and went beyond revision to include whole new chapters on evidentiary rules, disciplinary rules and general procedural requirements. See *Davar*, 29.9.27, p. 3.
14 On the history of the Hebrew Law Society, see Assaf Likhovski (1998) "The Invention of 'Hebrew Law' in Mandatory Palestine," *American Journal of Comparative Law*, 46(2), pp. 301–335. The Hebrew Law Society received the blessing of Norman Bentwich, the Mandatory government's Legal Adviser; Gad Frumkin, the most senior Jewish judge in the Mandatory administration, served as president. The Hebrew Law Society saw the tense cooperation of orthodox and secular enthusiasts: Simcha Assaf, Asher Gulak, Paltiel Dickstein, Mordechai Eliash, Kalman Friedenberg and Shmuel Eisenstadt, among others.
15 *Ha'Mishpat Ha'Ivri*, 1, 1926, pp. v–vi.
16 Weber, op. cit., pp. 657–658.
17 Ibid., p. 874.
18 Ibid., p. 886.
19 Ibid., p. 886.

20. Ibid., p. 887, fn 23: H. Isay 1929.
21. J. Herget and S. Wallace (1987) "The German Free Law Movement as the Source of American Legal Realism," *Virginia Law Review* 73, pp. 399–455, 407.
22. Weber, op. cit., p. 867.
23. Herget and Wallace, op. cit., p. 407.
24. Ibid., p. 415, citing Fuchs.
25. See annotations to Weber's text at 897, fn 20.
26. Weber, op. cit., p. 887, fn. 24, referring to Ehrlich's position.
27. See Eisenstadt reference to Kohler's work in Shmuel Eisenstadt (1931) *Ein Mishpat: Sefer Shimush Bibliography le-Sifrut ha-Mishpat ha-Ivri (The Fountain of Law: A Bibliography of Hebrew Law)* (Repertorium Bibliographicum) Mishpat: Jerusalem, pp. xix–xxvi.
28. See a report on the convention of the Hebrew Law Society and a summary of Dickstein's public speech in *ha'Mishpat ha'Ivri*, 2, 1926, 234.
29. Paltiel Dickstein (1925) "On the Hebrew Law of Peace," in: P. Dickstein (1925) *The Hebrew Law of Peace*. Hebrew Law of Peace Publishers: (1925), Tel Aviv.
30. Likhovski, op. cit., p. 318.
31. Paltiel Dickstein (1927) "The Revival of Law is at Our Hands," *Ha'Aretz*, 1.6.27, p. 2.
32. The appeal of wide discretionary powers, modeled on the Soviet example, was also articulated by Yisrael Bar Shira, a Zionist socialist activist who worked to promote workers' justice tribunals (see chapter 7). Bar Shira thus proposed to model the judicial process on the basis of article 4 of the Russian civil procedure code, which advised judges to use discretionary powers "in line with the general politics of the farmers' and workers' government." Bar Shira, in turn, suggested revising the phrase to guide judges to use discretion "in line with the general politics of the leadership of the Hebrew Federation of Labor." Yisrael Bar Shira (1930) "Lecheker Mahuto shel Mishpat haHaverim" (The Substance of the Comrades Law), *Hamishpat*, 4(3), pp. 103–113, 107.
33. An unknown writer, using the byline "A Lawyer," published "Law and Morality," in the daily *Davar*, 17.7.27, p. 2.
34. Shmuel Eisenstadt (1967) "On the History of Hebrew Law," in: *Zion with Justice*. Hamishpat: Tel Aviv, pp. 11–30.
35. Paltiel Dickstein (1922) "Law and Equity in the Hebrew Law of Peace," *ha'Poel ha'Tsair*, 33, pp. 5–7, 7.
36. Thurman Arnold (1934) "Trial by Combat and the New Deal," *Harvard Law Review*, 47, April, pp. 913–947, 922.
37. An unknown writer, using the byline "A Lawyer," published "Law and Morality," in the daily *Davar*, 17.7.27, p. 2. Another lawyer-activist, an enthusiast for 'workers' law' suited to the needs of the working class, also elaborated on the role the enlightened judge could be expected to play, along lines reminiscent the legal realists' approach to administrative forums: "Our fundamental goal is to find the truth. One should acknowledge the nature of the litigants who address us: Workers who do not possess legal education and lack legal understanding, not to mention legal sophistication. Exhausted

after a hard day's work, they arrive at night to assert their rights and to confront their peers. And if the other party's lawyer, or the other party himself, if talented, wishes to confuse the worker and to trap him in legal argumentation, he would always be able to do it ... We must therefore prevent the judge from becoming a passive observer of a competition in which he plays no part, but rather transform him into an active and conscious instructor. The judge must advise the weaker party who is not erudite in formalities and he must abstain from becoming a slave of formality himself." Yisrael Bar Shira (1930) "Lecheker Mahuto shel Mishpat haHaverim" (The Substance of the Comrades Law), *Hamishpat*, 4(3), pp. 103–113, 113.
38 Paltiel Dickstein (1927) "The Revival of Law is at Our Hands," *Ha'Aretz*, 1.6.27, p. 2.
39 Edward Said (1994) *Culture and Imperialism*. Vintage Books: New York, p. 15.
40 Sally Merry (1995) "Sorting Out Popular Justice," in: Sally Engle Merry and Neal Millner (eds) *The Possibility of Popular Justice*. Michigan University Press: Ann Arbor, p. 40.
41 Menachem Mautner (1993) *The Decline of Formalism and the Rise of Values in Israeli Law*. Ma'agaley Da'at: Tel Aviv.

5 NATIONALISM AS A DISCIPLINARY REGIME

1 De Han was a Dutch ultra-orthodox and anti-Zionist Jew who was a member of the executive of Agudat Israel, the ultra-orthodox political organ. He was a known public figure in Palestine and publicly denounced Zionism in articles and letters. His assassins were members of a Zionist organization. Laqueur writes that "some of [De Han's] writings were plainly antisemitic: The Jews stood for world revolution and a Jewish world government ... he dressed like an Arab and used to address Jews in Arabic ... De Han was assassinated in the streets of Jerusalem on 30 June 1924." Walter Lacqueur (1972) *A History of Zionism*. Weidenfeld and Nicolson: London, p. 410.
2 The case had significance beyond the 'national' aspect. Donkelblum argued that he sued in order to protect his professional reputation. Donkelblum was formerly the lawyer who assisted Shenkar in registering his company and drafting the firm's regulations. In another case, however, he represented a party against Shenkar. Shenkar therefore accused him of ethical misconduct. Donkelblum wanted the court to vindicate him. The court, however, ruled that Shenkar, "given his subjective feelings and the custom of the land from which he came, could consider the representation of his opponent by his former lawyer as unethical. Thus, while fining Shenkar for using insults against Donkelblum, the court implied that Donkelblum's behavior had been questionable. Donkelblum, understanding the implications, appealed the decision. He argued that a conviction in honor cases had to be established objectively and not subjectively and that Shenkar's accusation objectively damaged his reputation as a young lawyer. His appeal was granted and Shenkar was fined an additional three Pounds." State Archive 76/P box 636, High Hebrew Court 26–27, file 295.

3   State Archive 76/P box 644, file no. 4585, 21.5.25 Mann vs. Agronski, Municipal Hebrew Court of Peace, Tel Aviv.
4   The defendant was strongly reprimanded by the court for making these accusations and the judges resolved to emphasize that "monopoly over the Hebrew language was not at the hands of one person but rather at the hands of the entire Jewish Federation of Labor." State Archive 76/P box 644, file no. 1256, 26.3.24.
5   Yaffe vs. Shtander, State Archive 76/P box 644, file no. 4674, 7.7.25.
6   Meir Shalev (1988) *A Russian Novel (Roman Rusi)*. Am Oved: Tel Aviv, p. 274.
7   Case 763, 1st Instance, 16.10.26, Lavon Archive 4–245–2–80.
8   Max Gluckman (1963) "Gossip and Scandal," *Current Anthropology*, 4, pp. 307–316; Sally Engle Merry (1984) "Rethinking Gossip and Scandal," in: Donald Black (ed.) *Toward a General Theory of Social Control*, p. 296.
9   Merry, ibid., p. 279.
10 Ibid., p. 288.
11 Public shame in general, and the social costs of gossip in particular, were routinely debated in the Hebrew Courts of Peace. See State Archive 76/P box 644, file no. 4741, 4674, 4344.
12 Community law privileges local involvements and in this sense subverts the interaction-across-distance principle of state law and state-backed sanctions. The Hebrew Law of Peace, in its movement from community to nation, tried to ground nationalism in circumstances of co-presence. (I use Giddens's terminology, invoked in another context, in: Anthony Giddens (1990) *The Consequences of Modernity*. Cambridge: Polity Press, p. 63.
13 Compare Carol J. Greenhouse, Barbara Yngvesson and David M. Engel (1994) *Law and Community in Three American Towns*. Cornell University Press: Ithaca. Outsiders, lacking discreet means of resolving disputes, resort to law and thereby reproduce their standing as outsiders. Variation in the uses of law constitute one's relative distance from the community's imagined core.
14 This legal sanction is reminiscent of other nationalistic 'non-legal' sanctions characteristic of Israel. An example that comes to mind is the long-standing practice of labeling Israeli immigrants to other countries as "*yordim*", literally "going down," but connoting a sense of their being defectors and lower-grade persons. The fact that the practice has lost much of its vitality in recent years is probably related to the crisis of the Israeli state and to the weakening collective grip of Zionism.
15 See, e.g., State Archive 76/P box 636, 1925–26, file 244 (Public Works Office vs. Engineer Y. Berlin); box 635, 1923–24, file 183 (re: Advocate Gershman). In one case, a person initially refused to litigate, but threatened with the sanction, he argued at court that he was as "committed to the Hebrew Law of Peace as to all other autonomous institutions," and that his refusal stemmed from the fact that the plaintiff turned to a Hebrew court after he had failed to establish his case in a state court. The defendant therefore asked the court to create a new category, of a "plaintiff-*Shirker*", in order to deal with such cases (box 635, file 143.)
16 In the next chapter, I analyze the jurisdictional claims of the Hebrew Law of Peace in terms of a "professional project." The appeals to public opinion,

from this perspective, are analyzed as claims "for the legitimate control of a particular kind of work": see Andrew Abbott (1988) *The System of Professions*. Chicago University Press: Chicago, p. 60.

17 Letters between Dickstein and officials of the PZE were exchanged on 13.4.26, 22.4.26 (cited above), 6.5.26, 28.5.26, 2.6.26, 30.6.26, 6.7.26. CZA S/1–544.
18 The Second Convention took place on 20–21 Sivan, TRPZ (1927). A summary of resolutions was published in *HaMishpat haIvri*, 2, 1927, pp. 335–336.
19 Paltiel Dickstein (1928) "Le'Veidat Orchei Haddon" (To the Lawyers' Convention), in: Yitzchak Oren (1975) (ed.) *Prof. Paltiel Darkan: A Collection of Essays and Studies*. Yavne: Tel Aviv, pp. 42–44, reprint from *Ha'Aretz*, 8.4.28.
20 State Archive 76/P box 636, file 183, 20.1.23.
21 State Archive 76/P box 636, file 214, 6.2.24.
22 State Archive 76/P box 636, file 244, 12.11.24.
23 For a key work on the national as an imagined community see Benedict Anderson (1983) *Imagined Communities*. Verso: London.

SALLE D'ATTENTE

1 H. C. No. 54/26, collection of Judgments of the Courts of Palestine 1919–1933, p. 727.
2 The narrow definition suggested by the court was particularly harmful because it meant that women, as 'dependents,' were not ratepayers in themselves and thus not eligible to vote. A lot of public outrage was voiced over this particular issue and a major effort was made to amend the constitution of Tel Aviv in order to avoid that result.
3 H. C. No. 54/26, delivered on 1.10.26. On the impact of these two decisions on the politics of Tel Aviv in general and on the town's plans to develop public housing schemes based on the 'red Vienna' model see: Iris Graicer (1989) "Red Vienna and Municipal Socialism in Tel Aviv 1925–1928," *Journal of Historical Geography*, 15(4), p. 385.
4 Benjamin Constant (1767–1830) (1988) *Political Writings*. Cambridge University Press: Cambridge, p. 214.
5 See chapter 8 on the relative absence of the urban middle class from mainstream Zionist historiography.
6 The conflicts over the unification of Tel Aviv have never been systematically analyzed. For a brief summary see "Greater Tel Aviv", *Tel Aviv Jaffa News Bulletin*, 1952, p. 26. The development of Tel Aviv may be appreciated by considering the following figures: The 'original' town of Tel Aviv had 550 people in 1911, 980 in 1913, 2,862 in 1921 and 5,506 in 1923. This town was overwhelmed by the unification: in 1923, the south neighborhoods had 5,666 residents, the east neighborhoods had 777 residents, the west 1,363 and the north 3,242. By the end of 1923, after unification, Tel Aviv had 16,554 residents. In 1923, 13,227 people lived in 1,474 homes (either owned or leased), 1,702 people lived in 331 huts, and 1,625 people lived in 587 tents. The 1925 census provides a picture of immense growth. There were 34,200 residents in Tel Aviv in the summer of 1925. Of this total number,

8,046 lived in privately owned homes, and 18,300 lived in leased homes, 5,533 owned huts and 2,027 leased huts, and 294 people lived in tents. Between 1924 and 1925, the number of home-owners increased by 31.4 per cent, from 1,759 to 2,312. Out of this latter number, 90 per cent owned one home, 8 per cent owned two homes, and the rest owned from three to eight homes. Sources: *Tel Aviv Council News Bulletin*, 1925–26, 7 and 8.

7 The total Jewish population of Palestine was estimated at 80,000 in 1922 (non-Jewish population at the time was estimated at 650,000). In 1926, following three years of massive immigration, the total Jewish population was estimated at 140,000.

8 To wit, nearly 11,000 urban workers (and bureaucrats), comprising 70 per cent of the General Federation of Labor's total membership, lived and worked in Tel Aviv by 1926.

9 See protocols of joint meetings of representatives of the Zionist Executive, the National Committee, Tel Aviv Town Council and the Home Owners Association in July 1926, Central Zionist Archives, J1/132, 1–4, 1–10.

10 *Yediot Iriat Tel Aviv*, 30.6.26, 17, pp. 5–6.

11 *Yediot Iriat Tel Aviv*, 30.6.26, 17, pp. 5–8; 21.7.26, 18, pp. 5–8; 4.8.26, 20, pp. 2–9.

12 See the public statements of 'The Neighbors Association,' 'The Northern Neighborhoods Association,' 'The Tel Aviv (female) Workers Council,' and 'The Jaffa Workers' Council,' reprinted in *Yediot Iriat Tel Aviv*, 20, p. 7.

13 (Yediot Iriyat Tel Aviv), 9.8.26; 10.8.26; 11.8.26; 17.8.26.

14 The lawyer for the petitioners was Horace Samuel. He had to suffer severe personal attacks over his role in the affair. One of the arguments he invoked at court – that some voters were not naturalized in Palestine – drew such ferocious attacks that Shoshani defended himself by saying that the lawyer had acted without consulting him first and he (Shoshani) immediately instructed Samuel to withdraw that particular argument.

15 *Ha'Aretz* 7.7.26, p. 2.

16 *Ha'Olam* 27.5.27, 21, pp. 404–405.

17 *Ha'Aretz* 6.9.26. An editorial in *Ha'Aretz* also referred to lawyers as "lacking in national consciousness." Adding fuel to the fire was another legal scandal. In 1926, the municipality of Tel Aviv issued an order outlawing the opening of Jewish-owned shops and restaurants on the Sabbath. A restaurateur by the name of Altshuler challenged the order, opened his business, and was subsequently fined. Zvi Eliahu Cohen, a lawyer, represented Altshuler and challenged the validity of the order on constitutional grounds. Cohen argued that Article 15 of the Mandate guaranteed freedom of conscience and religion and forbade discrimination on the basis of religion. A rare coalition of forces was formed in opposition to the legalistic challenge: the middle-class-oriented daily, *Ha'Aretz*, the orthodox *Ha'tor* and the working-class daily *Davar* bitterly criticized the subversion of the council's autonomy and, among other things, attacked those lawyers who were "ready to do anything for money." The case was ultimately resolved by the Palestinian High Court of Justice which nullified the order on constitutional grounds in 1928.

6 LAWYERING THE NATION

1. Nathan J. Brown (1995) "Law and Imperialism: Egypt in Comparative Perspective," *Law and Society Review*, 29(1), pp. 103–26, 104.
2. None of the speakers in that meeting defended the Hebrew Law of Peace. The general sentiment was that it was a redundant institution and that, at best, it had to be 'reorganized' along professional and budgetary lines. On the pressure exerted on the Hebrew courts to 'professionalize', see next chapter in detail. CZA S/100, protocol 21, 21.12.26.
3. Tuvia ha'Shiloni (1927) "Mishpat u'Pshara" (Law and Compromise), *Davar* 12.6.27, p. 3.
4. CZA S/100, PZE protocol 11.12.27.
5. CZA S/100, PZE protocol 11.12.27. The two lawyers present at the meeting were Van Vriesland, and Harry Sacher. The law firm of Sacher, Horowitz and Klebanoff also represented the Council of Tel Aviv in the Shoshani case (see Salle d'Attente) and was instrumental in drafting and negotiating the Township Order of Tel Aviv with the colonial government.
6. On the response of Dickstein to this instrumental approach, "preferring a few scores of Pounds" to national duties, see CZA S/100, PZE protocol 11.12.27. The debate was widely covered by the daily press. See *Davar* 12.5.27; 31.5.27; 22.8.27. Also see in Gabriel Strassman (1984) *Wearing the Robes: A History of the Legal Profession until 1962 (Otei ha'Glima)*. Lishkat Orchei Ha'Din, Tel Aviv. Also in CZA S/100, PZE protocol 21.5.24, Harry Sacher opining "we should make a maximum effort to ensure that the case will be dealt with by a court of the government and not by the Hebrew Court."
7. Report to the Palestine Zionist Executive from Mr Van Vriesland, 11.3.29. CZA A114/210.
8. CZA A114/210, Van Vriesland report, 11.3.29. See also note 4, above. Zigfried (Zadok) Van Vriesland (1886–1939) was a lawyer and a Zionist activist. In the 1920s, he served as the treasurer of the PZE.
9. Abraham Cordova (1980) "The Institutionalization of a Cultural Center in Palestine: The Writers' Association," *Jewish Social Studies*, 1980, pp. 37–62.
10. CZA S/25/9729 and CZA J1/47, 20.7.20.
11. Bernard Joseph "Ha'Yishuv ha'Ivri u'Batei ha'Din shel ha'Memshala" (The Hebrew Community and the Courts of the State), *Ha'Aretz*, 24.8.26, p. 2.
12. Ibid., p. 2. On the centralist paradigm in law, closely linked to positivism through its insistence on state unity, see H. W. Arthurs (1985) *Without the Law: Administrative Justice and Legal Pluralism in Nineteenth-Century England*. Toronto University Press: Toronto. Arthurs identifies two competing paradigms, two ways of thinking about law among legal professionals. One is a 'centralist paradigm' that postulates law as a singular, objective, and hierarchical formal system that exists as a thing apart from society, politics, or economics; the other is a 'pluralist paradigm' that conceives of law as stemming from a multitude of sources that may be diverse in method, "content, causes, and effects." Arthurs invokes this polarized model in his analysis of administrative justice in nineteenth-century England. In that particular context, the centralist paradigm adhered to by most lawyers posited that

"administrative law is not the law *of* the administration; it is the law directed *against* the administration, the law by which reviewing judges ensure that the administration does not overreach" (pp. 1, 3). Arthurs in turn invokes the marginalized pluralist paradigm as an alternative way of conceiving administrative law, its sources and its methods, as another system of law within the state that is not hierarchically ordered.

13 Van Vriesland alluded to the Russian background of both Dickstein and Eisenstadt and, in particular, to their presumed Bolshevik hostility to the apparatus of the state.
14 Michael Bakunin (1814–1876) (1990) *Statism and Anarchy*. Cambridge University Press: Cambridge, p. 198.
15 Partha Chatterjee (1986) *Nationalist Thought and the Colonial World*. University of Minnesota Press: Minneapolis, p. 26.
16 Ibid., p. 73.
17 CZA A114/210, Van Vriesland report, 11.3.29.
18 Pierre Bourdieu (1987) "The Force of Law: Toward a Sociology of the Juridical Field," *Hastings Law Journal* 38, pp. 814–853.
19 Advocates' Ordinance 1922, Official Gazette No. 71, 15.7.22, Article 5(ii).
20 Consider, for example, the Palestinian law firm of Harry Sacher, Solomon Horowitz and Jacob Klebanoff, with offices in Jerusalem and Haifa and correspondents in London. Harry Sacher, in particular, set an example as the new professional, trained in English law and familar with British culture. Sacher, himself an influential Zionist activist, had direct access to the Chief Justice and the government's senior legal advisers; his firm represented the Town Council of Tel Aviv and the Zionist Executive in their dealings and negotiations with the colonial administration – taking an active part in drafting the Local Township of Tel Aviv Order – and in consulting the authorities on matters relating to other pieces of nationally relevant legislation. They were also active in all types of lucrative commercial and civil litigation affairs. The Sacher firm, in short, provided a model and blueprint for professionalism in law, a model that encouraged those lawyers who did try to integrate a national motive into their work to invest in lobbying for the appointment of Jewish lawyers as judges in state courts, in writing memorandums urging all kinds of legal reforms on behalf of Zionist institutions, and in establishing professional and social ties with the colonial administrators. Thus, by the mid-1920s, there was already a strong link between the professional and social status of lawyers and their form of relations with the colonial administrators of Palestine.
21 From 1924 onwards, entry examinations were required of anyone who was not a graduate of the Jerusalem English College, a graduate of one of the two existing Hebrew Gymnasiums or who held a Palestinian Matriculation Diploma. The law school also expanded its obligatory classes program and in 1926, in a step designed to limit the number of graduates, first-year courses were offered only every other year: "Legal Education and Legal Science: The Law School of the Palestinian Government," *HaMishpat*, 1, 1927, pp. 132–133; H. Kantorowitcz, "Courses in Law," *HaMishpat ha'Ivri*, 1, 1926, pp. 145–146; also in Gad Frumkin (1954) *Derech Shofet Be'Yerushaliim (A Way of a Judge in Jerusalem)*. Dvir: Tel Aviv.

22 In 1937, commenting on the number of lawyers in Palestine, the Palestinian Royal Commission reported that there were 264 Jewish lawyers in Palestine and that "this number of advocates seems to be in excess of the needs of the country for strictly professional work" (ibid., p. 165).
23 Dr Z. Klinzler (1927) "On the 1922 Lawyers Ordinance," *HaMishpat*, 1, 1927, pp. 106–108. The author specified a number of proposals designed to protect the sought-after lawyers' monopoly: repressing illegal competition from individuals and various offices, expanding the professional jurisdiction of lawyers by restricting to lawyers transactions at the land registry, company registry and trademark registry, and by establishing minimum fees to be imposed by courts. Such views are common whenever lawyers are in the process of consolidating their jurisdiction or perceive it as threatened. For comparison see: Richard Abel (1989) *American Lawyers*. Oxford University Press: New York; Jerold Auerbach (1976) *Unequal Justice*. Oxford University Press: London.
24 Andrew Abbott (1988) *The System of Professions*. University of Chicago Press: Chicago, p. 54.
25 See Van Vriesland report, informing the Zionist Executive that Donkelblum, in his capacity as counsel of the PZE, refused to appear in Hebrew Courts of Peace. Also see the case of Donkelblum vs. Shenkar, in chapter 5. This latter case also seems to have contributed to Donkelblum's frustration with the Hebrew Law of Peace.
26 State Archive 76/P, box 643, file 250.
27 Letter of Donkelblum to High Court of Peace, 22.7.25 and attached letter from Bezalzel Yaffe on behalf of Geula to Donkelblum of 20.7.25. State Archive 76/P, box 643, file 250.
28 Barry Unsworth (1996) *After Hannibal*, Hamish Hamilton: London, pp. 48–50.
29 Max Radin (1935) "The Courts and Administrative Agencies," *Minutes of the Judicial Section of the American Bar Association (July)*. Unpublished typescript.
30 "In the Hebrew Law of Peace at Tel Aviv," *Davar*, 21.12.27, p. 3; The resolutions of the convention were published in *Davar*, 17.7.27, p. 5.
31 See chapter 8.
32 In the course of negotiating a new Order for the Municipality of Tel Aviv with the colonial government, Sacher's office notified its client that "Mr Horowitz endeavored to see the Chief Justice this morning, but could not do so. He will try to see him tomorrow morning." In another letter, the firm notified its client that Mr Sacher would see the Chief Justice and would ask him to expedite the decision in the matter of Shoshani (letters dated respectively 12.8.26 and 15.8.26. Tel Aviv Historical Archive 4–2834). Incidentally, the firm is still in practice and considered to be one of the country's biggest and most influential. It carries the name of Solomon Horowitz and its present senior partner is Amnon Goldenberg.
33 Frumkin, op. cit.
34 Max Weber (1978) *Economy and Society*, pp. 875–879, fn 24.
35 Magali Sarfatti Larson (1977) *The Rise of Professionalism: A Sociological Analysis*. University of California Press: Berkeley, p. 169.
36 It may be of interest to note the correspondence between practitioners'

struggles within the legal field and contrasting academic paradigms of law. In a 1991 review essay, Peter Just noted the shift from the early "rule-centered paradigm" in the anthropology of law ("concerned largely with law as an aspect of social control and the imposition of sanctions, and legal procedures as the means of enforcing social rules") (p. 374) to a paradigm that locates and analyzes law as a "meaning-centered 'total social context'" process in which one looks at the "cultural logic of dispute" (p. 375). It seems to me that this paradigmatic move follows on the heels of actual struggles among practitioners and carriers of law concerning its meaning, scope and direction. In this respect, it is not surprising that those concerned had first to look 'elsewhere' – outside the legal fields of the 'West' – in order to become sensitive to the contingent nature of a rule-centered legal field. Peter Just (1992) "History, Power, Ideology, and Culture: Current Directions in the Anthropology of Law," *Law and Society Review*, 26(2), pp. 373–411.

7 NATION-BUILDING AND THE CONTAINMENT OF LEGALITY

1. Fredric L. DuBow and Craig McEwen (1995) "Community Boards: An Analytic Profile," in: Sally E. Merry and Neal Millner (eds) *The Possibility of Popular Justice: A Case Study of Community Mediation in the United States.* University of Michigan Press: Ann Arbor, pp. 125–168, 134.
2. Ibid., p. 135.
3. Ibid., p. 135.
4. This letter, as well as the protocol of the council's meeting, was published in *Tel Aviv Municipal Bulletin*, vol. 24, p. 2, November 1926. One member of the council objected the appeal to the Hebrew Court on grounds that by entrusting it with the list of voters the council admitted its own incompetence. Yet the overwhelming majority praised the neutrality of the High Court, its apolitical status and its public legitimacy.
5. Paltiel Dickstein (1927) "Le'Harchavat Tafkido Shel Mishpat Ha'shalom Ha'ivri" (Expanding the Role of the Hebrew Law of Peace), *Hamishpat*, 1, pp. 154–158.
6. Tel Aviv Historical Archive, Unit 4, File 2828, a draft dated August 1926.
7. See letter of David Bloch to the High Hebrew Law of Peace, 8.8.26, Tel Aviv Historical Archive, Unit 4, File 2828.
8. See a letter from the Hebrew Law of Peace to the Municipality of Tel Aviv, accusing it of shirking, 9.2.27, Tel Aviv Historical Archive, Unit 4, File 4592.
9. Report of the Tel Aviv District Court of Peace to the Municipality of Tel Aviv, 28.12.28, Tel Aviv Historical Archive, Unit 4, File 2828.
10. Letter sent to Dr Lurie, Head of the Education Department, 20.7.20, CZA J1/50.
11. In principle, the Hebrew Courts of Peace were designed to maintain themselves through fees levied on litigants. Often, these sums were insufficient to cover the ongoing operations of the courts, and additional funding was provided by local municipalities and settlements and by the Palestine Zionist Executive. See letter of Daniel Auster to Va'ad Ha'Zirim, dated 3.8.19 and 18.8.19 (CZA S1/544,) explaining the importance of the courts. "There are

already places where the courts do not need funding any longer, like Jaffa, but in other places they still need help ... truly, the public itself should be responsible for sustaining the courts because it is the public who needs them and I hope that in the future it will so be, but in the beginning of such important tasks they must be supported ... without help, Hebrew Peace Courts in many places will have to be closed. I therefore ask for a monthly support of 40EP for the courts." A follow-up letter of 18.8.19 revealed that the funds had not been yet approved. The request was approved on 22.9.19. On 31.10.19 Auster asked for more funds and was declined in a letter of 20.11.19 in which he was advised to secure funds for peripheral courts either by diverting funds from the "courts of Jaffa and Haifa, or through the rich resources of the rich settlements of Petah-Tiqwa and Zichron Ya'acov" (20.11.19), thus seeking to secure funding by local communities as well. Yet Vaad HaZirim approved a monthly funding of 25EP on November 1919. Again, special funding for the Hebrew Court of Petah-Tiqwa was requested in 1920: "It is true that local communities should be responsible for the maintenance of these courts. But the situation in Petah-Tiqwa is different than in other settlements. *Some of the settlement's residents oppose the Hebrew Court on religious grounds and the general meeting of the settlement forbade the settlement's committee to provide funding to the Hebrew Court* ... without securing the requested fund (20EP) the court would be shut down while it is particularly important to maintain it in a place like Petah-Tiqwa" (emphasis added). In latter years, funding was secured either by municipalities and settlements on an autonomous basis or through the Zionist Executive. The latter became stricter over the years. In 1921, the National Council asked the Zionist Executive to approve a budget for the Hebrew Law of Peace which had been denied (PZE protocol 23.12.21). In 1922, the PZE approved a monthly budget of 10EP to the Jeusalem Hebrew Court of Peace (PZE protocol 10.1.22, CZA S1/544 and S100/16/21). Also see a letter of 29.10.26 from the PZE to the Hebrew Court of Peace, threatening not to cover future deficits: "There is a deficit of 107.917EP that was caused by the fact that you increased the salary of your general secretary by 5EP per month at a time when the general income of the court is in decline. We thereby announce that we have decided to cover this deficit because we think we should help the Hebrew Law pay its debts and keep its operation without difficulties. We are ready to do so only on condition that the Hebrew Court will take all measures to insure that there will not be any deficits in the future and that its expenses in the future will not exceed its income. We therefore ask you to clarify how you intend to prevent such deficits in the future." Also see PZE protocol of 14.6.26 on that issue. The Hebrew Law of Peace issued a detailed account and explanation in response, expressing the hope that the "transition period" would soon pass and that the Hebrew law would attain financial independence (29.11.26).

12 Resolutions of the Second Convention of Hebrew Law Judges, published in *Davar* 20.6.27, p. 1.
13 Protocol of PZE meeting 17.2.20, CZA L2/186/3. Also see memorandum to the 1927 XV Zionist Congress, CZA K11/361.
14 In one case, the Jewish National Fund had been involved in a monetary

dispute with a private lender. Subsequently, the PZE and the JNF were sued at a Hebrew Court of Peace. Lawyers for the defendants announced that they would not litigate without obtaining the prior consent of the Hebrew court to apply the principles of the British Mandatory law to the dispute. The case against the PZE and the JNF received considerable attention and was followed by a series of articles praising or condemning the approach taken by the PZE. See *Davar* 12.5.27 and 22.8.27; see also an article by Y. Shuchman: "There are institutions who are ready to use the Hebrew Court in cases where there are no chances of sucessfully pursuing them in the courts of the state, but they act as shirkers when they are sued at the Hebrew Law of Peace in matters where they have better chances to prevail at the courts of the state," *Davar* 31.5.27, p. 2.

15 PZE protocol of 21.5.24, CZA S/100, Protocol 53: Harry Sacher represented Arthur Rupin in a case against *Do'ar Ha'yom* and argued that "we should make a maximum effort to ensure that the case will be dealt with by a court of the government and not by the Hebrew Court."

16 When a former employee of the Zionist Executive claimed compensation in a Hebrew Law of Peace court, for example, the institution refused to litigate on grounds that it had its own internal mechanism for resolving such matters on the basis of its own constitution. In a letter sent to the Hebrew Law of Peace, the Zionist Executive further explained that its decision not to litigate had been a "purely administrative one" and had nothing to do with the "appreciation of the Zionist Executive to the national work carried out by the Hebrew Law of Peace." See letter of 6.7.26 about the case of Yitchak Shechter vs. Palestine Zionist Executive. This letter was the latest in a series of letters exchanged between these two institutions, in which heavy rhetoric was used in order to appeal to the national sensibilities of the Zionist Executive. See letters of 13.4.27; 22.4.27; 6.5.27; 28.5.27; 2.6.27; 30.6.27, in CZA S/100, PZE protocols.

17 The letter was sent to the editor of *Do'ar Ha'yom*. On 24.8.26, the General Secretary of the municipality of Tel Aviv sent a copy of the letter to the Mayor, see Historical Archive of Tel Aviv, Unit 4, file 2954.

18 Paltiel Dickstein (1927) "Le'Harchavat Tafkido Shel Mishpat Ha'Shalom Ha'Ivri" (Expanding the Role of the Hebrew Law of Peace), *Hamishpat*, 1, pp. 154–158.

19 Ehud Shprinzak (1986) *Every Man Whatsoever is Right in His Own Eyes, Illegalism in Israeli Society*. Sifriat Po'alim: Tel Aviv.

20 Sally Merry, encountering abortive attempts to recreate traditional communities through pre-colonial law in various post-colonial settings, suggests the following:

Reintroducing pre-colonial law into the vastly different social conditions of post-colonial countries is problematic. Many post-colonial countries, caught in the pattern of dependent development, are pressured by the economically dominant countries of the core to retain their Western legal systems. Post-colonial countries can rarely afford an extensive commitment to this endeavor, despite the political popularity of eliminating hated alien laws, which were frequently used to control the indigenous peoples for the benefit of colonial economic development. Sally Engle Merry (1995) "Sorting Out Popular Justice," in: Sally E. Merry and Neal Milner (eds) *The Possibility of Popular Justice: A Case Study of Community Mediation in the United States.* University of Michigan Press: Ann Arbor, pp. 31–66, 47.

Not only that the Hebrew Law of Peace never attained the status of a viable alternative, but the laws of the Mandatory state were adopted without even repealing the notorious Emergency regulations that were enacted by the British in an effort to quell the opposition of Jewish militant groups in the 1940s. Rather, these emergency regulations (mandating destruction of houses, deportation, administrative detentions and a plethora of infringements upon basic civil rights) were immediately invoked by the sovereign state of Israel against Palestinian Arabs, thereby affirming (at least symbolically) the dual-colonialist nature of the Palestine enterprise. But I digress: the point to make here is that the wholesale adoption of the colonialist state's law cannot be fully accounted for in terms of external structural pressures of the kind suggested by Merry. Rather, this adoption has to do with being content with the ordering capabilities of colonial law (serving general purposes, but not directly threatening spaces of illegality) on the one hand, and with the systematic dismissal of 'national' alternatives on the other hand.

21 Yonathan Shapiro (1984) *An Elite Without Successors.* Sifriat Po'alim: Tel Aviv, p. 26.
22 See Zeev Sternhell (1995) *Nation-building or a New Society?* Am Oved: Tel Aviv, p. 228.
23 The Comrades Law was founded on an amendment to the Histadrut's General Constitution which stipulated that "all members of the Histadrut must submit to the Comrades Law and to obey its rulings" (Article 14).
24 Moshe Greenberg (1926) "Comrades Law and the State," in: *Mishpat Ha'haverim.* Histadrut Klalit: Tel Aviv.
25 Yisrael Bar Shira (1930) "Lecheker Mahuto shel Mishpat haHaverim" (The Substance of the Comrades Law), *Hamishpat haIvri,* 4(3), pp. 103–113, 107.
26 In principle, it is plausible to argue that the coexistence of a Hebrew Law of Peace and a Comrades Law led to jurisdictional struggles and may have contributed to the decline of the Hebrew courts. However, I have found no evidence that such was the case. First, advocates of each system often expressed support for the goals of the other. Second, I have found a number of cases of practical cooperation and smooth transitions from one forum to another. Third, this argument is much weakened by the fact that both systems had lost importance by the end of the 1920s, thus ruling out a zero-sum-game situation (see for example draft of a revised constitution, article 9, ch. 1, in which it was suggested that "when the regulations are silent, the ordinary practices of arbitration and the Hebrew Law of Peace should be followed". Lavon Archive (4)–250–72–1–2479).
27 Bar Shira, op. cit., p. 106.
28 Ibid., p. 112. Also see Zalman Feller (1926) "On the Comrades Law,' *Davar* 26.11.26, p. 2.
29 Bar Shira, op. cit., p. 113.

30 Feller, op. cit., p. 2. Also see a letter from a lower-instance court to the High Comrades Court, 5.9.27, in response to a complaint by the Haifa Workers' Council in the matter of case 420/38, Clerks Association vs. Zvi Pasmenick. Lavon Archive, High Comrades Court 1.27–5.28, (4)–245–2–1.
31 Sally Engle Merry (1995) "Sorting Out Popular Justice," in: Sally E. Merry and Neal Millner (eds) *The Possibility of Popular Justice: A Case Study of Community Mediation in the United States*. University of Michigan Press: Ann Arbor, pp. 31–66, 42.
32 Lavon Archive (4)–250–54–205.
33 Trial No. 124, Lavon Archive (4)–245–2–79. In same file, also see Trial No. 13.
34 Letter from Jerusalem Workers Council, 9.3.26, Lavon Archive (4)–250–72–1–2396.
35 Letter from Jaffa Workers Council to the High Comrades Law, 12.7.26, and letter of response from Dr Zmora, on behalf of the Comrades Law, protesting the position of the Jaffa Workers Council, 28.7.26. Lavon Archive (4)–250–72–1–2396.
36 Lavon Archive (4)–208–1–106, 2.10.28; (4)–250–72–1–2398; Also in *Milchamtenu*: A Publication of Po'aley Zion, 12.1.28 and 3.2.28.
37 Case 168/420 Sara Agi vs. Jerusalem Workers Council, decision of 22.2.28. Lavon Archive, Decisions of the High Court 1.27–5.28, (4)–245–2–1.
38 In case 218/420, 15.5.28, the High Comrades Court dealt with a case in which a plaintiff was awarded more than he had asked for. However it was the plaintiff who, unsatisfied with the judgment on other matters, tried to convince the court to reconsider the case on grounds that the lower instance erred in breaching the rule according to which a judge must not award a party more than that party had asked for. The court dismissed the appeal and yet observed that the argument could have been valid had it come from the losing party. Lavon Archive, Decisions of the High Court 1.27–5.28, (4)–245–2–1.
39 State Archive, 76/P, box 635, file 212, 1923–24.
40 See Lavon Archive file (4)–208–1–48 a, b, c 1923–28.
41 Case 1/28 Solel-Boneh vs. Moshe Shadmi and others, 8.4.29. Lavon Archive 72–1–2399 and 208–1–48.
42 Letter of 21.8.29 from the Tel Aviv Comrades Court to the High Comrades Court; Letter of response from Dr Krongold of 23.8.29. Lavon Archive 4–250–72–1, file 2475.
43 Lavon Archive (4)–250–72–1, file 2399 Tel Aviv Workers Council 1929. The file contains hundreds of collection cases (also see (4)–250–72– 77–1999).
44 Lavon Archive (4)–250–36–1, file 1852, letter of 18.9.29.
45 See *Davar* 18.6.26, p. 3; 28.7.26, p. 3; 29.8.26, p. 3; protocol of 13.12.26 Lavon Archive (4)–208–1–48.
46 Lavon Archive (4)–208–1–106, Bar Shira, lecture 16.10.28; *Davar* 11.11.28, p. 2.
47 Lavon Archive (4)–208–1–106, Bar Shira, lecture 16.10.28. On the Comrades Law as moral activism see: De Vries, David (1994) "The Emergence of Workers' Morality in the Jewish Community: Comrades Law in the Urban Sector in the 1920s," *Proceedings of the XI World Congress of Jewish Studies*, Division B, vol. 2, Jerusalem, pp. 227–234 (in Hebrew).
48 Sternhell, op. cit.

8 DEAD LAW AND STATISM: A SUGGESTED LESSON

1. Gary Schwartz (1996) "Ars Moriendi: The Mortality of Art," *Art in America*, November 1996, pp. 72–75.
2. Peter Fitzpatrick (1995) "The Impossibility of Popular Justice," in: Sally Engle Merry and Neal Millner (eds) *The Possibility of Popular Justice*. University of Michigan Press: Ann Arbor, pp. 453–474.
3. Sally Engle Merry (1995) "Sorting Out Popular Justice," in: Sally Engle Merry and Neal Millner (eds) *The Possibility of Popular Justice*. University of Michigan Press: Ann Arbor, pp. 31–66.
4. Michel Foucault (1990) *The History of Sexuality*. Vintage Books: New York, p. 144.
5. The description of statist-nationalism as 'content-empty,' largely inspired by the way Jewish lawyers approached the question of law (see chapter 6), was offered to me by Neta Ziv.
6. Edward Said (1991) "Art and National Identity: A Critic's Symposium," *Art in America*, September 1991, pp. 80–81.
7. Eliezer Shvied (1972) *Leu'miut Yehudit (Jewish Nationalism)*. Zack: Jerusalem, p. 51.
8. For an elaborate discussion of the various trends and the positions of their respective carriers see: David Vital (1982) *Zionism: The Formative Years*. Clarendon: London. The thinker most clearly associated with cultural Zionism was Ahad Ha-Am, who argued for the need to establish a community in Palestine that would have become the spiritual center for the Jewish people as a whole. For him, the challenge was to create a 'true' Jewish state and not merely a state for the Jews. See *Kol Kitvei Ahad Ha-Am* (The Writings of Ahad Ha-Am) (1947). Dvir: Tel Aviv. Vital (p. 28) comments that "of the problem of the content and the direction of Judaism in the modern world in the face of the new secular and scientific culture, Herzl and his 'political Zionists' understood little or nothing ..." For a less sympathetic view see: Walter Lacqueur (1972) *A History of Zionism*. Weidenfeld and Nicolson: London, pp. 162–171.
9. Paltiel Dickstein (1925) "On the Hebrew Law of Peace," in: P. Dickstein (ed.) *The Hebrew Law of Peace*. Hebrew Law of Peace Publishers: Tel Aviv, p. 12.
10. Abraham B. Yehoshua (1997) *Voyage to the End of the Millennium*. Sifria Chadasha: Kibbutz Meuchad.
11. Eliezer Goldman (1996) "Exposition and Inquiries: Jewish Thought in Past and Present" in: Daniel Statman and Avi Sagi (eds) Y. L Magnes: Jerusalem, p. 78; Yaacov Katz (1960) *Ben Yehudim le Goyiim*. Bialik Institute: Jerusalem.
12. Bernard Joseph (1926) "Ha'yishuv ha'Ivri u'Batei ha'Din shel ha'Memshala" (The Hebrew Community and Governmental Court), *Ha'Aretz*, 24.8.26, p. 2.
13. Martin Buber (1998) *A Country for Two Nations*. Shoken: Jerusalem, p. 209 (Heb).
14. Baruch Kimmerling (1995) "*Dat ha'Leumiut Mul Dat ha'Ezrachim*" (The Religion of Nationalism Versus the Religion of the Citizens) *Ha'Aretz*, 29.9.95.
15. Amnon Raz-Karkutzkin (1993) "Zehutam Ha'dala shel Yehudei Yisrael"

(The Impoverished Identity of Israeli Jews) *Ha'Aretz*, 29.10.93; Amnon Raz-Karkutzkin (1994) "Hadat Shamra al ha'Am ha'Yehudi?" (Did Religion Safeguard the Jewish People?) *Ha'Ir*, 1.4.94, pp. 50–51. Also see: Amnon Raz-Karkutzkin (1994) "Galut be'Toch Ribonut: Lebikoret Shlilat ha'Galut ba'Tarbut ha'Yisraelit" (Exile within Sovereignty: A Critique of the Negation of Exile in Israeli Culture), *Teoria u'Bikoret*, 4, pp. 23–55, 5, pp. 113–130.

16 Zygmunt Bauman (1989) *Modernity and the Holocaust*. Polity Press: Cambridge, p. 39. On the relevance of this self understanding to the way Palestinian Arabs had often been depicted by Zionists see Nurit Gertz (1995) *Captive of a Dream: National Myths in Israeli Culture*. Am Oved: Tel Aviv, p. 43, and chapter 1 note 45, of this book.

17 In: *Tabenkin on the Negation of the Diaspora*. Yad Tabenkin: Ramat-Gan (1973).

18 Ahad ha'Am (1947)(1888) "Derech ha'Ruach" (The Way of the Spirit), in: *Kol Kitvey Ahad ha'Am*. Dvir: Tel Aviv.

19 See, e.g., Shmuel N. Eisenstadt (1996) "The Struggle Over the Symbols of Collective Identity and its Boundaries in Post Revolutionary Israeli Society," in Pinchas Ginosar and Avi Bareli (eds) *Zionism: A Contemporary Debate (Tsionut: Pulmus Ben Zmanenu)*. Ben Gurion University Press: Beer Sheba.

20 Zeev Strenhell (1995) *Nation-building or a New Society?* Am Oved: Tel Aviv.

21 Ibid., pp. 30, 235–237.

22 Yonathan Shapiro (1996) *Hevra bi'Shvi ha'Politika'im*. Sifriat Po'alim: Tel Aviv. Shapiro talks about a distinct 'political system' that preceded the state of Israel and controlled that state after independence. He argues that this system, dominated by hegemonic labor parties which managed the affairs of the JFL and its affiliated institutions, transcended conventional state/civil society dichotomies. Shapiro thus aims to show how the eventual capturing of state apparatuses by the political elites is the key to understanding the weakness of Israel's civil society.

23 A number of sociologists and historians, both 'conservative' and 'revisionist', have noted this absence in recent years but have not developed a research agenda in this direction. See, e.g., Ilan Pappe (1996) "Ha'Zionut be'Mivchan ha'Teoriot shel ha'Leumiut" (Zionism in the Context of Theories of Nationalism), in: Pinchas Ginosar and Avi Bareli (eds) *Tsionut: Pulmus Ben Zmanenu (Zionism: A Contemporary Debate)*. Ben Gurion University: Beer Sheva, pp. 223–263; Moshe Lissak (1996) "Soziologim 'Bikort'iim' ve'Soziologim 'Mimsadiim' ba'Kehila ha'Academit ha'Yisraelit: Ma'avakim Idiologiim o Si'ach Academi Inyani?" (Critical Sociologists and 'Establishment' Sociologists in the Israeli Academy: Ideological Struggles or a Substantive Academic Discourse?) in: Pinchas Ginosar and Avi Bareli (eds) *Tsionut: Pulmus Ben Zmanenu (Zionism: A Contemporary Debate)*. Ben Gurion University Press: Beer Sheva, pp. 60–98; Baruch Kimmerling (1993) "Yachasei Hevra u'Medina be'Yisrael" (State and Society in Israel), in: Uri Ram (ed.) *Israeli Society: Critical Perspectives*. Brerot: Tel Aviv, pp. 328–350; Anita Shapira (1992) *Land and Power: The Zionist Resort to Force 1881–1948*. Oxford University Press: New York.

24 Notable exceptions are Dan Gil'adi (1973) *HaYishuv Bitkufat ha'Aliyah*

ha'Reviit. Am Oved: Tel Aviv; Yigal Drori (1981) "Ha'hugim ha'Ezrachiim' ba'Yishuv ha'Eretz Yisraeli Bishnot ha'Esrim." Doctoral dissertation: Tel Aviv University. For a general critique, see Penslar, who writes that "the political history of the Zionist Labor movement was the object of the ... historiographical gaze" of scholars who had been "raised in the Labor movement and were steeped in its ideology." And it is only from the mid-1970s onwards that some works focused on the orthodox Jews of Palestine, the Zionist Right, the colonizing community's economic history and historical geography. Derek Jonathan Penslar (1995) "Innovation and Revisionism in Israeli Historiography," *History and Memory*, 7(1), pp. 125–146.

25 For a rather comprehensive compendium of statistics on the import, dispensation, and distribution of Jewish capital in Palestine see: Baruch Kimmerling (1983) *Zionism and Economy*. Schenkman: Massachusetts. Kimmerling writes that "the private capital flow was greater than the public (Zionist and other) capital recruitment, even though the latter was the only capital that was perceived as a tool for nation building. Between 1918 and 1937, for example, only 21 percent of the imported capital was public capital, the other 79 percent ... was private – out of the control of the major political institutions of the Jewish community" (p. 21).

26 Ibid., p. 28. Eric Cohen (1970) *Zionism and the City*. Hebrew University: Jerusalem. Cohen writes that cities had no place in the blueprint of the new society. The result was that while the city, especially Tel Aviv, was the de facto industrial, cultural, and political center of the colonizing community, the dominant ideology ignored its role and emphasized the leading role of collective and cooperative rural settlements.

27 See Kimmerling, ibid., p. 34. Drori, op. cit., also writes about the 'total contradiction' between the concentration of most means of production at the hands of the 'civil circles' and their political weakness.

28 Gil'adi, op. cit., and Drori, op. cit.

29 See Lissak, op. cit., p. 291 and Drori, who explicitly excludes such organizations from in-depth consideration.

30 Kimmerling, (1983) op. cit., p. 34; Gil'adi, op. cit.

31 For such a paradigmatic opening, exercised by following the career of one Zionist entrepreneur, see the work of Eli Shaltiel (1990) *Pinhas Rutenberg: 1879–1942, Life and Times*. Am Oved: Tel Aviv.

32 Partha Chatterjee (1986) *Nationalist Thought and the Colonial World*. University of Minnesota Press: Minneapolis.

33 Peter Fitzpatrick (1980) "Law, Modernization, and Mystification," in: Rita Simon and Steven Spitzer (eds) *Research in Law and Sociology*, 3, JAI Press: Greenwich Conn., pp. 161–180.

34 Lissak (1995), op. cit., p. 286.

35 Letter of August 12, 1926. Tel Aviv Historical Archive File 2834, 4.

36 Letter of August 12, 1926. Tel Aviv Historical Archive File 2834, 4.

37 Letter of September 2, 1926 from the Acting Chief Secretary; A reply of September 5, 1926 from S. Horowitz expressed gratitude for "the prompt and favorable consideration" given to the matter. However, further negotiation was still needed, and the firm handled a minute negotiation over the

wording of the amended Order, in fact instructing the Chief Secretary how to interpret the High Court's ruling. Tel Aviv Historical Archive File 2834, 4.

38 For a brief description of Sacher, Horowitz and Klebanoff as a 'model' Jewish–Palestinian law firm, see chapter 6.
39 Gross (1982), op. cit., p. 11. Arie Shenkar (1963) *Be'Emuna U'Be'Ma'as* (In faith and Action) Privately published: Tel Aviv. Yaacov Shavit (1992) *Textiles in Eretz Israel 1854–1956.* Israel Textile Association: Tel Aviv.
40 Gross, ibid., p. 13. Peel Report, p. 209.
41 The 1937 Peel Report noted that aside from creating significant employment opportunities for semi-skilled and non-skilled laborers, the Department for Public Works regularly contracted work on a tender basis. It also noted that the Jewish Federation of Labor had its own special department for applying for such contracts but that it had submitted only one tender offer in 1933–34. The report accounted for this disinterestedness by pointing out that extensive construction work (mainly in Tel Aviv) exhausted the JFL's capabilities to contract more work (p. 322).
42 Shapiro writes that not only clerks and managers, but also "the free professions, lawyers, physicians and journalists, were absorbed into bureaucratic organizations which were controlled by politicians" (1996, op. cit., p. 17.)
43 See Peel Report, pp. 318–319.
44 See the arguments of the Jewish Agency before the Peel Committee, Peel Report, p. 319.
45 Jacob Reuveny (1993) *The Administration of Palestine Under the British Mandate 1920–1948: An Institutional Analysis.* Bar Ilan University: Ramat Gan, p. 117.
46 Gertz, 1988, op. cit., p. 42.
47 See Aharon Kedar (1978) "On the Worldview of 'Brit Shalom'" in: *Ideology and Zionist Policy.* Shazar Center: Jerusalem, pp. 97–114.
48 See Eisenstadt in chapter 1.
49 Yitzchak Nofech (1925) "The Al-Hukuk Arab Legal Periodical," *Hamishpat Ha'ivri*, 1, pp. 169–171.
50 Gyan Prakash (1992) "Writing Post-Orientalist Histories of the Third World: Indian Historiography is Good to Think," in: Nicholas B. Dirks (ed.) *Colonialism and Culture.* University of Michigan Press: Ann Arbor, pp. 353–388, 359.
51 John C. Hawley (1996) *Writing the Nation: Self and Country in the Post-Colonial Imagination.* Rodopi: Amsterdam.

BIBLIOGRAPHY

Abbott, Andrew (1988) *The System of Professions*. Chicago University Press: Chicago.
Abel, Richard (1989) *American Lawyers*. Oxford University Press: New York.
Agnon, Sha'i (1976) *Me'Azmi el Azmi*. Shoken: Jerusalem.
Ahad ha'Am (1947)(1888) "Derech ha'Ruach" (The Way of the Spirit), in: *Kol Kitvey Ahad ha'Am*. Dvir: Tel Aviv.
Ahronson, Ran (1996) "Settlement in Eretz-Yisrael — A Colonialist Enterprise?" in: Pinchas Ginosar and Avi Bareli (eds) *Zionism: A Contemporary Debate (Tsionut: Pulmus Ben Zmanenu)*. Ben Gurion University: Beer Sheva, pp. 340–375.
Anderson, Benedict (1983) *Imagined Communities*. Verso: London.
Arnold, Thurman (1934) "Trial by Combat and the New Deal," *Harvard Law Review*, 47, April, pp. 913–947.
Arthurs, H. W. (1985) *Without the Law: Administrative Justice and Legal Pluralism in Nineteenth-Century England*. Toronto University Press: Toronto.
Auerbach, Jerold (1976) *Unequal Justice*. Oxford University Press: London.
Avneri, Yossi (1985) "Ha'Rav Avraham Yitzchak Hacohen Kook, Raba shel Yaffo, Tarsad-Tarad" ("Rabby Kook, The Rabby of Jaffa 1904–1914"), *Cathedra*, 37, pp. 49–82.
Bakunin, Michael (1814–1876) (1990) *Statism and Anarchy*. Cambridge University Press: Cambridge.
Bar-Shira, Yisrael (1930) "Lecheker Mahuto shel Mishpat haHaverim" (The Substance of the Comrades Law), *Hamishpat*, 4(3), pp. 103–113.
Bauman, Zygmunt (1989) *Modernity and the Holocaust*. Polity Press: Cambridge.
Ben Hilel Hacohen, Mordechai (1925) *Mishpat Ha'shalom Ha'ivri*. Tel Aviv.
Ben-Sasson, Hilel (ed.) (1976) *The Jewish Community in the Middle-Ages*. Zalman Shazar, Israeli Historical Society: Jerusalem.
Bentwich, Norman (1926) "Recognition of Hebrew Law in the

Constitution of Eretz-Yisrael," *Hamishpat ha'Ivri*, 1, pp. 129–136.
Biger, Gideon (1983) *A Crown Colony or a National Home: The Impact of British Rule on Palestine 1917–1930, A Historical-Geographical Account* (Moshavat Keter o Ba'iit Leumi: Hash'pa'at Ha'shilton Ha'briti Al Eretz Yisrael 1917–1930 Bchina Geographit-Historit). Yad Ben Zvi: Jerusalem.
Bourdieu, Pierre (1987) "The Force of Law: Toward a Sociology of the Juridical Field," *Hastings Law Journal*, 38, 814–853.
Brown, J. Nathan (1995) "Law and Imperialism: Egypt in Comparative Perspective," *Law and Society Review*, 29(1), pp. 103–126.
Chatterjee, Partha (1986) *Nationalist Thought and the Colonial World*. University of Minnesota Press: Minneapolis.
Cohen, Eric (1970) *Zionism and the City*. Hebrew University: Jerusalem.
Constable, Marianne (1995) *The Law of the Other*. University of Chicago Press: Chicago.
Constant, Benjamin [1767–1830] (1988) *Political Writings*. Cambridge University Press: Cambridge.
Cordova, Abraham (1980) "The Institutionalization of a Cultural Center in Palestine: The Writers' Association," *Jewish Social Studies*, 1980, pp. 37–62.
Dickstein, Paltiel (1922) "Law and Equity in the Hebrew Law of Peace," *ha'Poel ha'Tsair*, 33, pp. 5–7.
Dickstein, Paltiel (1925) "On the Hebrew Law of Peace," in: P. Dickstein (ed.) *The Hebrew Law of Peace*. Hebrew Law of Peace Publishers: Tel Aviv.
Dickstein, Paltiel (1927) "The Revival of Law is at Our Hands," *Ha'Aretz*, 1.6.27, p. 2.
Dickstein, Paltiel (1949) "Lesium Pe'ulot Batei Mishpat Hashalom ha'Ivri" (The End of the Hebrew Courts of Peace), *Hapraklit*, 6(1–12), pp. 156–159.
Dickstein, Paltiel (1964) *Toldot Mishpat ha'Shalom ha'Ivri (The History of the Hebrew Law of Peace)*. Yavne: Tel Aviv.
Dirks, Nicholas B. (1992a) "From Little King to Landlord: Colonial Discourse and Colonial Rule," in: Nicholas B. Dirks (ed.) *Colonialism and Culture*. University of Michigan Press: Ann Arbor, pp. 175–207.
Dirks, Nicholas B. (1992b) "Introduction," in: Dirks (ed.) *Colonialism and Culture*. University of Michigan Press: Ann Arbor.
Drori, Yigal (1981) "Ha'hugim ha'Ezrachiim' ba'Yishuv ha'Eretz Yisraeli Bishnot ha'Esrim." Doctoral dissertation: Tel Aviv University.
DuBow, Fredric L. and Craig McEwen (1995) "Community Boards: An Analytic Profile," in: Sally E. Merry and Neal Millner (eds) *The*

Possibility of Popular Justice: A Case Study of Community Mediation in the United States. University of Michigan Press: Ann Arbor.

Eisenstadt, Shmuel (1931) *Ein Mishpat: Sefer Shimush Bibliography le-Sifrut ha-Mishpat ha-Ivri (The Fountain of Law: A Bibliography of Hebrew Law)* (Repertorium Bibliographicum). Mishpat: Jerusalem.

Eisenstadt, Shmuel (1967) "On the History of Hebrew Law," in: *Zion with Justice.* Hamishpat: Tel Aviv.

Eisenstadt, Shmuel N. (1996) "The Struggle Over the Symbols of Collective Identity and its Boundaries in Post Revolutionary Israeli Society," in: Pinchas Ginosar and Avi Bareli (eds) *Zionism: A Contemporary Debate (Tsionut: Pulmus Ben Zmanenu).* Ben Gurion University Press: Beer Sheba.

Elam, Yigal (1975) *An Introduction to Zionist History.* Lewin-Epstein: Tel Aviv (Heb).

Elam, Yigal (1979) *HaDerech Ha'Zionit el ha'Ko'ach (The Zionist Way to Force).* Zmora Bitan: Tel Aviv.

Eliash, Shulamit (1985) "The Chief Rabbinate and Ha'Mizrachi During the Mandate," *Cathedra,* 37, pp. 123–148.

Elgazi, Gadi (1997) "Tavnit Nof Moladeto: Nicolaus Cusanus, the Farmers of the Mossel and Rural Law," in B. Z. Kedar (ed.) *Hatarbut.* Shazar Center: Israel, pp. 123–139.

Elon, Menachem (1988) *Jewish Law: History, Sources, Principles.* The Jewish Publication Society: Philadelphia.

Even-Zohar, Itamar (1988) "The Growth and Crystalization of a Local and Native Hebrew Culture in Eretz Yisrael 1882–1948," *Cathedra,* 16, pp. 23–38.

Evron, Boas (1988) *A National Reckoning.* Dvir: Tel Aviv (Heb).

Falk, Zeev (1961) *Marriage and Divorce.* Mif'al ha'Shichpul: Jerusalem.

Finkelstein, Louis (1964) *Jewish Self-government in the Middle Ages.* Philipp Feldheim: New York.

Fitzpatrick, Peter (1980) "Law, Modernization, and Mystification," in: Rita Simon and Steven Spitzer (eds) *Research in Law and Sociology,* Vol. 3. JAI Press: Greenwich, Conn., pp. 161–180.

Fitzpatrick, Peter (1995) "The Impossibility of Popular Justice," in: Sally Engle Merry and Neal Milner (eds) *The Possibility of Popular Justice.* University of Michigan Press: Ann Arbor, pp. 453–474.

Foucault, Michel (1972) "The Discourse on Language," in: *The Archeology of Knowledge.* Pantheon Books: New York.

Foucault, Michel (1990) *The History of Sexuality.* Vintage Books: New York.

Friedman, Menachem (1978) *Society and Religion (Hevra ve Dat: Ha'ortodoxia Ha'lo Tzionit Be'Eretz Yisrael 1918–1936).* Yad Ben Zvi: Jerusalem.

Friedmann, Daniel (1975) "Independent Development of Israeli Law," *Israel Law Review*, 10(4), pp. 515–568.
Frumkin, Gad (1954) *Derech Shofet Be'Yerushaliim (A Way of a Judge in Jerusalem)* Dvir: Tel Aviv.
Gertz, Nurit (1988) *Literature and Ideology in Eretz Yisrael During the 1930s.* Open University of Israel: Tel Aviv (Heb).
Gertz, Nurit (1995) *Captive of a Dream: National Myths in Israeli Culture.* Am Oved: Tel Aviv (Heb).
Giddens, Anthony (1990) *The Consequences of Modernity.* Polity Press: Cambridge.
Gil'adi, Dan (1973) *HaYishuv Bitkufat ha'Aliyah ha'Reviit.* Am Oved: Tel Aviv (Heb).
Gluckman, Max (1963) "Gossip and Scandal," *Current Anthropology*, 4, pp. 307–316.
Goldberg, Assaf (1954) "Mishpat, Am, ve'Lashon" (Law, Nation and Language), *Hapraklit*, 1, pp. 139–152.
Goldman, Eliezer (1997) *Exposition and Inquiries: Jewish Thought in Past and Present.* Dani Statman and Avi Sagi (eds). Y. L Magnes: Jerusalem (Heb).
Graicer, Iris (1989) "Red Vienna and Municipal Socialism in Tel Aviv 1925–1928," *Journal of Historical Geography*, 15(4), p. 385.
Greenhouse, Carol J. , Babara Yngvesson and David M. Engel (1994) *Law and Community in Three American Towns.* Cornell University Press: Ithaca, NY.
Gross, Nachum (1982) "The Economic Policy of the Mandatory Government in Palestine," *Discussion Paper 816.* Maurice Falk Institute for Economic Research in Israel: Jerusalem.
Hawley, John C. (1996) *Writing the Nation: Self and Country in the Post-Colonial Imagination.* Rodopi: Amsterdam.
Herget, J. and S. Wallace (1987) "The German Free Law Movement as the Source of American Legal Realism," *Virginia Law Review*, 73, pp. 399–455.
Holmes, John Hayes (1929) (1977) *Palestine To-Day and To-Morrow: A Gentile's Survey of Zionism.* Arno Press: New York.
Horowitz, Dan and Moshe Lissak (1978) *Origins of the Israeli Polity.* University of Chicago Press: Chicago.
Hunt, Alan (1992) "Foucault's Expulsion of Law: Towards a Retrieval," *Law and Social Inquiry*, 17(1).
Just, Peter (1992) "History, Power, Ideology, and Culture: Current Directions in the Anthropology of Law," *Law and Society Review*, 26(2), pp. 373–411.
Katz, Yaacov (1960) *Ben Yehudim le Goyiim.* Bialik Institute: Jerusalem (Heb).

Kedar, Aharon (1978) "On the Worldview of 'Brit Shalom'" in Ben-Zion Yehoshoua and Aharon Kedar (eds) *Ideology and Zionist Policy*. Shazar Center: Jerusalem, pp. 97–114.

Kedar, Sandy (1998) "Majority Time, Minority Time: Land, Nationality and the Law of Adverse Possession in Israel," *Iunei Mishpat* 21(3), pp. 665–746.

Kimmerling, Baruch (1983) *Zionism and Economy*. Schenkman: Cambridge, Mass.

Kimmerling, Baruch (1993) "Yachasei Hevra u'Medina be'Yisrael" (State and Society in Israel), in: Uri Ram (ed.) *Israeli Society: Critical Perspectives*. Brerot: Tel Aviv, pp. 328–350.

Kimmerling, Baruch and Joel S. Migdal (1993) *Palestinians: The Making of a People*. Free Press: New York.

Kolatt, Yisrael (1994) "Religion, Society and State at the Time of the National Home" in Shmuel Almog, Yehouda Reinhartz, Anita Shapira (eds) *Zionism and Religion*. Zalman Shazar: Jerusalem, pp. 329–372 (Heb).

Lacqueur, Walter (1972) *A History of Zionism*. Weidenfeld and Nicolson: London.

Larson, Magali Sarfatti (1977) *The Rise of Professionalism: A Sociological Analysis*. University of California Press: Berkeley.

Likhovski, Assaf (1995) "In Our Image: Colonial Discourse and the Anglicization of the Law of Mandatory Palestine," *Israel Law Review*, 29(3), pp. 291–359.

Likhovski, Assaf (1998) "Between a 'Mandate' and a 'State': On the Periodization of the History of Israeli Law," *Mishpatim* 29(2), pp. 1–34.

Likhovski, Assaf (1998) "The Invention of 'Hebrew Law' in Mandatory Palestine," *American Journal of Comparative Law* 46(2), pp. 339–374.

Likhovski, Assaf (1998) "Mishpat Ivri ve'Idiologia Zionit be'Eretz Yisrael ha'Mandatorit" (Hebrew Law and Zionist Ideology in Mandatory Palestine), in: Menachem Mautner, Avi Sagi and Ronen Shamir (eds) *Multiculturalism in a Democratic and Jewish State*. Ramot: Tel Aviv, pp. 633–659 (Heb).

Lissak, Moshe (1996) "Soziologim 'Bikort'iim' ve'Soziologim 'Mimsadiim' ba'Kehila ha'Academit ha'Yisraelit: Ma'avakim Idiologiim o Si'ach Academi Inyani?" (Critical Sociologists and 'Establishment' Sociologists in the Israeli Academy: Ideological Struggles or a Substantive Academic Discourse?) in: Pinchas Ginosar and Avi Bareli (eds) *Tsionut: Pulmus Ben Zmanenu (Zionism: A Contemporary Debate)*. Ben Gurion University Press: Beer Sheva, pp. 60–98.

Lissak, Moshe, Anita Shapira and Gabriel Cohen (eds) (1995) *The History of the Jewish Community in Eretz-Israel Since 1882, The Period of the British Mandate, Part Two.* Israel Academy for Sciences and Humanities and the Bialik Institute: Jerusalem (Heb).

Lockman, Zachary (1995) "Exclusion and Solidarity: Labor Zionism and Arab Workers in Palestine 1897–1929," in: Gyan Prakash (ed.) *After Colonialism.* Princeton University Press : Princeton, NJ, pp. 211–240.

Luz, Ehud (1985) *Parallels Meet Religion and Nationalism in Early Zionist Movement (1882–1904).* Am Oved: Tel Aviv (Heb.)

Malchi, Elieger (1953) The History of the Law of Palestine. Dinnim: Tel-Aviv.

Malouf, David (1994) *Remembering Babylon.* Vintage: New York.

Mautner, Menachem (1993) *The Decline of Formalism and the Rise of Values in Israeli Law.* Ma'agaley Da'at: Tel Aviv (Heb).

Mautner, Menachem "A Rabbinical Court at Netivot" in: Adi Ophir (ed.) *Fifty to Forty Eight.* Van Leer: Jerusalem, pp. 467–475 (Heb).

Merry, Sally Engle (1984) "Rethinking Gossip and Scandal," in: Donald Black (ed.) *Toward a General Theory of Social Control,* Vol. 1. Academic Press: Orlando, pp. 271–302.

Merry, Sally Engle (1988) "Legal Pluralism," *Law and Society Review,* 22(5), pp. 869–896.

Merry, Sally Engle (1995) "Sorting Out Popular Justice," in: Sally Engle Merry and Neal Millner (eds) *The Possibility of Popular Justice.* Michigan University Press: Ann Arbor.

Miller, Ylana N. (1980) "Administrative Policy in Rural Palestine: The Impact of British Norms on Arab Community Life, 1920–1948," in: Joel S. Migdal (ed.) *Palestinian Society and Politics.* Princeton University Press: Princeton, NJ.

Morag, Amotz (1967) *The Financing of the Israeli Government: Development and Problems.* Magnes: Jerusalem, pp. 1–28.

Oren, Yitzchak (ed.) (1975) *Prof. Paltiel Daykan: A Collection of Essays and Studies.* Yavne: Tel Aviv.

Palestine Royal Commission Report (July 1937), (Peel Report). Report Presented to Parliament by the Secretary of State for the Colonies by command of His Majesty.

Pappe, Ilan (1996) "Ha'Zionut be'Mivchan ha'Teoriot shel ha'Leumiut" (Zionism in the Context of Theories of Nationalism), in: Pinchas Ginosar and Avi Bareli (eds) *Tsionut: Pulmus Ben Zmanenu (Zionism: A Contemporary Debate).* Ben Gurion University Press: Beer Sheva, pp. 223–263.

Patai, Raphael (ed.) (1971) *Encyclopedia of Zionism and Israel.* McGraw-Hill: New York, p. 757–760.

Peel Report (1937), see Palestine Royal Commission.
Penslar, Derek Jonathan (1995) "Innovation and Revisionism in Israeli Historiography," *History and Memory*, 7(1), pp. 125–146.
Prakash, Gyan (1992) "Writing Post-Orientalist Histories of the Third World: Indian Historiography is Good to Think," in: Nicholas B. Dirks (ed.) *Colonialism and Culture*. University of Michigan Press: Ann Arbor.
Radin, Max (1935) "The Courts and Administrative Agencies," *Minutes of the Judicial Section of the American Bar Association (July)*. Unpublished typescript.
Raz-Karkutzkin, Amnon (1994) "Galut be'Toch Ribonut: Lebikoret Shlilat ha'Galut ba'Tarbut ha'Yisraelit" (Exile within Sovereignty: A Critique of the Negation of Exile in Israeli Culture), *Teoria u'Bikoret*, 4, pp. 23–55, 5, pp. 113–130 (Heb).
Reuveny, Jacob (1993) *The Administration of Palestine Under the British Mandate 1920–1948: An Institutional Analysis*. Bar Ilan University: Ramat Gan.
Rousseau, Jean-Jacques (1712–1778) (1985) (trans. Willmoore Kendall), *The Government of Poland*. Hackett Publishing: Indianapolis
Said, Edward (1978) *Orientalism*. Penguin Books: London.
Said, Edward (1991) "Art and National Identity: A Critic's Symposium," *Art in America*, September 1991, pp. 80–81.
Said, Edward (1994) *Culture and Imperialism*. Vintage Books: New York.
Samuel, Edwin (1957) *British Traditions in the Administration of Israel*. Anglo-Israel Association, Vallentine, Mitchell: London.
Schwartz, Gary (1996) "Ars Moriendi: The Mortality of Art," *Art in America*, November 1996, pp. 72–75.
Shachar, Yoram (1995) "History and Sources of Israeli Law," in: Amos Shapira and Keren C. DeWitt-Arar (eds) *Introduction to the Law of Israel*. Kluwer Law Int'l: The Hague, pp. 1–10.
Shafir, Gershon (1989) *Land, Labour and Origins of the Israeli–Palestinian Conflict 1882–1914*. Cambridge University Press: Cambridge.
Shafir, Gershon (1993) "Land, Labor and Population in Zionist Colonization: General and Specific Aspects" in: Uri Ram (ed.) *Israeli Society: Critical Perspectives*. Breirot Publishers: Tel Aviv, pp. 104–119 (Heb).
Shalev, Meir (1988) *A Russian Novel (Roman Rusi)*. Am Oved: Tel Aviv.
Shaltiel, Eli (1990) *Pinhas Rutenberg: 1879–1942, Life and Times*. Am Oved: Tel Aviv.
Shamir, Ronen (1996) "Suspended in Space: Bedouins under the Law of Israel," *Law and Society Review*, 30(2), pp. 231–257.

Shapira, Anita (1992) *Land and Power: The Zionist Resort to Force 1881–1948*. Oxford University Press: New York.
Shapira, Anita (1995) "Political History of the Yishuv, 1918–1935," in: Moshe Lissak, Anita Shapira and Gabriel Cohen (eds) *The History of the Jewish Community in Eretz-Israel Since 1882, The Period of the British Mandate, Part Two*. Israel Academy for Sciences and Humanities and the Bialik Institute: Jerusalem.
Shapiro, Yonathan (1984) *An Elite Without Successors*. Sifriat Po'alim: Tel Aviv.
Shapiro, Yonathan (1996) *Hevra bi'Shvi ha'Politika'im*. Sifriat Po'alim: Tel Aviv (Heb).
Shenkar, Arie (1963) *Be'Emuna U'Be'Ma'as* (In Faith and Action). Privately published: Tel Aviv.
Sherman, A. J. (1997) *Mandate Days: British Lives in Palestine 1918–1948*. Thames and Hudson: London.
Shprinzak, Ehud (1986) *Every Man Whatsoever is Right in His Own Eyes: Illegalism in Israeli Society*. Sifriat Po'alim: Tel Aviv.
Shvied, Eliezer (1972) *Leu'miut Yehudit (Jewish Nationalism)*. Zack: Jerusalem.
Sternhell, Zeev (1995) *Nation-building or a New Society?* Am Oved: Tel Aviv (Heb).
Strassman, Gabriel (1984) *Wearing the Robes: A History of the Legal Profession Until 1962 (Otei ha'Glima)*. Lishkat Orchei Ha'Din: Tel Aviv.
Unsworth, Barry (1995) *Morality Play*. Norton: New York.
Unsworth, Barry (1996) *After Hannibal*. Hamish Hamilton: London.
Van Vriesland Report, unpublished report of 11.3.29, CZA A114/120.
Vestreich, Elimelech (1998) "Polygamy and Forcing a Woman to Divorce in the Rulings of Ashkenazi Scholars in the Eleventh and Twelfth Centuries," *Mechkarey Mishpat*, 6.
Vital, David (1982) *Zionism: The Formative Years*. Clarendon: London.
Weber, Max (1978) *Economy and Society* (Max Rheinstein ed.). University of California Press: Berkeley.
Yadin, Uri (1962) "Reception and Rejection of English Law in Israel," *International and Comparative Law Quarterly*, 11, January 1962, pp. 59–72.
Yehoshoua, Abraham B. (1997) *Voyage to the End of the Millennium*. Sifria Chadasha: Kibbutz Meuchad.
Zerubavel, Yael (1995) *Recovered Roots: Collective Memory and the Making of Israeli National Tradition*. University of Chicago Press: Chicago.

INDEX

Achdut Ha'Avoda 135, 159
Advocates ordinance 115–16
Ahad Ha'Am 33, 158; *see also* cultural Zionism
Arabs 13–16, 19–25, 28–9, 107–8, 155, 171–2
   and the Hebrew Law of Peace 170
   perception of 19–21, 23, 25, 27–8, 169–71
   see also Jewish–Arab relations
Arbitration, ordinance 31–2, 61, 121, 134
Auster, Daniel 60–1, 84, 178n1, 184n26, 184n28
autonomy, legal 34–6, 83

Balfour Declaration, the 10
Bar-Shira, Yisrael 136–7, 143–4, 188n32
Bebkov, Arie 181n39, 183n22, 187n13
Belkovski, Zvi 84, 181n39
Ben-Gurion, David 142, 184n39
Bentwich, Norman 60–2, 64, 115
Benvenishti, Meron 8, 10
Berlin, Eliahu 84, 184n26, 184n28, 187n13
Bloch, David 128
Bourdieu, Pierre 114, 121
Brit Shalom 170
Brown, Nathan J. 7, 108
Buber, Martin 154–5, 170
Bugrashov, Menachem 104
Caro, Yosef 34, 73
Chatterjee, Partha 24, 113, 163
Chief Rabbinate 47–8, 64–6, 69–70

civil society 135–7, 145, 152, 159–60
Cohen, Eliahu Zvi 132–3, 192n17
colonialism
   and law 7, 27, 108, 118, 163
   dual 18–19, 23, 25
   theories of 16–19, 23–5
Common Law 7, 12, 54, 80, 85–6, 105, 118, 163
community justice 36, 42–5, 48, 52, 55–7, 62–3, 67–8, 70, 72, 76, 78, 88, 90, 95–7, 137, 150, 154; *see also* popular justice; lay justice
Comrades Law 94–5, 127, 135–45, 154
Constable, Marianne 54–6

democracy 134, 135
Diaspora 35, 43, 151–4, 156–7; *see also* Jews-in-exile
Dickstein, Paltiel 33, 46, 48, 56, 58, 71, 77–88, 82–5, 88, 98, 105–7, 133, 152, 187n13
Donkelblum, Menachem 101, 114, 119–20, 178n1, 189n2

Eisenstadt, Shmuel 36, 71–2, 82, 85–6, 105, 170
Eliash, Mordechai 77, 178n1
Elon, Menachem 34, 40–1, 43–4, 56
English law 25, 101
Epstein-Halevi, Eliahu 181n39
excommunication 37–9, 59–60, 66–8, 112
exile *see* Jews-in-exile; Diaspora
Foucault, Michel 51, 53, 74
Fitzpatrick, Peter 163
Frumkin, Gad 122

German
  free-law 41, 79–83, 85–6, 89
  historical school 71, 80–5, 89
  legal education 84
Ghosh, Amitav 23–4

Ha'Cohen, Ben-Hilel Mordechai 181n39
Haifa 46, 58, 138
Halakhah 34, 40, 42, 44, 46
Ha'Mishpat 77
Ha'Mishpat Ha'Ivri 77, 170
Ha'Mizrachi 39, 48, 64
Ha'Poel Ha'tzair 135
Hebrew
  language 7, 33, 94
  law 7, 29, 40–1, 43, 63, 90; see also Jewish law
  Law Society 77
  new person 14, 25, 42
High Court of Justice (Supreme Court) 66–8, 91, 101, 122, 127
Histadrut see Jewish Federation of Labor
Home Owners Association 94, 102–4
honor disputes 92–3
Horgin, Haim 181n39
Horowitz, Dan 15, 18–19
Horowitz, Solomon 121–2, 164, 194n20; see also Sacher law firm
Hoshen Mishpat 73, 78, 83, 119, 186n7

India 13, 23–4, 27, 114, 163
Israeli–Arab conflict see Jewish Arab relations
Israeli law 25, 91

Jerusalem 9, 46, 58, 139, 140
Jewish
  Arab relations 14–18, 166–71
  Federation of Labor (Histadrut) 94, 127, 135–45, 160–1; Acting Committee (Va'ad Ha'Poel) 136–7, 142, 144
  immigration 11, 18, 20, 58, 103, 161, 167
  law 31, 34–6, 40, 43, 56, 65–6, 72–4, 78, 86, 90, 146, 153–4; see also Hebrew Lawyers Association 76, 99
  middle class 58, 84, 102–3, 160–8
  National Fund 92, 110, 130, 197n14
  orthodoxy 31, 33, 35, 39–42, 45–6, 63–70, 71, 144–6, 154, 158
Jews-in-exile 24–5, 34, 42–3, 45, 152, 154–7, 168; see also Disapora
Joseph, Bernard 112–13, 154–5, 157, 162, 168
jurisprudence 71, 75, 78–9

Keizerman, Yossef 85
Kimmerling, Baruch 155–6
Keren Kayemet Le'Yisrael see Jewish National Fund
Klebanoff, Ya'acov 85, 122, 164
Kohler, Josef 83
Kook, Avraham Y. Ha'Cohen 32, 46
Krongold, Haim Dr 141

labor
  disputes 138–43
  market 17, 138
  movement 160–1
land
  acquisition 94
  colonial policy 13
  disputes 94
  transfer ordinance 13
law
  and community see community justice
  as culture 33, 63, 83, 85, 101, 106–7, 111, 152
  see also Mandatory law, Hebrew law
lawyers see legal profession; Jewish Lawyers Association
lay justice 43, 46, 78, 148
legal
  creativity 35–6, 82, 85
  positivism see positivism in law
  profession 74–6, 86, 88, 98–9,

105–6, 108–9, 112, 114,
115–16, 118–24, 145–6, 166–7
realism 81, 86
sanctions against shirking 57–8,
95–100; *see also* shirking
Likhovski, Asaf, 41, 84
Lissak, Moshe 15, 18–19

Maimonides 34, 56, 73
Majele *see* Ottoman law 115, 118
Mandatory law 6, 12, 112, 117
Mandatory state 7–9, 14, 25, 112; *see also* colonialism
Mani, Yisrael 178n1
Manufacturers Association 165
Meir, Shalom 181n39
Merry, Sally Engle 55, 90, 96, 138
middle classes *see* Jewish middle class

National Council (Va'ad Leumi)
30, 48, 103–4, 113–14, 124,
130–1, 155, 163
nationalism 92–3, 159
and Jewish orthodoxy 68–70
in law 97–8, 113–14, 124, 160
see also statism
Nofech, Yitzchak 170

orthodoxy *see* Jewish orthodoxy
Ottoman
law 12, 84, 86, 110, 115
rule 6, 8, 21, 23, 64, 116

Palestine Zionist Executive (PZE)
94, 98, 109–10, 122, 130, 196n11
Peel Report, the 18
Pen, Shmuel 183n19
personal status 39, 48, 64–7
popular justice 51, 72, 76, 90, 138,
149–50; *see also* community
justice, lay justice
positivism in law 26, 52, 54–6, 66–8,
79–82, 91, 111, 122, 152
anti-positivism 35, 83
Prakash, Gyan 24, 171

rabbinical courts 32, 39, 45–7,
63–70, 127, 133, 146, 152
Raz-Karkutzkin, Amnon 155–6
Remez, David 142
Rosenboim, Shimshon 84, 181n39, 187n13
Rosenthal, Haim 84, 181n39
Ruppin, Arthur 108–9

Sacher, Harry 109, 121–2, 142,
193n5
law firm 121–2, 142, 164, 193n5,
194n20
Said, Edward 88, 151
Samuel, Herbert 11
Samuel, Horace 105, 192n14
San Francisco Community Boards
126
secularism 32–3, 35–6, 39–42, 64–6,
69, 71, 153, 155–8
and religion 48, 69–70, 158
Segev, Tom 8, 10
Set Table (Shulchan Aruch) 34, 36, 73
sexual harassment 140
Shafir, Gershon 16–17
Shapira, Anita 11, 70
Shapiro, Yonathan 134, 160, 166, 168
shirking 58, 59, 60, 95–8, 100, 130;
see also legal sanctions against
shirking
Shiv'at Tovei Ha'Ir 38, 43, 48
Shmeterling, Haim 84, 181n39
Shoshani, Affair 100, 106, 112,
127–8, 131, 164
Shoshani, Sa'adia 100–4, 112, 127,
128, 131, 164
Shulchan Aruch see Set Table
socialism 159–163
and statism 156–60
socialist law 136–7, 145
Solel Boneh 142–3
Soviet Socialist Republic 85
Civil Procedure Code 136
law 85
statism 26, 29, 63, 65, 74, 118, 124,
150–3
and nationalism 156–8

INDEX

and socialism 156–70
anti-statism and non-statism 35, 56, 63, 67–8, 74, 90–1, 149, 154–6, 160, 169
Sternhell, Zeev 159

Takanot Ha'Kahal 43
Tel Aviv 28, 46, 58–9, 93–4, 101–3, 127–30, 132, 161, 164
  and Hebrew Law of Peace 127–30
  Municipal Council of 94, 101, 103, 122, 128
  population 103
Thon, Yaacov 178n1

Unsworth, Barry 49, 51, 120

Va'ad Ha'Poel *see* Jewish Federation of Labor Acting Committee
Va'ad Ha'Zirim 60, 130, 196n11
Va'ad Leûmi *see* National Council
Van Vriesland, Zigfried 109–10, 113–14, 193n5
Weber, Max 78–80, 82, 122
Weinshel, Avraham 85

Weizman, Chaim 8, 21
World Zionist Organization (WZO) 46

Yaacobson, Moshe 183n22, 187n13
Yehoshua, Abraham B. 37–9, 153–4

Zerubavel, Yael 39, 69
Zionism
  and law 109, 134–5, 145–7
  and statism 159–60
  cultural 33, 46, 63, 151, 170; *see also* Ahad Ha'Am
  historiography 6, 8–9, 18–19, 160–2
  political 150
  post-Zionism 16–17, 171–2
Zionist
  attitude to Hebrew Law of Peace 110
  Executive *see* Palestine Zionist Executive (PZE)
  Palestine Office 30, 108–10
Zmora, Moshe 141–3

Lightning Source UK Ltd.
Milton Keynes UK
UKHW012343290119
336442UK00011B/142/P